# Beyond the Contingent

# Beyond the Contingent

*Epistemological Authority, a Pascalian Revival,
and the Religious Imagination in Third Republic France*

KATHLEEN A. MULHERN

*With a Foreword by Martha Hanna*

◆PICKWICK *Publications* · Eugene, Oregon

BEYOND THE CONTINGENT
Epistemological Authority, a Pascalian Revival, and the Religious Imagination in Third Republic France

Copyright © 2011 Kathleen A. Mulhern. All rights reserved. Except for brief quotations in critical publications or reviews, no part of this book may be reproduced in any manner without prior written permission from the publisher. Write: Permissions, Wipf and Stock Publishers, 199 W. 8th Ave., Suite 3, Eugene, OR 97401.

Pickwick Publications
An Imprint of Wipf and Stock Publishers
199 W. 8th Ave., Suite 3
Eugene, OR 97401

www.wipfandstock.com

ISBN 13: 978-1-60899-370-3

*Cataloging-in-Publication data:*

Mulhern, Kathleen A.

Beyond the contingent : epistemological authority, a Pascalian revival, and the religious imagination in Third Republic France / Kathleen A. Mulhern ; with a foreword by Martha Hanna.

xviii + 212 p. ; 23 cm. Including bibliographical references and index.

ISBN 13: 978-1-60899-370-3

1. France—History—Third Republic, 1870–1940. 2. Pascal, Blaise, 1623–1662. 3. Duhem, Pierre Maurice Marie, 1861–1916. 4. Blondel, Maurice, 1861–1949. 5. Laberthonnière, Lucien, 1860–1932. 6. Religion and science. 7. Church and state—France—History—19th century. 8. Catholic Church—France—History—19th century. I. Hanna, Martha. II. Title.

DC337 M70 2011

Manufactured in the U.S.A.

*To Steven C.*
*by way of Goethe*
*because of "l'unique nécessaire."*

# Contents

*Foreword by Martha Hanna / ix*

*Acknowledgments / xvii*

1  Introduction / 1
2  A *Fin-de-Siècle* Scaffolding / 13
3  Pascalian Perceptions / 44
∞  Interlude I: *Providentissimus Deus* (1893) / 74
4  Knowing and Imagining / 82
5  Reversing Epistemological Methodologies / 106
6  Wagering on *Fin-de-Siècle* Probabilities / 128
7  Telling Stories about Authenticity / 154
∞  Interlude II: *Pascendi Dominci Gregis* (1907) / 189
8  Conclusion / 195

*Selected Bibliography / 203*

*Index / 209*

# Foreword

CULTURE WARS ARE NOT unique to contemporary America. Indeed, a culture war as divisive, acrimonious, and apparently interminable as the one that currently pits Creationists against Darwinians and "red states" against "blue states" characterized late nineteenth-century France, and for many of the same reasons. The spiritual heirs of the French Revolution of 1789 believed that the very future of France depended upon securing once and for all the foundations of a democratic and secular republic that respected science, consigned superstition (and all its irrational manifestations) to the past, and minimized what they were convinced was the pernicious influence of organized religion in politics, culture, and everyday life. Outraged and appalled by the prospect of a Godless and mindlessly materialist revolutionary modernity, social conservatives championed a moral order predicated on the preservation or restoration of everything that the Revolution of 1789 had worked to eradicate from French life: hierarchy, obedience, faith. This culture war did not originate in the 1880s and 1890s—it had been evident since the Revolution itself—but three important developments of the late nineteenth century brought the divide into ever-sharper relief. The unambiguous triumph of republicanism in the elections of 1879 meant that a monarchical restoration, still a possibility through the 1870s, was henceforth most unlikely; the increasing dominance of science in intellectual life threatened to undermine or render irrelevant the religious truths that had persisted in spite of Revolutionary anticlericalism; and the failure of the Vatican's efforts to seek a working reconciliation with French republicanism—through the stillborn venture in 1892 of the *Ralliement*—combined to alienate conservative Catholics from the Third Republic, to intensify Republican anticlericalism, and to create a political and cultural chasm in French public life that seemed well nigh unbridgeable.

This, at least, is how we have long understood the political and cultural history of late nineteenth-century France: two spiritual families eternally at odds with one another, incapable of seeking common ground, indifferent in fact to the very possibility of doing so. And yet, as Kathleen Mulhern reveals in *Beyond the Contingent*, this vision of a profoundly, irrevocably divided nation—in which men of faith stood on one side looking contemptuously at the men of science on the other, and the men of science looked, with equal contempt, upon their benighted, religiously befuddled intellectual adversaries—doesn't quite tell the whole story and certainly doesn't do justice to those who genuinely hoped to achieve an intellectual rapprochement that would allow men of true faith to respect the real accomplishments of modern science while affirming the existence of God.

The scholars examined in *Beyond the Contingent* were united in their belief that such a rapprochement was sorely needed in the crisis years of the *fin-de-siècle* and they were convinced that the ideas of Blaise Pascal, the seventeenth-century mathematician, philosopher, and man of faith, held the key to succeeding at this intellectual project. Indeed, the neo-Pascalians whose philosophical reflections constitute the core of this book's analysis—Pierre Duhem (1861–1916), Maurice Blondel (1861–1949), and Lucien Laberthonnière (1860–1932)—embraced Pascal's philosophy of knowledge precisely because it seemed uniquely equipped to address the challenges and transcend the obstacles that confronted Catholic intellectuals at the end of the nineteenth century. Pascal had affirmed a hierarchy of "orders of knowledge" that acknowledged the legitimacy of science, reason, and faith. Pascal did not reject science or deny the utility of knowledge derived from scientific, empirical inquiry; rather, he merely affirmed its limits. Science could know many things; but it could not know everything. Nor could reason, the second order of knowledge, inspire definitive and certain knowledge of God. Ultimately, Pascal contended, individual faith in the existence of God comes neither from science, nor from reason, nor from accepting unthinkingly the dogma affirmed by the Church. Rather, faith comes from within, from the "reason of the heart." Why these Pascalian principles resonated for a community of French Catholic intellectuals at the end of the nineteenth century and why their efforts to constitute a philosophical system that simultaneously respected the accomplishments of science, affirmed the existence of God, and honored the autonomy of the individual conscience ultimately failed is the story that *Beyond the Contingent* unpacks with admirable rigor.

*Foreword* xi

The late nineteenth century was a challenging age for French Catholic intellectuals, and most especially for those who aspired, in Kathleen Mulhern's words, to "the renewal of the Church through the reconciliation of modern thought with Catholic tradition" (p. 2). Many, but not all, of the challenges that confronted Catholic scholars, were generated by the progressive political agenda and intellectual character of the Third Republic (1870–1940). Forged in the tumultuous circumstances of military defeat and challenged by threats of monarchical restoration throughout the 1870s, the Third Republic secured in 1879 the political victory that allowed it in the following decade to root republican principles so firmly in the soil of the national psyche that the Revolutionary ideals of liberty, equality, and fraternity—a secular trinity to which the Republic was fundamentally committed but which the nation had only intermittently honored since 1789—would at last thrive. Once armed with the requisite political authority, Republican politicians dedicated themselves to the creation of a moderate but avowedly secular republic that would banish the memories and avoid the excesses of the Reign of Terror (to which all republican regimes in France were inevitably compared), while de-fanging the twin perils of working class radicalism and conservative authoritarianism. Thus the Republic cultivated an ethos and established a legislative agenda that combined relentless anticlericalism with triumphant scientism. By liberating France from the shackles of religious orthodoxy (the most loyal indomitable ally of political conservatism since the Revolution) and by encouraging material progress grounded in scientific innovation, the Third Republic resolved to fulfill at last the promise of 1789.

The Third Republic neither disguised nor apologized for its anticlericalism. Jules Ferry, the architect of educational reform in the 1880s, famously boasted that he dreamed of establishing "humanity without a God and without a King" and although the anticlericalism of the 1880s was neither as acerbic nor as unforgiving as that which would follow twenty years later, it was nonetheless resolute. The goal of Ferry and his allies in the "Opportunist Republic" of the 1880s was to wean the people of France from their lingering loyalty to the Catholic Church and to win them over instead to a secular catechism of duty-driven patriotism. The patriotism of the Third Republic was to be forged, first and foremost, in the nation's school-houses, catechized by an army of republican schoolteachers who taught the children of France to read, to write, and to recognize themselves as citizens of a secular, progressive, and egalitarian Republic. This pedagogy of patriotism proved fundamental to the identity and, indeed, the very survival of the Third Republic, as the Great War would demonstrate, but it required the removal of priests and nuns from the classrooms of republican France and the excision of religion from the national curriculum. It is not surprising that devout Catholics perceived at the very heart of the Third Republic an unsettling animosity that raised real doubts about the possibility of Catholic-Republican "co-habitation."

French Catholics could (and in many instances, did) accommodate themselves to the patriotic ethos of the secular republic; as the First World War made evident, Catholics proved themselves as willing to die for France as their agnostic comrades-in-arms. They certainly could have participated fully in national elections without compromising their faith. This, at least, was the belief that inspired Leo XIII's effort in 1892 to initiate a *Ralliement* between Catholics and republicans. More fundamentally incompatible with Catholic belief and hence more corrosive of Catholic confidence in the Third Republic than its overt anticlericalism, however, was the pervasive scientism that informed its intellectual life. The Republic did more than simply celebrate the legitimate accomplishments of scientific enterprise; it made the scientific method the keystone to all intellectual inquiry. Convinced that France's inadequate attention to science had contributed directly to the nation's humiliating defeat in 1870, when Prussia's newly developed technical acumen had combined so potently with its long-standing military expertise, the Republic devoted itself to the cultivation of scientific inquiry and to the veritable canonization of the scientific method. Scientific success, however, threatened—in ways direct and indirect, large and small—to challenge the long-standing authority of Church and faith by demystifying everyday life and by stressing, to the detriment of all other systems of thought, the centrality of materialist ontology.

No one contributed more to France's national infatuation with science than Louis Pasteur: an observant Catholic himself, Pasteur not only called upon the nation, in the aftermath of 1870, to apply itself more seriously to the study of science but demonstrated through his many brilliant successes how much was to be gained by doing so. His most celebrated scientific victory came in 1885 when he first used a rabies vaccine to save a nine-year-old boy, bitten by a rabid dog, from certain death. Heretofore, the power of science to persuade ordinary people of its efficacy had been limited at best: although Pasteur had made significant advances prior to 1885 that protected the wine, beer, and silk industries of France, the capacity of science to make a real difference in the lives of ordinary people remained unproven. 1885 changed all of that. In one dramatic moment, science demonstrated its almost miraculous powers and acquired an almost mystical authority.

Had France's reverent regard for the power of the natural sciences and the application of scientific method been confined to the admirable and awe-inspiring conquests of Louis Pasteur's laboratory, few would have complained. As *Beyond the Contingent* makes clear, the neo-Pascalians (and many other critics of Republican materialism) wanted neither to condemn scientific inquiry nor disregard science's real accomplishments. What they objected to, however, was the pervasive—and, to their way of thinking, pernicious—penetration of the materialist worldview that grounded the natural sciences in every corner of intellectual inquiry. By the early 1890s, the very spirit of intellectual inquiry in France was marked by what admirers and detractors alike called "scientism." Proponents of "scientism" believed that the empirical method and ontological presuppositions of the natural sciences should become the foundation of all intellectual inquiry: if the careful accumulation and categorization of factual data constituted the key to predictive certainty about the natural world, might it not also become the key to understanding the human past? At its most expansive and most hubristic, this ethos of scientism dominated scholarship in history, literature and (as *Beyond the Contingent* demonstrates) biblical hermeneutics. Indeed, the most avid proponents of the scientific method made no bones about what they hoped to accomplish by adopting the methods of science to the study of human nature and culture: "the almost religious love of scientific truth raises minds that are otherwise rather ordinary above themselves and communicates to them a grandeur which they would seem incapable of at first glance."[1] Nor did they ignore the political implications of an intellectual culture grounded in the methods and principles of the natural sciences: the triumph of democracy depended, they insisted, upon the triumph of rational, egalitarian scientific inquiry.

Scientism had powerful advocates within the French university system, but it also confronted serious (and, in some instances, well-

---

1. Croiset, "L'Unité des principes dans l'enseignement public," as cited in Keylor, *Academy and Community*, 196.

situated) critics who denied that the scientific method was appropriate to all fields of intellectual inquiry and doubted that it was capable of providing satisfactory answers to all the questions that from time immemorial had begged for answers. Among those who gave voice to this anti-scientistic backlash of the 1890s were neo-Kantians in the nation's faculties of Letters, neo-Thomists in the marginalized Catholic universities, and the neo-Pascalians who constitute the heart of this study. All shared a belief that science alone could not answer all the questions that needed to be answered. But unlike the neo-Kantians who secured for themselves a comfortable and respected niche in the very heart of the French university system; unlike the neo-Thomists who found favor with the Vatican; the neo-Pascalians were ostracized by the former and ultimately anathematized by the latter. Their failure was not a failure rooted in inadequate intellectual rigor: as *Beyond the Contingent* demonstrates, the neo-Pascalians took a backseat to no one in that regard. Rather, their failure derived in part at least from contingent circumstances over which they had, at best, only minimal control.

If the emergence by the 1890s of a more skeptical attitude towards the hegemony of science augured well for those like the neo-Pascalians who were willing to accept the legitimate accomplishments of science but were loathe to accede to its exclusively materialistic worldview, the decade presented other challenges—from an increasingly anticlerical Republic, on the one hand, and an ever more authoritarian Church, on the other—that ultimately proved their undoing. In the little more than a decade that constituted the neo-Pascalian moment, they fell under the hostile gaze of republicans ever more suspicious of and antagonistic towards the Church. As independent-minded Catholics, whose theology veered dangerously close to crypto-Protestantism insofar as they dared to believe that "the pursuit of truth would lead the individual back to the Church, but that this process began not with the authority of the Church but with the autonomy of the human soul" (p. 24), they encountered ever more vigilant resistance from the Church hierarchy, culminating in 1907 with the promulgation of the papal encyclical, *Pascendi Dominici Gregis*.

Even more than during the 1880s, the last years of the century, punctuated by the Dreyfus Affair and its attendant animosities, made it seem unlikely that one could be both a loyal son of the Church and a loyal defender of democratic republicanism. Superficially at least, the Dreyfus Affair had nothing to do with science and little to do with religion. It certainly shed no new light on the knotty epistemological questions that absorbed the intellectual heirs of Pascal at the end of the nineteenth century, and thus should not have mattered much to the neo-Pascalians or compromised in any serious way the legitimacy of their cause. But insofar as the Affair separated defenders of hierarchy, obedience, and the privileges of state from those who championed the rights of man and insisted upon the proper administration of justice, it effectively divided France into two hostile, mutually acrimonious camps that situated Catholics almost automatically in the anti-Republican ranks. Unlike the Dreyfusards, whose dedication to the Revolutionary principles of the rights of man and the citizen compelled them to demand justice for Alfred Dreyfus, the Jewish officer whom the Army had wrongly convicted and then systematically persecuted, the anti-Dreyfusards were animated by an overarching respect for authority (whether military or religious) and a narrow, and intensely bigoted nationalism that prompted them to defend the Army, deny its misdeeds, and countenance the persecution of a man who could not, they contended, be a true son of France. In the aftermath of the Affair, a newly invigorated and increasingly assertive anticlerical spirit prevailed in Republican France and the Catholic Church became its most prominent victim. Religious orders were expelled, religious property confiscated and, in 1905 the ministry of Émile Combes formalized the Separation of Church and State, thus bringing to an end the settlement of the Concordat, which had governed Church-State relations in France since 1802.

*Beyond the Contingent* makes the case, however, that the neo-Pascalians failed not primarily because they fell victim to the acerbic anticlericalism of Émile Combes, but because they fell afoul of Vatican orthodoxy. Unjustly characterized as modernists who rejected outright the authority of the Church, they—like the real modernists of the day—were silenced by the severe hand of papal authority. And thus after 1907 the neo-Pascalian option was no longer available as a means for bridging the cultural chasm that now more than ever divided believers from nonbelievers.

Their best efforts notwithstanding, the neo-Pascalians failed to bridge the cultural chasm that divided *fin-de-siècle* France. But is that the end of the story? Is it possible that Pascalian principles about the order of knowledge might offer some direction out of the cultural trenches of the present day? To the extent that the contemporary world thinks about

Blaise Pascal at all, it would seem (tragically) to be only as the author of his most famous epigram: "The heart has its reasons that reason does not know." Yet as *Beyond the Contingent* makes evident, perhaps Pascal deserves to be remembered for more than a clever phrase now consigned to highbrow Valentine's Day cards. Perhaps his insights on science and faith deserve another look. Certainly the issues that absorbed his attention are issues that continue to engage reflective thinkers: Is it possible to reconcile science and faith? If so, what place should be given to each enterprise? Should those who define themselves as believers reject out of hand the evidence and conclusions of empirical science? And should those who define themselves as rational beings dismiss religious faith as nothing but ignorant superstition? Does there exist today the possibility for building a community of scholars willing and able to build a bridge across the ravine created by our contemporary culture wars, a bridge that would unite in fruitful dialogue people of faith and people of science? And if such a possibility does exist, what inspiration might they find in the insights and philosophical reflections of a French mathematician and philosopher who died more than three hundred years ago?

Martha Hanna
University of Colorado, Boulder

# Acknowledgments

THE YEARS OF STUDY, research, and writing culminating in this book were made possible by a community of personal friends, academic mentors, and enthusiastic family members. The constant guidance and support of my advisor, Martha Hanna, and her colleagues at the University of Colorado, were invaluable. I am especially grateful for the Emerson/Lowe Fellowship, which made my research possible. The sacrificial support of my husband and children cannot be overestimated. They have been full of grace and good humor.

# 1

# Introduction

## THE PROBLEM AND ITS SIGNIFICANCE

IN ALL THE POLITICAL and social turbulence of *fin-de-siècle* Europe, the arcane discourses of a handful of Catholic thinkers publishing protracted articles for an elite audience hold a surprising relevance to a contemporary understanding of France's experiences during its Third Republic (1870–1914). These authors had neither the profile nor the literary flair of an Émile Zola thrusting "*J'accuse*" into the face of a stunned public; they lacked the poetic intensity and élan of a Paul Claudel or a Charles Péguy; they offered no easygoing spirituality for a curious public, as had Ernest Renan. Many of the published conversations of this handful of intellectuals simply gather dust in forgotten corners of libraries while the works of their more popular contemporaries are bound in leather and shelved prominently. Nevertheless, these men believed they offered a unique solution to the dilemmas of late nineteenth-century French Catholic intellectual thought, dilemmas that issued from the crossroads of scientific hubris, political volatility, and religious anxieties.

This book addresses the religious imagination of those Catholic intellectuals of France's *fin-de-siècle* who sought inspiration in Pascalian thought. These individuals were particularly challenged by the epistemological conflict created, on the one hand, by the escalating centralization of religious power in the papacy (most clearly evident in the declaration of papal infallibility, 1870) and on the other hand, by the parallel centralization of political and social authority in scientism, the belief most famously expressed in Ernest Renan's claim that "science alone can resolve for man those eternal problems for which his nature imperiously demands the solution." Their position was also made more complicated by the unsettling political realities of France during the last decade of the nineteenth century and the first decade of the twentieth—namely, the Dreyfus Affair, Émile Combes' anticlerical administration, and the thrust toward the separation of Church and State (effective in the Law of 1905). The pressures made on Catholic intellectuals in general by an increasingly anticlerical culture forced these neo-Pascalians to express their ideas in a manner relevant to secular concerns.

The opposing demands of ecclesiological objectives and secular ambitions, both directed toward moral authority, generated a flurry of Catholic intellectual discussions about the renewal of the Church through the reconciliation of modern thought with Catholic tradition. Many were concerned about the marginalization of Catholic thought that had been caused, as they believed, by the Church's attitude of entrenchment and its stubborn refusal to engage with contemporary developments in science and politics. Pope Pius IX's Syllabus of Errors (1864), which listed eighty political, educational, and cultural errors of modern society, is one notable example of this attitude. In the period under consideration, two Catholic responses struggled for supremacy. The one, neo-Thomism, advocated a rejuvenation of Catholic authority through philosophical consent to the supremacy of reason and its appropriation for the purposes of a traditional Catholic apologetic. The second, modernism, argued for an engagement with modern developments in science, historical studies, and philosophy that granted external credence to their claims while retaining a religious structure bereft of any of the problematic claims of Church dogma and tradition, claims about the historical veracity of scripture and the supernatural character of ecclesial authority.

The neo-Pascalians offered a third approach, though history has lumped them together with the modernists whose voices, like those of all who were not advocates of neo-Thomism, were silenced in 1907. By carefully examining the contributions of these ardent neo-Pascalians, we are given insight into the deep concerns that motivated Catholic intellectuals in *fin-de-siècle* France to try to salvage the Church's reputation and to justify its participation in the governance of the secular state. Indeed, this analysis of the discourse and subsequent defeat of the neo-Pascalians suggests the possibility that intra-Catholic dissension, so rancorous and deeply divisive in the debate surrounding the modernists and the Pascalisants, might be a more important factor in contributing to the

Law of Separation than scholars have previously realized. Had French Catholics been more ideologically unified in the early years of the twentieth century, the anticlerical impulses of the post-Dreyfusard Republic might have encountered greater resistance, making the Separation less likely.

Through this study, we are also afforded a more nuanced understanding of the last years of the Church-State relationship, an affiliation that had continued in some form for nearly as many years as the French nation had existed; and most importantly, we gain a better understanding of one group's desperate attempt to circumvent the growing authoritarianism of the Roman Catholic Church via a spiritual Gallicanism that directed attention to the priority of the individual.

## THE FRAMEWORK

The last three decades of the nineteenth century were a critical juncture in the development of French Catholic thought, especially as it related to developments in the natural sciences. The increasingly divergent and antagonistic relationship between science and religion is, of course, a matter of the first importance in the history of modernity, and perhaps especially so in the history of the nineteenth century. Nowhere was this more evident than in France, where the dominant Catholicism of the nation, challenged by the secularism of revolutionary culture since the end of the eighteenth century, came under sustained assault during the early decades of the Third Republic. The multiple administrations of the Third Republic, particularly in the years before the Law of Separation, were fully given over to the defense of science and its methodologies as an ideological strategy. At the same time, they grew ever more wary of any religiously inspired or directed involvement in State (or secular) affairs.

By the early 1890s, French Catholics had been called by Pope Leo XIII (1878–1903) to reconcile themselves politically to the Republic; intellectuals were particularly encouraged to recapture science, which had, largely through positivist trends, strayed from the religious moorings that had once afforded the Church moral authority in the social realm. The tension that issued from the search for intellectual respect from religious skeptics and the deference due to Catholic dogma and direction stimulated the Catholic intellectual imagination. Catholic scientists and philosophers had to imagine new ways of harmonizing their religious beliefs and loyalties with their rational convictions and the evidence presented by the scientific world.

The escalating ideological debates at the turn of the century moved in overlapping spirals, always contesting the nature of the human being, the origin and destiny of humanity, and the individual's powers of knowledge and choice. In the years under study, these spirals began with questions about the historical veracity of scripture, issuing from the textual criticism begun in German theological circles and rooting themselves in the French culture most notably in the work of Alfred Loisy (1857–1940), priest, biblical scholar, historian, theologian, and professor at the Institut Catholique. This conversation about the authenticity of scriptural history was held in the context of the academy's keen interest in the scientific model of doing history. And from that debate stemmed the question about whether or not science was real knowledge. The epistemological chase culminated in the question about the relationship between knowledge and truth. Was scripture history? Was history science? Was science knowledge? Was knowledge truth? And finally, did truth result in power? And for whom?

Each level of debate demanded new levels and methods of interpretation. "Facts" no longer seemed objective or certain; they were appropriated and deciphered, rendering meanings that were widely disputed. Theories imposed their order on the facts, and such hermeneutical theories became keys to understanding the present and charting a course for the future. Who had the authority to dictate these theories? To compel the action required by their conclusions? While the political leaders of late nineteenth-century France were calling for the civic responsibility of the individual and ostensibly wished to make possible a greater participation in the governance of the social community, the Church, hoping to stem the tide of attrition that had built in the years after the Council of Trent (1545–1563) and erupting in earnest during the French Revolution, was seeking ways to restrict lay empowerment and enhance hierarchical authority, thus precluding an individualism that would lead to heterodoxy, relativism, and finally apostasy. Conciliar governance waned, and clerical authority in local settings became a mere base upon which rested the centralized power of the pope.

It was a difficult time to keep both faith and intellectual integrity afloat. Both required a certain level of confidence, and in both spheres such confidence was on the defensive. Scientific circles were recognizing the loss of certainties. Intellectuals grasped for new ways to interpret an unmanageable profusion of empirical evidence, to make meaning of collapsing structures of knowledge. The ideas of contingency—that political and social relationships and the construction of knowledge were not random developments (as the Darwinists insisted) but the deliberate actions of an external interpretive element, i.e., God, which would render meaning out of what seemed paradoxical—were failing. Both Church and State wanted objectivity. For the Church, a clear access to a rational faith that built on the evidence of God in the external world seemed the only path to moral (and perhaps temporal) authority. The State demanded unchallenged positive realities, cleansed of all metaphysical underpinnings and conclusions, which could justify its claim to governance.

Many struggled either to eliminate the tension generated by these polarizing forces or to resolve it. Some of those who thought to eliminate the tension found a happy solution in the dichotomization of intellectual matters into two distinct and separate compartments, leaving their intellectual work out of their religious beliefs and their private beliefs out of their public work. Such, like Louis Pasteur (1822–1895), were able to pass under the radar of suspicion, both from political watchdogs and religious overseers. Those who sought resolution to the tension were authorized by a papal mandate (the encyclical *Aeterni Patris*, 1879) to do so by means of the scholastic methods issuing from the work of the thirteenth-century Angelic Doctor, Thomas Aquinas. Leo XIII's advocacy of Thomism made Aquinas's scholastic method the Catholic philosophical position *de rigeur*. Among those who sought to resolve the tension were the modernists who, with their apparent willingness to challenge religious claims that were clearly incompatible with contemporary discoveries, defied the prevailing neo-Thomism until their suppression in 1907.[1]

There was another alternative, one that, instead of elimination or resolution, called for a methodology that juxtaposed the tensions and held them together in a careful equilibrium that yielded neither to positivist reductionism nor to religious authoritarianism. Those who sought this third way found inspiration in the scientific and metaphysical reflec-

---

1. Such claims, as we shall see, included the ability of natural reason to extend to supernatural knowledge; the transparent historical reality of biblical events; and the subordination of the individual to the dictates of an elite *magisterium*.

tions of Blaise Pascal (1623–1662), a pre-Enlightenment French scientist and mathematician, devout Catholic and Christian apologist. In Pascal they found a mentor who could guide them through the delicate relation between natural and supernatural knowledge, who could offer them a pattern of resistance to inappropriate papal authoritarianism, and who could justify their neo-apologetic efforts that were focused on the power of the individual.

## PARAMETERS OF NEO-PASCALIAN THOUGHT

As a young adult, Pascal had experienced a personal religious awakening within the context of Jansenism, a reform movement within the Catholic Church based on the Augustinian reflections of Cornelius Jansen. Jansenism encouraged a more rigorous personal spirituality and stressed man's need of divine grace. Pascal's exposure to Jansenism, combined with his creative and meticulous scientific thinking, led him to reflect deeply on the relationship between reason and revelation, between faith and science. Most notably, Pascal rejected the efficacy of natural revelation in conversion and sustained faith. This ran contrary to the course of natural theology, which bids any observer to discover truth—about God, about humans, about creation—through the study of nature. For Pascal, faith was grounded on an internal experience of revelation rather than an external one.

Among other things, Pascal addressed the uncertainty of all scientific theories. Though based on experimentally derived fact, each such theory could only serve as truth as long as every phenomenon conformed to its expression. The occurrence of even one contrary phenomenon could disprove the theory, and no scientific experiment, or even a lifetime of such experiments, could address every possible combination of components to any equation or theory. Thus, a level of uncertainty about science and its claims had to remain. Because of these ruminations, Pascal was often labeled a skeptic, and because he remained devout in the face of such skepticism, he was also labeled a fideist (one who abandons all reason in the workings of faith and makes a "blind leap" of belief).

Nevertheless, Pascal was neither a skeptic nor a fideist, despite the complaints of his opponents. For against the calculated claims of science, claims constructed by means of what he called an *esprit de géométrie*, Pascal posed the unqualified powers of the *esprit de finesse*, a way of knowing truth that did not rely on reason. Pascal argued that there were two different orders of knowledge, the one dealing with matter, and the other dealing with mind (agreeing with Cartesian thought). These two orders could not be collapsed into one unified theory.

Such ways of thinking were surprisingly consistent with the speculations of many late nineteenth-century thinkers, and their reflections resonated with Pascalian thought. Pascal had never entirely disappeared from view. The Jansenist community in Port-Royal published his works in 1670, and Voltaire, finding him a pleasant subject to vilify, kept his name in the public eye through his *Remarques sur les Pensées de Pascal* in 1734. Condorcet reissued the *Pensées* in 1776, an edition that served until an 1835 release by Frantin. Victor Cousin proposed a new edition in 1842, one which would return to the original manuscripts rather than to the Port-Royal version of them. Faugère published this in 1844, and further editions followed throughout the next sixty years, including editions by Vinet (1848), Sainte-Beuve (1848), Havet (1852), Droz (1886), Michaut (1896), and Brunschvicg (1904).[2] As a recognized literary genius, Pascal's popularity waxed through the nineteenth century, but as the century grew old it was not his literary prowess, but his epistemological claims that caught the imagination of young Catholic intellectuals.

For as the turn of the century neared, some scientists and intellectuals recognized with astonishment the inadequacies of positivistic science. Many found Pascal's skeptical attitude toward the certainty of knowledge relevant to the waning nineteenth century's awareness that scientific knowledge was receding in absolute terms faster than discovery and understanding could progress. Very little was as germane to the discourses of the *fin-de-siècle* as were ideas about human nature, its origin and destiny, the power of reason, the role of faith in public life, the value of "proof," the possibility of absolute knowledge, and, most interestingly in view of the gritted-teeth optimism of the positivist mentality, the inexorable condition of human misery.

Pascal also offered a radically different perspective of the human experience, a perspective that had been lost to rationalist conceit during the Enlightenment years, particularly under the piercingly derisive comments of Voltaire. Contemporary historian Lucien Goldmann called that perspective tragic, but we shall see that it is anything but tragic. Nevertheless, it was certainly a perspective deeply incompatible with the relentlessly optimistic claims of late nineteenth-century positivistic sci-

2. Hubert, *Pascal's Unfinished Apology*, 27.

ence and the entrenched belief in the human experience of unremitting progress.

## THE PASCALISANTS

Throughout the second half of the nineteenth century, intellectuals of every ilk were finding Pascalian thought increasingly stimulating. This was due in large measure to new editorial reviews of the original Pascalian manuscripts, particularly the *Pensées*, and their appropriation by a variety of authors, most notably Victor Cousin, who popularized many of his ideas. By the end of the century, however, a small group of Catholic intellectuals were rallying around Pascalian thought in the hopes of deriving from it an intellectually compelling apologetic and a clerically acceptable alternative to the rigors of neo-Thomism.

The work of these Pascalisants, as Victor Giraud, editor of the *Revue des deux mondes* names them (or "disciples of Pascal" as another described), can be found most intensely expressed in the years between two key papal encyclicals, *Providentissimus Deus* (1893) and *Pascendi* (1907). The former focused on the role and authority of scripture, which had become a key battleground in Catholic epistemological controversies and an entrée to the threatening possibilities of dissenting thought. The latter summarized and condemned the liberal threat of modernism, an effort to reconcile Christianity with the methods and ideas of the modern world. The first encyclical set the parameters within which the dialogue between science and faith could continue; the latter closed the door on dissenting compromises.

Pascalisants worked out their thoughts primarily in a handful of the many journals being produced at the end of the century. Certain of these journals were more conducive to heterodox thought than were others. Four of these journals—*Revue de philosophie, Revue des questions scientifiques, Revue des deux mondes*, and *Annales de philosophie chrétienne*—were particularly amenable, for a time, to the works of these authors. We will focus on three of these authors, three whose work is most prolific and most closely tied to Pascalian thought: Pierre Duhem, Maurice Blondel, and Lucien Laberthonnière. The journals, along with the key books written by the Pascalisants during this period, will illuminate our inquiry into the discourse of these men who strove to remain Catholic in name and in spirit while exploring avenues of intellectual freedom.

While it is not hard to contextualize the efforts of these neo-Pascalians within the dynamics of Church dialogue, we should not overlook the secular milieu within which they worked. Each of these writers was active politically and each was an academic product of and participant in the work of elite secular institutions. We will take a closer look at the educational world in order to understand the discourses that shaped their arguments. As academicians, they needed to contribute professionally to their fields in ways that would garner the respect of a largely unsympathetic audience. As apologists, they spoke to two audiences: one secular and political, their academic and literary colleagues; and one ecclesiastical, their religious superiors and fellow Catholics. Every apologist seeks both to communicate dogma persuasively to an unsympathetic listener while simultaneously satisfying the guardians of the doctrine he or she promulgates. I make no attempt to gauge the success of their persuasive abilities; whether their apologetic efforts actually won anyone over is beyond the scope of this study. We will, however, make a careful examination of the arguments they found most compelling and the reception of those arguments in their religious circles. All of them emphasized method before substance, the hermeneutic of the individual over the mandates of the hierarchy, and the inaccessibility of faith by means of reason alone. Neo-Pascalians countered the loss of the contingency argument, found primarily in natural theology, with a focus on an inner contingency, that of the individual's need to explain his or her experience of life.

Pierre Duhem (1861–1916) was one of France's most brilliant theoretical physicists and prolific scientific writers. He was also a *Catholique avant tout*, a devout Catholic who refused to hide his spiritual piety, his loyalty to the Roman Catholic Church, or his Legitimist (pro-monarchy) leanings. These overt predilections cost him career advancement, but nothing prevented him from contributing notably to the fields of thermodynamics, electricity, and magnetism; he also wrote extensively on the philosophy and history of science. A graduate of one of France's premier academies, the École Normale Supérieure (ENS), Duhem went on to teach at universities in Lille, Rennes, and then Bordeaux. Duhem, who identified himself as a scientist, not a metaphysician or apologist, nevertheless incorporated Pascalian thought throughout his work. One of his colleagues described Duhem's Pascalian passion thus: "He never stopped appealing to the example of Pascal, never gave a lecture, never wrote a chapter, without citing the *Pensées*..."[3] That such a notable figure in the French scientific academy could integrate Pascalian thought into all his work testified both to its usefulness to his scientific philosophy and its profile in the French intellectual community.

Duhem's work will show us the philosophical nuances Pascalian thought brought into scientific inquiry. With Pascal, Duhem insisted on the careful separation of physics from metaphysics; Duhem brought in a discussion of the inability of mechanical theories to demonstrate the symbolic nature of true scientific claims. He made repeated use of Pascal's theory of orders to differentiate between epistemological methodologies (natural and supernatural) and to demonstrate the mere theoretical status of the knowledge produced by science. Duhem reiterated Pascal's rejection of the efficacy of natural theology, thus also rejecting neo-Thomist principles, and also used Pascal to cast doubt on the scientific status of historical studies, pointing out the ways that they too demanded a hermeneutic.

Maurice Blondel (1861–1949) was a highly regarded French philosopher who, while linked by many to the modernist movement, rejected that movement's reliance on historical criticism and the redefinition of orthodoxy. Another graduate of the ENS, Blondel's best-known work, *L'Action: essai d'une critique de la vie et d'une science de la pratique* (1893), was also his thesis. From his youth, Blondel had aspired to reintroduce Christian thought as a valid intellectual option to those in the secular academic world who had discarded it. In his thesis, which was first rejected because of its suspiciously nonphilosophical subject matter (human action rather than human thought), Blondel explored the nature of human will and desire and the full integration of reason and religion in the expression of that nature. Blondel drew heavily on Pascalian discourse about human nature and teleology, finding in his philosophical predecessor's reflections on the antinomies of human existence (what we are versus what we wish to be) the key to his own arguments about human destiny. He also made extensive use of Pascal's case regarding the properly delimited role of natural reason in the human effort to believe in supernatural revelation.

Lucien Laberthonnière (1860–1932), French priest, philosopher, and editor of one of France's most widely distributed journals of Catholic philosophy, *Annales de philosophie chrétienne*, was a graduate of the

---

3. Martin, *Pierre Duhem*, 59.

University of Paris. A member of the Order of the Oratory, Laberthonnière was especially interested in ecclesiastical authoritarianism and its deadening effect on genuine Catholic spirituality. He was convinced that the heavy burden of clerical elitism and the parallel diminution of lay participation in matters of faith made spiritual vitality impossible. For Laberthonnière, the individual was key to the revitalization of the Church, and any system that bypassed the individual's own experiences of faith and revelation was doomed to fail. Thus, Laberthonnière made careful use of Pascal's emphasis on inner reality versus objective truth as the source of authority.

Even more than Blondel, Laberthonnière is often most closely associated with the modernist movement and he suffered more than any of the others in the outcome of the *Pascendi* encyclical. Nevertheless, he rejected modernism's skepticism regarding the historicity of scripture, and defended Christian history by making use of the Pascalian definition of revelation as an inner knowledge. Pascal's insistence that certain knowledge only comes when the human spirit moves past the point of reason's effectiveness informed Laberthonnière's efforts to circumvent what he perceived to be stultifying religious tyranny.

Many others found Pascalian thought useful for a variety of intellectual arguments. Writers as diverse as Henri Poincaré (non-Catholic scientist) and Ferdinand Brunetière (literary critic, journalist, editor, and later Catholic convert), among many others, found Pascalian thought an inspiration in their endeavors to understand and interpret contemporary philosophical, scientific, and spiritual developments. They, along with Duhem, Blondel, and Laberthonnière, have been addressed in many intellectual histories. These include most notably the works of Donald Miller, Stanley Jaki, R. N. D. Martin, and Armand Lowinger on Duhem; Alec Vidler, Darrell Jodock, Lester Kurtz, and Harvey Hill on the modernists (including Laberthonnière and Blondel); and Harry Paul, Gerald McCool, and John McManners on the larger issues of the relationship between science and religion in late nineteenth-century France. Darrell Jodock has brought together a powerful series of essays on Catholicism and modernity, which together carefully position the conflict in the political, philosophical, academic, social, and theological discourses of the time. There is, however, no mention of Pascal or his influence in these essays.

Dorothy Eastwood has contributed an excellent study of Pascal's relation to modern French thought. She, and the others insofar as they touch on Pascalian ideas, argue for the relevance of Pascalian "skepticism" about science, of his focus on the individual personality, and of his apologetic methodology to late nineteenth-century experience. None of these historians, however, has explored the relationship between neo-Pascalian thought, the narrow imperatives of Catholic authoritarianism, and the dynamics of Third Republic politics.

Pascalisants recognized that reliable knowledge about the moral order and human society could only come from a true interpretation of the human individual. Such a hermeneutic could not, however, be subject to the methods and purposes of rationalism, whether that rationalism was found in religious neo-Thomism or positivistic science, because reason alone failed to deliver authentic knowledge about God, the self, and the human community. Reason alone, the Pascalisants would argue, was a dead end, and both the sterility and attrition of Church life and the moral ambiguities and scientific disillusionments of secularism testified to its futility. Pascal, dangerous as his Jansenist connections made him, offered a way to circumvent the religious and scientistic absolutism of their day. Pascal's orthodox yet challenging expressions of faith gave these intellectuals avenues of Catholic non-cooperation in their relationship with the Church. Pascal's scientific prowess and philosophical depth gave them mental structures on which to build their own theories of order differentiation. And Pascal's deep spiritual faith gave them resources with which to resist the demythologization of the skeptics and the modernists. Nevertheless, *Pascendi's* closed door made such creative perceptions nearly impossible.

# 2

# A *Fin-de-Siècle* Scaffolding

Each of the intellectuals under consideration wrote under highly charged social, political, and religious conditions. These writers were born in the early 1860s, reaching an age of awareness just as the Second Empire fell apart, and their worldviews were shaped by crisis and reconstruction, by political and social uncertainties. Just as Karl Popper's falsification theory of scientific knowledge makes positive theoretical proofs impossible, so it would be beyond the scope of any historian to state unequivocally that any particular event or current of discourse had no measurable effect on the thoughts or actions of any historical figure. Nor should we assume that any thoughts or actions were merely reactive. Nevertheless, we need to realize that the currents of historical circumstance in some measure contributed to the emphases each intellectual makes. The intellectuals under examination were more than nominal Roman Catholics; they were men whose passion could be found in their religious convictions and whose scholarly labors were geared toward the reconciliation of those convictions with the transitional times in which they lived.

In describing the political temper of *fin-de-siècle* France, we need to focus on the threats—perceived or actual—made against traditional Roman Catholic perceptions of moral order and claims to authoritative truth. Most of these gauntlets were thrown down in the intellectual arena, and the increasingly antagonistic relationship between the Church and the Republic often made scholarly success a tumultuous affair. The authors we will be examining were the last products of the mid-nineteenth-century Catholic educational privileges granted by the 1850 Falloux Law (which permitted the Church greater involvement in primary and secondary education), and their matriculation in secular schools of higher education introduced them to intellectual and religious challenges unique to their generation. These pressures generated multiple apologetic efforts by Catholic traditionalists (expressed in neo-Thomism), by modernists, and by the Pascalisants. Political challenges were complicated for these intellectuals by the Vatican's affairs of state and its machinations, which in turn were triggered in part by the actions of secular governments and by the epistemological discourses current at the time. In these discourses, lingering positivists with hardened mid-nineteenth-century certainties wrestled for legitimacy with forward-thinking scientists and philosophers who were imagining a world with more paradox. In order to understand the concerns and proposed solutions of the Pascaliants, each of these issues needs to be described in full.

## THE MARGINALIZATION OF CATHOLICISM

Whatever socio-political vision lay beneath the madness and myth of the French Revolution remained buried for the greater part of the nineteenth century. It was "a great event which lay at the back of all nineteenth century reflections on religion, politics and society."[1] Condorcet, Mirabeau, Marat, and Danton, along with their partners in dismantling royal structures of privilege and excess, aspired to something that was seemingly beyond their reach. Though historiographical interpretations about the causes and results of the Revolution are prolific, it remains undisputed that the fullness of political reform, as imagined at the time, was aborted. The muse of republicanism bided her time, whispering memories and prophecies throughout the Terror, the Directory, the Empire, the Restoration, and the July Monarchy. She awakened briefly during a few short years of republican striving after the upheavals of 1848, but was quickly silenced again by Louis-Napoleon's coup d'état in 1851 and subsequent imperial reign of nearly two decades.

Not until Prussia's invasion and France's humiliating defeat in 1870 did the republican muse stir herself, and even then she could only do so disguised as a temporary fix of the imperial collapse while the monarchists could resolve their differences and place someone on the throne. Nevertheless, temporary became permanent. Adolphe Thiers (a long-time political statesman, Orléanist, and the first elected executive

---

1. Wilson, *God's Funeral*, 57.

of the newly-formed Third Republic) kept a tight grip on the Republic in its first years, making possible a number of elections whereby vacancies in the Assembly were filled in large measure by republicans. Even so, republicanism came in many flavors, and finding a consensus that would bear the weight of so many differences, from far-left Radicals to bourgeois centrists, was neither easy nor quick. Monarchism, in a variety of forms, festered and nagged through most of the 1870s, and it was not until 1877's elections that the French roundly defeated monarchists and fully legitimized the republican cause. More than eighty years after the first movement of Revolution, the ideals of reform, republicanism, and secularization began to incarnate themselves again in democratic structures.

But the monarchists continued to hope, and this seemingly unquenchable hunger for royal restoration infused all relations between republican leaders and Catholics with suspicion and rancor. Though the Bourbon heir, the Comte de Chambord, was gone from the scene by 1883, the other pretender to the throne, the Orléanist Comte de Paris, remained through the dwindling years of the century as a faint reminder of an *ancien régime* that had afforded certain moral guarantees that, to many, seemed lost forever. Monarchist yearnings, despite their increasing futility and the simultaneous social castigation that, in some circles, accompanied such leanings, lingered long in many Catholic homes and conversations.

In the last decades of the nineteenth century, the French government was a veritable revolving door of leadership and ministries as Radicals, Opportunists, and moderates sought both to define themselves and understand their positions vis-à-vis the shifting sands of social reform and cultural innovation that took hold of the French imagination. The fractured political scene made dissatisfaction for some of the people all of the time inescapable. Nothing could appease the spirits of nostalgia and discontent bred by such wildly diverse groups as frustrated Catholic royalists and emerging socialist fermenters. The constant changes in coalitions and cabinets fractured the republican façade. In the late 1880s, many die-hard monarchists and some old Bonapartists hoped that General Georges Boulanger could restore an authoritarian government that would make France safe from the Radical rabble. The threat of a coup d'état dissipated even as it presented itself, ending with Boulanger's flight and a quick scattering of his followers.

Nevertheless, for a non-event it lingered mightily in the psyches of French republicans whose suspicions about Catholic loyalties had been largely proved true, echoing their earlier betrayal of the Second Republic when they had so overwhelmingly supported the Bonapartist takeover.[2] Though in the wake of the Boulanger affair the Opportunists retained power and did so with greater stability than ever before, hostility for authoritarianism in all its forms became part and parcel of French republicanism in a far deeper way. The right, however, hungrier than ever for authoritarian certainties, assumed the strident spirit of aggressive politicking, vitriolic protests, and pro-military support.[3]

This divisive mentality continued to exacerbate relations between the political leadership and this rising right, most of whom were Catholics. Though the intellectuals under review in this study were not all monarchists, they were all high-profile Catholics, and their work put forward strong arguments for the role of the Catholic faith in the resolution of the challenges facing their culture. Insofar as political mistrust infused the Republic's opinion of the Catholic community, republicans in leadership positions—whether governmental or academic—sought to hem in those who challenged their ideas of secularism. The efforts to laicize the educational system demonstrate this marginalization.

A major goal of the Third Republic was to raise up a new generation of French citizens, men and women who believed wholeheartedly in the Republic and were ready to assume positions of civic responsibility, including compulsory military service for men. Certainly, it was feared, the youth who continued to be fed Catholic sentiment in the nation's public schools were potentially unreliable participants in the system. The evidence of treasonous undercurrents, dragged into the open over and over again through a century of republican struggle, was too great to ignore.

In fact, many republicans in the latter part of the nineteenth century believed that the strife and suffering of the century behind them confirmed the theories of Auguste Comte (1798–1857), founder of positivism. Positivism, which we will examine more closely at a later point,

---

2. Louis-Napoleon had publicly declared his support for Pius IX's claim to Rome, a long-standing sore point for many republican French who believed French troops should not be used to prop up a religious establishment. France had been involved in the Italian peninsula since 1849, and troops were not brought home from Rome until the Prussian invasion in 1870.

3. Wright, *France in Modern Times*, 237.

had become, by this time, a system widely known throughout Europe. Though its rigid ideology had become muted by the last decade of the century, still its principles of human progress and the sequential rejection of earlier ways of knowing—from theological to metaphysical and finally to positive/scientific—retained their appeal, particularly to the leaders of the Third Republic, many of whom were scientists in their own right.[4] According to positivist thought, civilization needed to push past the theological and mystical/metaphysical nonsense of earlier generations and find more solid ground on which to establish the strength of a nation. That solid ground was the certain knowledge afforded by scientific methods. Yet society had not yet managed to loose itself from the shackles of theology and metaphysics, and worse, it persisted in passing them on, most effectively through the school systems.

In 1850, before Louis-Napoleon abandoned all pretense of republicanism, he had allowed the Assembly to pass the Falloux Law proposed by the Catholic constituency. The Falloux Law made possible a resurgence in Catholic faith by establishing a parallel system of Catholic secondary schools, the *collèges*, schools that became highly popular among the burgeoning bourgeois, whether Catholic or no, because of the quality of education and the inculcation of a reliable moral foundation. The Falloux Law also granted Catholic orders greater freedom of involvement in the public primary schools, going so far as to require religious education classes.

It never ceased to rankle the left that the Catholic Church continued to exercise such a dominant influence over the minds of France's youth. By allowing the Catholics to keep a tight grip on the national educational systems, republicans felt they were condoning the Catholic claim to moral authority. By the early 1880s, once the Republic was securely in place, republicans were ready to remedy this situation, and Jules Ferry was the man to do it. Under his sponsorship and over a period of several years, the National Assembly led a crusade against Church involvement in the public school system—revoking the rights of religious orders to teach in public schools, eliminating the religious education requirements, and repealing the university status of Catholic higher educational institutions. In place of religious education, students were required to

---

4. These included Paul Bert, physiology; Marcelin Berthelot, chemistry; Charles de Freycinet, engineering; Paul Painlevé, mathematics; and Émile Combes and Georges Clemenceau, medicine. See Paul, "The Debate," 300.

take civics courses. Such actions ignited even greater animosity between Catholic authorities and their republican antagonists, an animosity that seeped into multiple levels of national and local experience.

The hostility between the republican politicians and the Catholic communities generated its own caricatures. While Catholics were not a homogeneous community, they became cardboard cutouts of the Republic's enemy.[5] Republicans, too, were a more diverse group than the adversarial positions would allow, yet they managed to assume a near-religious posture of their own. Unwilling to be satisfied with a merely secular public order, republicans developed an ideological credo of their own. Utterly convinced that devout Catholics were incapable of either national loyalty, faithful as they were to the directives of the Pope, or of objective thought, republicans became increasingly anticlerical. Their antireligious posture was linked inextricably to a dogmatic substitute for the authority that had been exercised by the Catholic Church. That substitute was science, positivistic science.[6] In tying itself so symbiotically to scientism, French republicanism could only view religious challengers as political challengers as well, a perspective that many Catholics did all they could to corroborate. Catholics, on the other hand, could only view "the politico-religious mythology of the establishment"[7] as a defiance of religious faith and an aggressive effort to exclude Catholics from the public sphere, a perspective that many republicans worked to reinforce. Many republicans came to believe in their own self-created religion, and their brazen confidence in the absolute power of science to grant progress and order in both public and personal spheres was easily translated by means of the laic laws of the 1880s to the generations of French citizens coming into roles of civic responsibility. "The reverence once accorded to the pronouncements of theologians was now revived, but transferred to those of scientists, and from 'science' something resembling a new 'religion' was born."[8] Out of this conceit, the State not

---

5. As Maurice Crosland points out, there were gradations of Catholicity that provoked lesser and greater hostilities in French circles. A Catholic *avant tout* was a Catholic who aggressively infused his or her public work with religious ideologies; others, equally devout, practiced more discretion and consequently faced less antagonism. See Crosland, *Science under Control*, 197.

6. For more information on the irreligious positions of republican leadership during this period, see Acomb's *The French Laic Laws*.

7. Paul, "The Crucifix and the Crucible," 202.

8. McManners, *Church and State in France*, 16.

only took over education, but removed the Church from control of poor relief, permitted divorce, appropriated burial rituals, claimed Church property, and established new holidays.⁹

Anticlericalism, however, was not born under the watch of the Third Republic. Late nineteenth-century hostility to organized religion had a long history to build on. John McManners suggests that this hostility existed even before the Revolution (as many of the Enlightenment writers made evident), and that that violent upheaval and its clerical resistance had merely calcified the opposition. The clergy's role as moral police and its usurpation of authority over the family, particularly evident during the nineteenth century in its influence on women, all served to instill a silent societal resentment toward clerical superiority that had only been kept in check by kings and emperors who recognized the value of the Church in maintaining the social order that kept them in place.¹⁰

Nor was anticlericalism restricted to the educational sphere. The tenuous international relationships of the end of the century were also exacerbated by the role of the Church. In search of a measure of security, France engaged in high-profile diplomatic negotiations intended to compensate for the isolation it felt in the face of European power struggles. Many of these international dialogues were complicated by the ongoing Roman Question. Though Rome's status as the capital of a united Italy was secure by 1871, the claims of the Vatican to territorial sovereignty festered, not to be resolved until the Lateran Treaty of 1929. In the years after France's 1870 abdication of its role as protector of the Papal States, many French Catholics mourned their loss and lobbied for a renewed French interest in their recovery. The Vatican became a symbol of diplomatic suspicion on both sides of the republican-Catholic divide as well as a pawn in the larger international affairs around it. Otto von Bismarck's interest in the affairs of the Roman Catholic Church confused French republican attitudes toward the Vatican. Surely a Protestant nation could care nothing about the pope's temporal authority, and Bismarck's *Kultur* wars certainly had not endeared him to the papacy. Yet by the mid 1880s, Bismarck was courting the pope in hopes of gaining Catholic votes against a democratic order in Germany, and the pope enjoyed this

---

9. Acomb, *The French Laic Laws*, 193–207.
10. McManners, *Church and State in France*, 14.

diplomatic role, viewing his position as "the grand international arbiter."[11] Papal cooperation with Germany made France even more nervous.

As late as 1892, French publications were releasing articles that argued that the pope was still playing the diplomatic field with the singular goal of recovering temporal power. The arguments included charges that the pope's unrelenting efforts to press the Vatican's case for restoration of the Papal states had caused Italy to seek military alliances in the event that some nation—perhaps France—would intervene on the pope's behalf. All this once again churned up, within the Catholic community, nostalgia for the monarchy: "If the Count de Chambord had reigned, he would have restored the temporal power [of the Vatican]."[12] More than a decade after the Republic had secured political power, monarchism needled the republican ranks, and clearly that monarchism was Catholic driven. The Roman Question, as trifling as it may seem in view of the larger national and international affairs of the day, remained within French political and cultural discourses as an ongoing example of Catholic interference in the work of the Republic.

While the Republic argued about the perceived political threat posed by the Vatican, many Vatican leaders themselves argued about the perceived political threat posed by its own members, the Pascalisants among others, who "betrayed" the goals and methods of Catholic traditionalists. These traditionalists, many of whom called themselves "integralists," found the multiple threats at the end of the century to be of one piece. Political, social, moral, and religious authority was a single tightly woven fabric, and any loose thread jeopardized the integrity of the whole. Rome was preeminent, and from its authority, the integralists argued, would issue the directives that could keep the faithful committed and compel the unfaithful to recognize and submit to its moral supremacy. While the Vatican argued for the restoration of the Church as the social and moral arbiter of truth, the Pascalisants, as we shall see, placed the responsibility for that discernment on the individual. Devout Catholics that they were, they remained convinced that the pursuit of truth would lead the individual back to the Church, but that this process

11. de Voqüé, "Affaires de Rome," 826.

12. "Si le comte de Chambord eût régné, il l'eût restauré, lui, le pouvoir temporel." Benoist, "La France et le Pape Léon XIII," 425. Benoist's article dispelled these papal-political fears and concluded with a shrewd observation that the pope did not want France to restore Rome, but that the pope wanted France itself.

began not with the authority of the Church but with the autonomy of the human soul. The Roman Question was more than a political conundrum; it was also a methodological challenge to those who recognized the role of volition.

The period of our inquiry experienced the peak of this ideological warfare. Public discourse about the proper role of the Church in the governance of the State (and the involvement of the State in the governance of the Church) filled popular journals and occupied much of the legislators' time in debate. By the 1880s, republicans were free to express the fullness of their resentment, and they worried the Catholic position until, with the Law of Separation in 1905, they permanently expelled the Catholic Church from any formal tie to the Republic. As we consider Blondel's philosophy of action and his defense of Tradition, Duhem's provoking thoughts about the nature of knowledge, and Laberthonnière's call to an absolute truth, we need to recognize that they wrote in defense of Catholic faith as a posture of authentic knowing that could both inform State strategy, which had lost its moral bearing, and revitalize the Catholic community, which had succumbed to vacuous theology and a lack of genuine devotion. The Republic worked to restrict such opinions to the private life, eliminating them from the public sphere. And, as we will see, their defense was equally repugnant to Catholic traditionalists, to whom the Pascalisant approach suggested anti-authoritarian individualism.

By the early years of the twentieth century, Émile Combes (premier from 1902–1905), and the anticlerical crusade against the Church that he set in place effectively disentangled the State from Church involvement in every level of civil order. Henceforth, a Catholic identity no longer posed such an immediate political threat and republican hostilities consequently waned in the subsequent generations.

## THE ROMAN CATHOLIC EXPERIENCE AND RESPONSE

Surely the century of losses and transitions experienced by the Roman Catholic Church during the late eighteenth and nineteenth century rivals its most remarkable accounts of tumultuous change in the Great Schism of the eleventh century and the Protestant Reformation and religious wars of the sixteenth and seventeenth centuries. From the Civil Constitution of the Clergy in 1790 and the Concordat of 1802 through the escalating conflicts with Italian nationalists in the early 1800s to the expulsion from Rome in 1848 and final loss of the papal states in 1870, the papal throne had been forced to relinquish whatever hegemonic shreds of temporal power it had left.

Its political losses were nothing, however, compared to the diminution of its cultural and spiritual authority, an authority that had been waning for more than a century. Ralph Gibson points out the ways that the Council of Trent (1545–1563) and its subsequent reforms had already been alienating the laity long before the papal rejection of the Civil Constitution of the Clergy severed so many ties. Tridentine faith was primarily penitential and punitive. Catering to the initiated, the elites and intellectuals, it was incomprehensible at the popular level, and offered a repressive rather than inspiring message, one of clerical distinction and lay worthlessness.[13] With its new commitment to purify Catholic rituals and practices from the many popular superstitions and semi-pagan cultural traditions and its emphasis on correct theology and morality, particularly in view of the Jansenist challenges of the seventeenth and eighteenth centuries, Tridentine theology led to a sense of frustration and discord among many nominal believers that easily fed into the chaos of the Revolution.

In the ensuing confusion and divisiveness, the Revolution also estranged many priests from their bishops and people from their priests. Napoleon's Concordat was an Erastian solution to the problem, but did little to help mend the Church's internal fractures. Gibson goes on, however, to point out that in the years following the Revolution, more and more clergy came from the lower classes and thus had greater rapport with the common people. Such a demographic shift created a clerical class with far fewer educational advantages and an increasingly unsophisticated attitude.

Eugen Weber describes the developing antipathy between the people and the hierarchy's morals, the utilitarian nature of the rites and sacraments, the growing awareness of the Church's focus on the upper classes, and the declining popularity of priesthood as a vocation. Yet in the 1870s, ninety-eight percent of France's thirty-six million citizens called themselves Catholic.[14] What was there to complain about? Maurice Larkin points out the difficulties involved in understanding the historical definition of Catholic membership. What had been a matter

---

13. Gibson, *Social History of French Catholicism*, 15, 24.
14. Weber, *Peasants into Frenchmen*, 339–74.

of course ever since the Revocation of the Edict of Nantes in 1685—a unity of identity between nation and religion—was by the 1880s long undone. Nominal Catholicism was all about social participation, evident in stage-of-life rituals and educational choices.[15] In certain areas of the country, namely the northwest and a diagonal strip that extended from the northeast to southwest, piety flourished, but for many the Catholic Church no longer offered the answers sought to such pressing issues as class suffering, the challenges to the family, and the seeming futility of long-established rituals in view of the greater success of new technologies. Industrialism with its rewards and reprisals spoke with an ever more vociferous voice, while the Church became increasingly more onerous in its demands and duties with fewer and fewer meaningful compensations. "As supernatural interpretations crumbled under the impact of materialism, and even more before the puritanical expurgations of the clergy, the basis for the belief itself, where simple minds made simple associations, also crumbled."[16]

A diminishing attendance at confession and Easter Mass, fewer marriages in the Church, and a growing enrollment in public schools meant one thing: attrition, a losing battle for the hearts and souls of the French people. All this was exacerbated by the Church's growing identification with the upper classes, which were still choosing Catholic schools and were more vested in the kind of stability and order that the Catholic Church promised.[17]

The fear of lay attrition was echoed in the decline of religious vocations. Members of orders had been ousted from their public roles in schools thanks to Ferry, but their disenfranchisement was nothing compared to the growing isolation of the secular clergy. Local priests had become the teachers' nemeses, making the vocation less appealing. Fewer and fewer men presented themselves for holy orders until, on the eve of the Separation, there was approximately one priest for every 740 practicing Catholics.[18]

One good priest in a rural setting might count for a lot, but many of the priests in the late nineteenth-century had little or no meaningful education. Seminaries were shockingly backward, as Ernest Renan

---

15. Larkin, *Religion, Politics and Preferment in France since 1890*, 5.
16. Weber, *Peasants*, 370.
17. Ibid., 360.
18. Ibid., 371.

(1823–1892), perhaps France's most infamous priest-in-training turned apostate, had experienced. They offered nothing in the way of science or current developments in philosophy, sociology, or psychology. According to Abbé Duchesne (1843–1922), Catholic priest and professor of ecclesiastical history at the Institut Catholique and later the director of the École des Hautes Études, the French episcopate was "composed of imbeciles" and French Catholic laypeople hardly knew there was a Bible. Seminary education was largely useless and included only the most superficial and arcane content.[19]

Duchesne's laments reflected the dire state of institutional Catholicism during the late nineteenth century in France. The brilliant piety of Thérèse of Lisieux (1873–1897), herself a representative of rural devotion, shone all the more brightly because of its rarity. Much more common were the jaded intellectuals, the hardened and desperate urban workers, the smartly smug Freemasons, and the confident and materialistic positivists. By the end of the nineteenth century, French Catholicism in many circles was indeed in very deep trouble.

Yet we not must underestimate the efforts made by Rome to stem what it took to be a tide of impiety. The nineteenth century was not only a century of tumult, but a century of fortification as well. The Church took several measures to counter the challenges to its authority. The sense of disequilibrium generated by political and social turmoil fed a hunger for spiritual security that only Rome seemed able to offer.[20] Religious Gallicanism, the ancient belief in the relative independence of French bishops from the authority of the Pope in matters pertaining to the administration of the Church in France, granted by the Four Gallican Articles of 1682, was effectively put to rest, and the loyalties of French Catholics were increasingly directed not to their local leadership but to Rome and the pope himself. Gerald McCool suggests that Rome's failure to retain hold of the political authority it had exercised in national governments provoked its decision to take a more hard line approach with the local churches and their leadership. "Rome intervened in almost every serious theological controversy during the nineteenth century and, in almost every case, the intervention was influenced by

---

19. O'Connell, *Critics on Trial*, 92–97.
20. Desan, *Reclaiming the Sacred*, 219.

the Church-state tensions."²¹ Ultramontanism, the assertion of papal authority over international Church affairs, flourished.

If the right hand of the Church elevated the authority of the pope, its left hand was busily rejecting the authority of the State, most especially in its increasing appropriation of the right to define and determine the progress of society. Innovative attempts to Catholicize the reforms initiated by the Revolution, such as Félicité Robert de Lamennais's goal of "baptizing the Revolution," had come to naught in the early decades of the century, in spite of his advocacy of ultramontanist spiritual authority. Pope Gregory XVI's 1832 encyclical, *Mirari Vos*, rejected Lamennais's call to popular sovereignty and reiterated papal temporal authority, called science "impudent" in its epistemological and social claims, and denounced the "liberalism and religious indifferentism" that plagued society. He followed that up with the 1834 encyclical, *Singulari Nos*, in which he "deplored the fact that, where the ravings of human reason extend, there is somebody who studies new things and strives to know more than is necessary, against the advice of the apostle."²²

Pius IX (1846–1878), who had for a time entertained ideas of political and liberal reform, took a sudden reactionary turn, understandably, perhaps, in view of his alarming experiences during the 1848 revolutions. In France, the economic distress of 1846–1847 triggered bourgeois anxieties and working-class rage. When French leaders of the Second Republic terminated the National Workshops (a relief system for the poor), workers revolted, validating bourgeois opinions of their instability. Archbishop Affre tried to intervene and reason with the revolutionaries, but was killed in the fray. His death convinced both the bourgeoisie and the Catholics that the working class and their radical compatriots were dangerous and in need of a strong hand. The fruit of this was a "de-Christianization of the masses and a re-Christianization of part of the bourgeois."²³ At this same time, two years of exile (from November 1848 to August 1850) under the Roman Republic, Italy's early attempt at national unity, succeeded in convincing Pius IX that liberalism was of the devil. From that point on, he worked tirelessly to eradicate the notions of democracy and the claims of modernity from both the inner workings of the Church and from the political structures of Catholic nations.

21. McCool, *Catholic Theology in the Nineteenth Century*, 25–26.
22. *Papal Encyclicals*, vol. 1, 249–51.
23. Moody, *Church and Society*, 147.

Pius IX worked carefully to augment the growing ultramontanist movements. In 1853, he wrote *Inter Multiplices*, calling for the recognition that "This chair [of Peter] is the center of Catholic truth and unity, that is, the head, mother, and teacher of all the Churches to which all honor and obedience must be offered." "They [the faithful people of France] should execute whatever the See itself teaches, determines, and decrees."[24] Three years later, in *Singulari Quidem*, a missive to the Austrian Church, he condemned rationalism as "a spreading disease" and insisted that "Faith bases itself not on reason but on authority." "We must also believe, in addition, that there is nothing else to believe and to seek once we have found and believed what was taught by Christ."[25]

Pope Pius IX's most notable efforts to squelch liberal movements included the encyclical *Quanta Cura* (1864) and its Syllabus of Errors, a list of eighty errors being promulgated in political, educational, and cultural arenas. In this statement, the papacy clearly declared the authority of the Catholic Church over "nations, peoples, and their sovereign princes." It rejected naturalism, that "impious and absurd principle," and called the right of liberty of conscience an "insanity." Communism and socialism were equally excoriated.[26] This assertion of religious authority over the political order was matched by the pope's claim to unchallenged spiritual authority, culminating in the First Vatican Council of 1870 and the declaration of papal infallibility in all matters of faith and dogma. Dissenting French bishops, such as Félix-Antoine-Philibert Dupanloup of Orléans (1802–1878), felt that such a declaration served to place authority in the institution and remove it from scripture.[27] It also presumed the essential spiritual and temporal ignorance of the common person who was no longer given permission to judge truth for him or herself. "Do not reason, decide nothing, content yourself with being docile and humble."[28]

Pope Leo XIII continued Pius IX's work of enhancing papal authority, extending his reach into affairs such as theological education that had traditionally been left to local bishops. His 1879 encyclical, *Aeterni Patris*, made the Thomistic philosophical model required for

---

24. *Papal Encyclicals*, vol. 1, 315–18.
25. Ibid., 339–45.
26. Ibid., 381–85.
27. Tavard, "Blondel's *Action* and the Problem of the University," 154.
28. Dechamps, *L'Infaillibilité et le Concile Général*, 39.

all Christian philosophers. His 1888 encyclical, *Libertas*, addressed the growing political liberties throughout European societies, declaring them nothing but avenues to license were they granted without spiritual authority. Individuals who believed that their own will was the highest authority and that civil society could be grounded on the will of the majority, exercising its collective reason, were deceived and had paved "a road leading straight to tyranny."[29] Leo XIII was not disparaging democracy, merely insisting that "the Catholic doctrine be maintained as to the origin and exercise of power."[30]

These Vatican declarations, infused into a French religious culture that, as we have seen, felt it was fighting a rearguard action against the dispossession of all its traditional values—alliance with a monarchy that established a symbiotic relationship between spiritual and temporal authority over families, village life, and national order—contributed to the larger discourses of reactionary elitism and the shape of French citizenship and moral order.[31] Catholic intellectuals were painfully aware of the discrepancies between the nature of knowledge as proposed by secular education and the nature of knowledge accepted by the Church. While neo-Thomists insisted on incorporating and subsuming the former into the latter, modernists and Pascalisants sought a different kind of reconciliation, one that recognized the separate validity of scientific knowledge. This common goal, though pursued in two very different ways, would earn the Pascalisants the indiscriminate condemnation of *Pascendi*.

The century's Catholic story can be told another way, however. For despite the dechristianization of the Revolution, culminating decades of indifference,[32] and the authoritarian developments of Roman thought, the nineteenth century also witnessed a flowering of both intellectual advocacy and popular Catholic sentiment. Early nineteenth-century writers struggled to recapture the glory of traditionalism. Joseph de Maistre (1753–1821), Louis de Bonald (1754–1840), and Louis Bautain (1796–1867) all promoted the necessary role of the Church in politi-

---

29. Leo XIII, *Great Encyclical Letters*, 146.

30. Ibid., 162.

31. The increasingly dichotomous definitions—liberal and republican versus conservative and reactionary—eventually became the chasm into which flowed the acerbic arguments of the Action française.

32. Vovelle, *Revolution against the Church*, 6.

cal and social affairs because they believed that it alone could provide the common tradition necessary for the establishment of proper order. They sought to "reduce Christianity to faith, revelation, and historical tradition."[33]

The Marian miracles of the 1850s and 1860s with their consequent pilgrimages and ongoing injections of devotion renewed faith.[34] This kindled a return of the bourgeoisie to its Catholic roots, bringing a new intellectual flavor into the French circles. This return first became evident in the work of a variety of authors who embraced many of the ideals of Romanticism. A celebration of the common man, the criticism of urban society in favor of a more idyllic rural setting, the celebration of nature and a fascination with the past all fed into romantic reappropriations of Christian faith. François René de Chateaubriand captured this synthesis of Catholicism and Romanticism in his *Génie du Christianisme* (1802), an early nineteenth-century work that sustained several generations of bourgeois Catholic piety. Though this early revival waned as naturalism and positivism dispelled some of the mists of Romanticism, it later yielded a second flowering of Catholic piety.

This second renewal of devotion had a completely different feel to it. It issued not out of the hopes of restoration and renewal, as had Chateaubriand's work, but out of reaction against and the rejection of prevailing currents of scientific and irreligious thought. Thus the Catholic writers who captured this revival tended to be more anti-rational, mystical, and hostile to modernizing movements. They posited revelation against reason, tradition against discovery, and simplicity against complexity.[35] Such authors included poet and playwright Paul Claudel (1868–1955), poet and essayist Charles Péguy (1873–1914), novelist Paul

---

33. McCool, *Catholic Theology*, 35.

34. These Marian miracles had been preceded by a mission movement in the 1820s that had forcefully linked a popular Catholic faith to the monarchy. In this movement, carried by the enthusiasm of the restoration of the Bourbon king, participants went from village to village evangelizing and raising a cross in each village that often had a *fleur-de-lis* carved into it. Their mission canticle was: "Vive la France! Vive le Roi! Toujours en France, Les Bourbons et la Foi!" The violent eruption of rage at the onset of the July Monarchy, a civil disturbance during which many angry bourgeois tore down those crosses, contributed to the rise of the Bourgeois Monarchy and that social class's concessions to the utilitarian functions of the faith. See Phayer, "Politics and Popular Religion," 349.

35. Griffiths, *Reactionary Revolution*, 21.

Bourget (1852–1935), poet Paul Verlaine (1844–1896), and novelist J.-K. Huysmans (1848–1907).

Besides the renewal of the literary world, the second half of the nineteenth century also experienced a regeneration of Catholic thought in non-literary intellectual circles. Though Pope Leo XIII was not a liberal and continued his predecessors' rejections of such modern notions as freedom of the press and the rights of the individual conscience, his own bent for intellectual inquiry issued in a cautious encouragement of biblical and scientific research, philosophical renewal (as long as it corresponded to Thomistic thought), and social progress. His 1885 encyclical, *Immortale Dei,* directed the Church to "recognize in all truth that is reached by research a trace of the divine intelligence."[36] Between 1888 and 1900, five Catholic congresses were convened for the sole purpose of investigating the relationship between scientific discoveries and Catholic truth.

The rector of the Institut Catholique in Paris, Msgr. Maurice d'Hulst (1841–1896) argued in 1885 that the weakening of the faith was due in large measure to the sorry status of Catholic intellectual thought. In his judgment, those who were best educated in the philosophies and natural sciences were atheists. D'Hulst's solution, echoing Leo XIII's ambitions, involved the reinstatement of the Catholic mind at all levels of societal order, particularly in fields of science and their applications.[37]

Making a foray into a scientific/societal field, in 1891 Leo XIII released *Rerum Novarum,* an encyclical addressing the injustices of industrialism and advocating fair wages and trade unions. In a grand effort to reenter and recapture the political field, Leo XIII issued *Au milieu des sollicitudes* in 1892, encouraging French Catholics to abandon their royalism and embrace the Republic as a government capable of rendering justice and establishing necessary societal order. This *ralliement*, considered by many a matter of too little, too late, may have failed in its overt attempt to reinvest a Catholic voice in republican discourses, but it actually boosted the profile of moderate republicans and further diluted the abrasive monarchist clamoring.[38] We will have occasion to reexamine the *ralliement* later.

---

36. Leo XIII, *Great Encyclical Letters*, 128.
37. Paul, *Edge of Contingency*, 2.
38. Wright, *France in Modern Times*, 239.

Perhaps the oddest channel of Catholic renewal in French history was the contribution made by Charles Maurras (1868–1952) through his leadership of the Action française. While his time of greatest influence was in the years after our period of inquiry, his work at the end of the century begins to represent the tangled web of responses to the diverse philosophical and political pressures of the day. Maurras epitomized an amalgamation of attitudes: rationalist/positivist mingled with remnants of a strong appreciation of classical, Greco-Roman legacies; anti-Semitic, pro-Catholic, and anti-republican. In a twenty-first-century world, the mix sounds bizarre and illogical, but in Maurras, a literary critic and journalist, it perfectly embodied many of the longings of a frustrated generation of men and women, from whom time and transition were leeching all the dearest ideals of their heritage. Maurras's methods were wholly pragmatic, aimed entirely at the restoration of lost institutions, systems, privileges, and values. Such pragmatism is most evident in his relationship with the Catholic Church, for though Maurras was an atheist, he believed the Roman Catholic Church was indispensable to France's future. He stirred up a new zeal for Catholic identity, redefining it along the way, that refused to fight a rearguard action of defense and instead asserted the very notion that Catholic monarchism expressed the truest form of French nationalism. Eugen Weber points out that the longing for stability and a growing sense of meaninglessness that issued out of sterile scientific claims created a vacuum that Maurras' rhetoric filled. "Many people, tired of religious strife and parliamentary finagling, were looking for a force that could heal social and intellectual rifts and in some way discipline the national energies. The contemporary revival of interest in the Catholic Church appears as a result of the same reaction. It was part of a trend in favor of authority, hierarchy, and discipline, rather than a search for ultimate truth, which did not seem nearly so interesting."[39]

Maurras built on and extended the bloc of upper crust French society that had turned with increasing zeal to a sort of crusading Catholicism through the efforts of Louis Veuillot. Veuillot took over the editorship of *L'Univers*, a Parisian newspaper, in 1842 and used that platform to generate a new conservatism that denigrated any liberal or progressive element in French society, including republicanism and social or educational reform. Veuillot found allies in the Assumptionist

---

39. Weber, *Action Française*, 16.

Fathers, a Catholic order that raised its profile in the 1870s. Gordon Wright points out that their approach was anything but intellectual or rational. On the contrary, they promoted a religio-political order that was "mystical, emotional, fanatical." They were the ones who managed to place the guilt for the 1870 defeat on the nation, many of whose citizens paid for the building of Sacré Coeur as a penance.[40] Their publication, *La Croix*, afforded them a popular entrée into the homes of Catholics who were, perhaps, wondering what was left of their Catholic identity. In the fall out from the Dreyfus Affair, this radical right would find new structures in the Camelots du Roi, a pseudo-paramilitary group affiliated with the Action française and its nationalist proclivities. The fact that these disparate spirits of Catholicism were developing in the last decade of the nineteenth century and yet remained unchallenged by the Vatican until 1926 hints at the Vatican's internal appetite for the exercise of social power and its focus on the stemming of membership attrition rather than on the issues that concerned the Pascalisants—genuine Catholic renewal built on an intellectual grappling with the modern developments within scientific and philosophical circles.

## IMPRESSIONS AND INSTITUTIONS OF FRENCH INTELLECTUAL CULTURE

Having laid the table with all the place settings, such tangible, direct pieces of human history, we now turn to dinner conversations, a subject of much greater ambiguity and subjectivity. Who was talking about what? How possible is it really to give labels to individuals and trains of thought that were surely an amalgam of convictions and persuasions and suggestions and nuances?

What has become evident about late nineteenth-century France is the fervent quest for sources of moral order and political stability and the extreme claims made by diverse groups to have the answers. We have briefly considered Auguste Comte's positivist arguments and pointed out the ways that, though the details of the system had fallen away, the sense of confident empowerment that the system gave afforded powerful weapons against the reactionary forces of Catholicism, traditionalism, and royalism. Comte's *Course of Positive Philosophy*, received with great alacrity during the July Monarchy, gave Third Republic leaders the am-

---

40. Wright, *France in Modern Times*, 228.

munition they needed to justify exorcising religion from public policy. The careful accumulation of facts, the objective interpretation of laws, and the relentless rejection of supernatural speculation or reasoning became standard procedure in republican circles. All phenomena, positivists argued, should be managed according to strictly scientific practices, and the purer the application, the sooner the last vestiges of the metaphysical and theological handicaps would be eradicated and true happiness be attained.[41]

Naturalism, a corresponding extension of positivism, argued that nature expressed the whole of reality, and that any speculations beyond or outside of the realm of nature were irrelevant for the structuring of human thinking. Teleological models of human origin and destiny were deemed improper guides for human knowledge since they could be neither proved nor falsified and could provide no answers about cause or effect, the only genuine measurements of reality. Naturalism, more than positivism, became a prevalent attitude within circles extending beyond political/intellectual ones, largely through the naturalist writings of eminent authors who did their best to support the republican ambition. With Émile Littré's *Conservation, Révolution et Positivisme* (1852) and Hippolyte Taine's *Les Philosophes classiques du XIXème siècle en France* (1857), the groundwork for a naturalist movement in literature was laid. Naturalism invited the reader to understand human nature, society, and the course of history using scientific methodologies. The Goncourt brothers, Guy de Maupassant, Anatole France, J.-K. Huysmans and others created worlds in which science illuminated the human experience. Émile Zola could imagine, in his novel *Travail* (1901), a time when "at last religion was dead, with the last priest, saying the last mass, in the last church."

It was an ironic twist of fate that a young man who had diligently pursued the priesthood became a spokesman for the abandonment of traditional Catholic faith. Ernest Renan (1823–1892) discovered that a seminary education seemed to have no connection to the world as it was. It afforded no answers, no certainties that stood up under the tests of the day; it apparently did not even ask the right questions. Though Renan shied away from the positivist label, his journey from faith to agnosticism, from Catholicism to humanism, from God to Science made him positivism's poster boy. His two central works, *Vie de Jésus* (published in

---

41. Gay and Webb, *Modern Europe since 1815*, 638.

1863) and *L'Avenir de Science* (written in 1849 but not published until 1889), offered a reinterpretation of Christianity that omitted the supernatural element and substituted for it a religion of science.

And yet, just as positivism neared its triumph, undercurrents of something new stirred in both scientific and literary circles. Henri Bergson (1859–1941), French philosopher, began to explore spiritual dimensions within evolutionary structures; his *Essai sur les données immédiates de la conscience*, published in 1889, signaled a sea change that had been waiting its chance for some time. Bergson challenged the notion that intellectual thought, of any kind, could entirely capture or measure truth as found in life, experience, memory, feeling, and intuition. Novelist Maurice Barrès (1862–1923), with his *Le Culte du moi*, redirected thought to the self, to the immanent recesses of the human mind and heart; the symbolists (e.g., Mallarmé, Verlaine, Rimbaud, Laforgue), explored associations and intuitions, none of which was fair game for a realist, naturalist, or positivist. Paul Bourget's novel, *Le Disciple* (1889), which suggested that positivism was an inadequate source of moral knowledge, became enormously popular in its advocacy of traditional values, an influence that did not fail to gain the attention of the positivists. Harry Paul points out that Renan's *L'Avenir de Science*, gathering dust in manuscript form for more than forty years, was released as a positivist reaction to Bourget's novel.[42]

These ventures beyond the strictures of scientism were echoed in the work of scientists who began to toy with an abandonment of strict empiricism with its positivist conclusions. Henri Poincaré (1854–1912), French physicist and mathematician, began to explore the possibilities that scientific solutions and equations are no more than approximations of reality, not actual dimensions of reality. Actual reality cannot be determined without theory, and theory is a human appropriation and arrangement of "the facts." Another irritant was his insistence that intuition had a role to play in mathematics and the outworking of science.[43] In his later works, he contributed to Einstein's work on the theories of relativity and prepared the field for chaos theory and ideas of indeterminism. This rejection of the tidy boxes generated by strict positivism signaled for many Catholic intellectuals the end of science's claims to absolute truth and moral adequacy.

42. Paul, "The Debate," 324.
43. Eastwood, *Revival of Pascal*, 27–28.

Ferdinand Brunetière (1849–1906), literary critic and editor of *Revue des deux mondes,* reviewed Bourget's *Le Disciple* and expressed his suspicion that science's moral vision of endless human progress had imploded. By 1895, Brunetière was ready to argue that science was morally bankrupt and that Catholicism offered a fuller and more certain future than that of republican scientism. The field was wide open, and a variety of options presented themselves, including those of the Catholic traditionalists (integralists), the modernists, and the Pascalisants.

The evidence of the influence of both "old-school" positivists and a new spirit of openness to alternative ways of thought can be found in France's system of higher education and its focus on the debates about philosophy and epistemology. The university system at the end of the nineteenth century was still shaped largely by the work of the Revolution. The National Convention (1792–1795) had created several specialized schools to address the new nation's need for qualified leaders in engineering, education, military science, and more. The École Normale Supérieure and the École Polytechnique, two lasting institutions, joined earlier *grandes écoles* that had been established in the mid-eighteenth century by the throne, and the even older schools, such as the Collège de France and the Academy of Sciences.[44]

Conservatives in the early years of the Third Republic gained for the Catholics the right to establish their own university system, though the State reserved the right to grant degrees.[45] The five Catholic universities created in 1875—Paris, Lyons, Lille, Angers, Toulouse—and their quick establishment of scientific faculties (rather than theological) indicated the Church's concern for the management and production of "secular" knowledge, knowledge that would influence the course of government. Though the rights granted to these institutions were revoked by 1880, the five years of foundational work thrust Catholics into the academic world in new ways, drawing attention to the Church's renewed efforts in the academic world.

Joseph Moody describes the revamping of the university system after the French defeat of 1870. The Prussian success was attributed in large part to German models of education, and the decades after the fall of Sedan were years of organizing higher education around a scientific model. "They would replace the ethical neo-Kantianism that informed

---

44. Smith, *École Normale Supérieure and the Third Republic,* 6.
45. Moody, *French Education since Napoleon,* 92.

all teaching with an impersonal objectivity that admitted a single moral principle—the unity of science and democracy."[46] Nevertheless, as we have seen, just as the positivist mentality seemed to gain the upper hand, a counterculture was brewing in the depths of the university system, particularly in Paris.

In many ways, the burgeoning field of historical studies, a "new science" in the French university system, became a flashpoint for the conflict between positivist certainties and the growing uncertainty triggered by the loss of confidence in scientistic methodologies. William Keylor argues that the elimination of religion from public education had led to a vacuum that left France vulnerable to truth claims from hostile sources. Victor Duruy (Minister of Education, 1863–1869) had earlier addressed the need for a retelling of the French story, a focus on historical studies that told the glorious truth about France. While many of his initiatives failed, he did supervise the creation, under Napoleon III, of the École Pratique des Hautes Études, an institution devoted to the replication of German successes in scholarship.[47] The scientific model of doing history gained preeminence in the last two decades of the nineteenth century, particularly in the Sorbonne and the École Normale Supérieure.[48]

During the restructuring of the Sorbonne in the 1890s and the accompanying incorporation of the various free-floating faculties into a unified university system,[49] the thrust of the scientific method, beginning with the greater honor accorded the "hard sciences" (applied and theoretical) and the infusion of their methodologies into the "soft sciences" (including history, social science, literature, and philosophy), informed the faculties of every school.[50] Martha Hanna also recognizes the moral void left by the scientistic model and argues that neo-Kantianism became the republicans' philosophical alternative of choice. "Kant's emphasis on the moral obligation and—by extension—civic responsibility of citizens"[51] made possible the Republic's goal of infusing the educa-

---

46. Ibid., 114.

47. Keylor, *Academy and Community*, 25.

48. Ibid., 65.

49. The last autonomous school was the École Normale, which was absorbed in 1903. See Keylor, *Academy and Community*, 64.

50. Hanna, *Mobilization of Intellect*, 32.

51. Ibid., 34.

tional system with an epistemology that circumvented the randomness of scientistic naturalism.

Neo-Kantianism was especially pronounced at the École Normale Supérieure (ENS). The primary thrust of the ENS was to train teachers and fill the educational system with loyal republicans. Napoleon's reorganization of the University system had made room for a broader scholarly education that led to the ENS's reputation for educating the nation's intellectual elite. Robert Smith points out that, during the Third Republic, the *normaliens* gained both political and academic status and influence. They had become recognized "interpreters" of the quickly changing social order.[52] As philosophy interacted with scientistic presuppositions, the result was less of a fusion and more of a confusion. The antipositivist movement pushed through the cracks created by the Kantian questions about objectivity, and growing minorities within the university system voiced doubts about the preeminence of the scientific method.

The ENS (alma mater of both Maurice Blondel and Pierre Duhem) was one institution where the acceptability of philosophical dissent was most recognized.[53] The school had developed a tradition of broad liberalism, making room for a variety of opinions and positions.[54] Smith suggests that the infusion of scientism had certainly affected the course of the school's curriculum, but that "they could not eliminate the persistent and widespread Pascalian sensibility which hesitated to generalize about individuals and human affairs and which proceeded by intuition and an *esprit de finesse* rather than by geometric logic ... The priority and independence of the mind remained the central strand of Normale's intellectual tradition during the Third Republic."[55] Though the dominant sensibility at the ENS was republican, it was also generous. While the students were largely anticlerical, they were also tolerant of individual religious beliefs.[56] This suggests that by the turn of the century, spirituality was already becoming relegated to the personal, private sphere, and that institutional religion had lost a voice among the intellectual elite. As

---

52. Ibid., 17.

53. In the ongoing effort to streamline and systematize France's university system, the ENS was incorporated into the University of Paris, Laberthonnière's alma mater, in 1903. See Weisz, *Emergence of Modern Universities in France*, 283.

54. Smith, *École Normale Supérieure*, 64.

55. Ibid., 77–78.

56. Ibid., 92–93.

we examine the efforts of the Pascalisant intellectuals, their struggle to position themselves carefully in the shifting ideological ground of the academies becomes further complicated by the concurrent ecclesiastical challenges of acceptable intellectual freedom of inquiry and philosophical dissent. As we shall see, the Church's traditional posture of openness to philosophical systems was radically retracted as its authority was truncated. "In the nineteenth century, in [the Vatican's] assaults on every development in scientific knowledge, every glimmering of light shed in the field of biblical scholarship, every advancement of technical skill (it even issued condemnations of the electric light), the Vatican was the great powerhouse of reaction, posing very grave difficulties for those who wished to practise the Catholic faith without committing intellectual suicide."[57]

## THE INTELLECTUAL AND RELIGIOUS ENVIRONMENT OF NEO-PASCALIAN THOUGHT

In their introduction to the work of Maurice Blondel and his philosophical challenges to both scientism and Church authoritarianism, Alexander Dru and Illtyd Trethowan begin their story with the Revocation of the Edict of Nantes in 1685 and the long-standing inter-Catholic religious feuds of the seventeenth and eighteenth centuries. The Revocation served to bind more closely the Church/State relationship, and defined French identity as thoroughly Catholic. Dissent went underground, not merely in a political sense, but in a psychological sense as well. The Revocation had eliminated the possibility of being French while clinging to heterodox practices.

The Church at that point entered into a dispute that still echoed in the late nineteenth century, a dispute regarding the potential of the individual to entertain God in the depths of the human soul. The struggle between Catholic orthodoxy and Protestant "subjectivity" was not primarily one of doctrine or structure, but of the nature of the Christian life, its practices, and its relationship to authority—biblical and ecclesiastical. The famed argument of 1699 between Bossuet and François Fénelon over quietist practices (the belief that the human soul most perfectly experiences the presence of God in its most passive, individual state of contemplative reception, a one-on-one encounter with God out-

---

57. Wilson, *God's Funeral*, 222.

side of sacrament, priestly mediation, and dogmatic rectitude) invited intervention by Pope Innocent XII and ultimately condemnation of the practice as a heresy. Madam Guyon, who spent time in prison on and off from 1688 to 1703, and Miguel de Molinos, a Spanish priest who had found favor with Pope Innocent XI, had introduced quietism into the broader stream of Catholic mysticism, and Fénelon, royal tutor, had endorsed many of these ideas in his 1697 publication, *Explication des maximes des saints*. Bossuet won the battle, and, Dru and Trethowan argue, an unnatural split in the life of the Church resulted, a split between reason and sentiment. "As a result of the fear of Quietism spirituality itself was externalized into 'devotions' and the emphasis was placed on outward expressions of religion."[58] This "extrinsicism" (Blondel's term for a religious outlook that shuns the interiority of feeling, sentiment, and individual experience) rejected the kind of internal appropriations of faith and religious expression that Pascal, as we shall see, had advocated so forcefully. This extrinsicism, purportedly objective, was not a capitulation to rationalism, but a rejection of it in its eighteenth-century form in favor of an authoritarianism linked to the Church.

Those of the nineteenth century who retained an appreciation for the inner experience of faith found themselves assailed by two shrill voices demanding recognition. The liberal Catholics of the century built on the enthusiasm of Lamennais and the Romanticism of Chateaubriand. Their values would eventually issue in the pursuit of modernism, both in its uniquely ecclesiastical sense (of which more will be said below) and in its broader meaning as a general reconciliation of Catholic belief with modern ideas. Conservative, classicist Catholics listened to the traditionalism of de Maistre and Bonald, whose arguments built on the spiritual and temporal authority of the Church, and by the end of the century this ultramontanism would calcify in rigid structures of integralism,[59] a unified and rigid approach to orthodoxy that recognized Catholic dogma as a wholistic piece that was greater than the sum of its parts. Integralism was a defensive posture, an effort to pull up the drawbridge and bar the gates so that enemies could not penetrate the citadel. Any moderation regarding intellectual freedom, previously considered acceptable, threatened the security of the keep.

---

58. Dru, "Introduction," 23.
59. Ibid., 24.

The fear concerned the apparent futility of an inner experience as a deterrent to rationalism. Inner experiences were, by nature, subjective, unrelated to the mind or to reason, irreproducible and therefore non-scientific, and, most dangerously of all, beyond the long arm of orthodox authority and supervision. Inner experiences smacked of fideism, an irrational leap of faith over reason or knowledge or objective revelation, a position that had been rejected by the Church.

The Church desperately needed to find a solid place to stand, its former broad terrain diminished first by Humean empiricism and skepticism, and then by Kantian rationalism. The eighteenth-century Scottish philosopher David Hume had made empirical knowledge all-sufficient and had set aside any possibility of knowing causation. Immanuel Kant had banished the reality of things-in-themselves to a realm beyond the reach of human reason. The Cartesian self-reflection of an earlier century now became infused with these subsequent challenges to intellectual capabilities, producing a theory of knowledge that invited a larger role for an internal intellectual intuition. This epistemology was fundamentally opposed to an orthodox Catholic interpretation of knowledge as natural revelation understood by human reason and perfected through supernatural revelation made accessible and certain through historically verifiable signs and miracles.

"The act of faith, as Catholics understood it, was an intellectual assent to an historical word of revelation made under the illuminating influence of grace," so theologians were required to defend the intellectual integrity of such a decision in a way that was epistemologically possible, but not logically required (because of its supernatural character).[60] This essential act of assent must then lead into a systematic theology, which imparts a scientific, objective, rational character to the positive theological content. Hegel, McCool points out, had insisted that such systems were impossible. "You could have either positive revelation or systematic knowledge, since religion and philosophy operated upon different levels of intellectual consciousness. But you could not have both simultaneously."[61] Integralists needed, somehow, to subjugate reason by means of reason, banish skepticism by means of speculation, and demand an internalized faith *sans* the individual's contribution.

---

60. McCool, *Catholic Theology*, 33.
61. Ibid., 34.

The late nineteenth-century integralists were the legatees of French traditionalism. French traditionalists had avoided all this mess by dismissing the power of individual human reason altogether. The individual, according to such thinkers as Joseph de Maistre and Louis de Bonald, was hopelessly inept in the spiritual realm, and only through the infallible transmission of divine revelation through the auspices of the Church could any truth—religious, moral, or social—be made known. Ultimately, in 1855 the Church's Congregation of the Index rejected traditionalism because it failed to take into account natural revelation, diminished the role of human reason in the generation of faith, and rejected the "proofs" made available to humanity through miracles. All of these factors were pivotal in Catholic integralism and were given dogmatic status in 1870 at the First Vatican Council.

Yet the kind of reasoning integralists advocated was not that of rationalism. As Lamennais pointed out in his 1817 *Essai sur l'indifférence en matière de religion*, atheism, deism, and Protestantism—the three heresies that destroyed faith—all rested "on a single postulate, either stated or implied: that knowledge is reached by *individual* reasoning and action approved by the *individual* conscience."[62] Lamennais's emphasis lay in the role of authority, that it alone could direct human reason in proper channels and that without it the individual had no hope of discovering anything true about God or about the self. The senses mislead; circumstances can change sentiment; reasoning can be manipulated. The foundations of authority are the only sure bases for knowledge. The individual's job is one of submission.[63] Submission alone could grant faith, and it alone could determine safe paths for reason.

The First Vatican apostolic constitution *Dei Filius*, addressing the Church's teaching on the relationship of faith and reason, declared: that God's existence and divine attributes "could be known with certainty by natural reason"; that faith is reasonable, but because it is supernatural it is not a moral necessity; that miracles imparted a certainty to faith, as did the existence of the Church itself; and that there were two orders of knowledge—faith and reason, and these were mutually complementary. "Right reason demonstrated the foundations of faith, and reason, enlightened by faith, acquired scientific knowledge of divine reality."[64]

62. Reardon, *Liberalism and Tradition*, 69. Italics added.
63. Ibid., 76.
64. McCool, *Catholic Theology*, 218.

As the century progressed, it became evident that doctrine needed to rein in epistemology and its handmaidens, philosophy and science. Prior to Leo XIII, a "philosophical eclecticism" prevailed in Catholic intellectual circles.[65] Leo recognized that a systemic overhaul was necessary in order to bring the kind of structure to epistemology and all the intellectual forays that issued from it into a path of fidelity to the purposes of the Church. Despite his predecessor's Syllabus of Errors, liberalism, individualism, and rationalism ran rampant. Leo turned to the tidiness of Thomism and its scholastic configurations to ground Catholic theology and give proper boundaries to intellectual work.

Leo XIII's 1879 encyclical, *Aeterni Patris*, mandated a return to Thomistic philosophy in all Catholic teachings on the relationship between reason and faith. To that end, he directed the Gregorian University in Rome to use Thomism solely and he appointed Désiré Mercier as 'Professor of Philosophy according to St. Thomas' at the Catholic University of Louvain. Unfortunately, thirteenth-century scholasticism, with all its scientific limitations and archaic cultural associations, made a difficult transfer into a near-twentieth-century world. Yet its claims served Leo's purposes: a commonality of thought and a faithful adherence to Roman authority. The only authorized textbooks for use in Catholic seminaries were those issued by Rome and were written in Latin to avoid misinterpretations, resulting in what Daly calls a virtual "Italianization of the Roman Catholic Church."[66] The issue of language also resulted in an increasing alienation of the laity who had little or no familiarity with Latin and with the scholastic methodology. "Rome, while not explicitly approving of Mgr. Talbot's view that the laity should stick to hunting, shooting, and entertaining, was undoubtedly happier when they did so. 'Lay' theology is apt to be a trifle adventurous and its practitioners insufficiently moulded in the methods of the Schools."[67]

On the other hand, scholasticism afforded a happy return to the certainties so prolific in the world before the Scientific Revolution and the Enlightenment. The painful skepticism and empty rationalism of the day were captured in the word coined by Thomas Huxley in his stumping for Darwin—*agnosticism*, the very opposite of what the Church claimed to be possible, that is, the knowledge of God and of God's will for the

---

65. Daly, *Transcendence and Immanence*, 10.
66. Ibid., 12.
67. Ibid., 13 n. 11.

human community. The scholastic scientist, on the other hand, was one who could "rise to a higher order than the order of the natural sciences in order to truly understand the nature and ordering principles of the corporeal world." Scholasticism alone could "overcome the dangers to public order and to religious and moral life, created by false modern notions of liberty and authority... The weakness of modern philosophy, on the other hand, could be traced to its subjectivity and individualism. Responding to the traditionalists and the post-Kantian theologians, *Aeterni Patris* linked the individualism of modern philosophy to the religious individualism of the Protestant reformers who had rejected the public authority of the modern Church."[68]

Oddly enough, the Church's positivist foes agreed with them about the fickleness and subjectivity of the individual. Their conviction that reason, and reason alone, could determine truth and true courses of action led them to disparage the role of the individual insofar as that individual allowed his or her personal preferences or convictions to interfere with the pure work of reason. "To the rationalist, disinterestedness is the keynote of intellectual probity. All desires must be silent when the reason speaks. It is as spectators, refraining from the slightest intervention, that we must assist at the inner conflict of ideas. The production of truth ... is an objective phenomenon, independent of ourselves, taking place within us, but outside us. The mind in its reflection of reality must be a clear pool unruffled by desire, as passive and impartial as a mirror."[69] Only with the turn-of-the-century stirrings of scientific uncertainty and the suspicions that science was not bringing about all the progress it had promised did this obsession with pure objectivity begin to wane.

All of these discourses came to a head in the last decade of the nineteenth century. By the early 1890s, many voices clamored for supremacy—all of them challenged by the uncertainties and vacillations brought on by the erosion of strongholds that had carefully been built over decades of antipathy between reactionaries and republicans, positivists and papists.

The Church's course of action involved recovering lost territory, regaining intellectual capital. In his 1895 article, "Après une visite au Vatican," Ferdinand Brunetière sided with the Roman Catholic Church when he challenged the pretentiousness of science and its practitioners who had promised the end of mystery. He tells his readers that only one

68. McCool, *Catholic Theology*, 231–32.
69. Eastwood, *Revival of Pascal*, 14.

question mattered: "Jesus Christ: Is he or is he not God?"[70] In the minds of Roman Catholic leadership, this question went to the heart of the dispute about authority. The historical identity of Christ issued from the teachings of the Church, which were founded on the witness of scripture and were ratified by the signs and miracles recorded in that scripture. Brunetière points to the two historical questions: is scripture history? And is history science? From there, we can observe the argument move to the epistemological questions: Is science knowledge? And is knowledge truth? And out of that debate emerged the question of authority and the role of the individual: Does truth grant power, even in and to the individual? These anxieties, these seemingly unanswerable questions, reflected the growing suspicion that the utopian promises of science—social stability, ease and prosperity, the end of human suffering—were fading and that there was an essential darkness in human experience, a chasm between aspiration and achievement, between the potential and the possible.

This elemental darkness came not from the natural world around them, for that world and all that it contained continued to reveal itself in layer upon layer of wonder, invention, exploration, and discovery. Yet for all this bounty, the individual of the late nineteenth century faced even greater antinomies than one of the seventeenth century: greater possibilities, greater freedoms, greater challenges, greater failures, greater suffering. The ideas of contingency—that Church, society, political and social relationships, and the very construction of knowledge were not logical and determined extensions of natural "laws" but were in fact effects of both divine and human causes that required an interpretive element—were reappearing in new forms. The "gaps" that natural theology and, later, scientific positivism had filled were breaking open again, and the sense of the paradoxical troubled the individual's inner world.

The Pascalisants—scientists, philosophers, mathematicians, journalists, professionals—all recognized this elemental darkness, this central experience of antinomies, as a confirmation of Pascal's interpretation of the affliction of the human soul and the hiddenness of God, both of which were at the core of the human dilemma. Human knowledge had gone from paradox to positivism and was now returning to paradox. The Pascalisants felt convinced that Pascal had understood something that could now help them in this reappropriation of internal contingencies.

---

70. "Jésus-Christ est-il ou n'est-il pas Dieu?" Brunetière, *Questions Actuelles*, 20 n. 1. According to the Preface, this book consists of essays written between 1895 and 1905.

# 3

## Pascalian Perceptions

THE QUERY: WHAT DID Blaise Pascal (1623–1662) contribute to intellectuals whose worldview had been revolutionized, in more ways than one? This is a scientist gone from the scene twenty years before Newton's *Principia Mathematica*, one hundred years before Joseph Priestley's work on electricity, one hundred fifty years before Lamarck's early works on evolution, and two hundred years before Jean Bernard Léon Foucault measured the speed of light. This is a philosopher whose work would be overshadowed by the likes of his contemporary René Descartes; Gottfried Leibniz of the next generation; David Hume and Immanuel Kant of the next century; and then misunderstood and summarily dismissed by many of the thinkers of the nineteenth century— Comte and Cousin, Taine and Renan. This is a Christian apologist whose memory bore two stigmas, that of his apparent skepticism and that of his reputed Jansenism, neither of which made him useful to the Church, particularly in her late nineteenth-century neo-scholastic frenzy. This is a royal subject, unsuspecting of the power of revolution and the possibilities of republican politics, incapable of conceiving of life without a throne or a crown, and without the ever-present religious leaders bending to speak into the royal ear.

The diversity of Pascalian thought—scientific, religious, philosophical—manifested itself in the ways it was appropriated by the intellectuals of the late nineteenth century. Different thinkers found different emphases useful in their attempts to make sense of the epistemological perplexities that dogged philosophical, historical, scientific, and biblical fields of study. In this chapter, we will examine certain critical Pascalian principles that show up two hundred years later in the arguments of the Pascalisants. We will begin by considering some of Pascal's scientific work and his reflections on natural philosophy. In his experimental and mathematical studies, Pascal introduced his ideas about epistemological boundaries, the existence of *a priori* knowledge, and the proper methods of building on that tacit knowledge in order to produce usable scientific knowledge. These ideas became the modus operandi of Pierre Duhem's scientific philosophy.

We will then turn to Pascal's reflections on metaphysical knowledge and the limits of reason in the search for supernatural truth. Pascal delved deeply into his contemporaries' struggles with skepticism and developed his theory of orders, which became the basis of his claims to certain knowledge apart from dogmatism, skepticism, and rationalism. These theories, along with Pascal's responses to the religious authoritarianism of his day (evident in Jesuit/Jansenist disputes) served to inform Blondel's and Laberthonnière's focus on philosophical authenticity and the role of the individual. Finally, Pascal's great theme of the *Deus absconditus*, the hidden God, with its accompanying ideas about the role of history and scripture in the outworking of human destiny gave Blondel and Laberthonnière the inspiration they needed to imagine a renewed Catholicism that incorporated the best of contemporary thought with the treasures of Catholic tradition.

## PASCAL ON NATURAL PHILOSOPHY

Pascal's empirical accomplishments earned him a permanent place in the annals of scientific knowledge. A child prodigy, he was not yet twenty years old when he published his *Essai pour les coniques* on conic geometry. Assisting his father in tax assessment motivated Pascal to invent a calculating machine, earning him the contemporary honor of having his name identify a computer language.

Pascal wrestled famously with one of the conceptual impasses of that period—the impossibility of a vacuum. His work on this concept helps us identify some of his unique contributions to the dialogue that would occupy the thoughts of many at the end of the nineteenth century. We shall see that this significant empirical study demonstrated Pascal's rejection of both rational theory and traditional authority when they are inappropriately used in the construction of knowledge. These boundaries became important to the Pascalisants.

Two prevailing understandings of the vacuum existed in Pascal's day. Some adhered to Aristotle's concept of a continuum, that all that existed did so in a seamless whole, all things in relationship to one another without any rupture or barren space. The four elements—earth, air, fire, and water—blended and cooperated in such a way that every piece of nature moved into its suitable place of relationship with all the other pieces of nature and fit just as it should. Earth's motion was downward. The heavenly bodies, however, retaining their circular orbits, moved through a fifth element, the ether, which sustained all matter as an unobservable medium. Aristotle's system retained a great deal of popularity, particularly throughout the Middle Ages, and remained ensconced in much scholastic thinking. Such thinking gave far more credence to the authorities and traditions taught in the schools and sanctioned by the Church than to the possibilities generated by new methods of study.

Descartes offered a new way of explaining the impossibility of a vacuum. Descartes's system worked from a mechanical model, an approach that relegated empirical evidence to the peripheral role of verification rather than giving it the central role of discovery. For Descartes, there were only two substances in nature—physical matter defined as extension and mental matter defined as thought. There was no room in his system for a void, and therefore a necessary ether, an invisible physical matter, stretched between all other visible extensions of substance. Descartes worked out of theory rather than out of experiment.

Pascal rejected both theory and authority in favor of experimentation and the results it afforded. He explored the work of Evangelista Torricelli (1608–1647), Galileo's last secretary, and his barometric pressure experiments. Pascal's 1646 experiment verified Torricelli's hypothesis that when the mercury in a glass tube dropped leaving an empty space at the top of the tube an actual vacuum existed; no ether having been present when the tube was full, none could now occupy the empty space. Thus, apparently, nature did not abhor a vacuum. In his publication, *Expériences nouvelles touchant le vide*, Pascal rejected the idea that a presupposition, such as the existence of an undetectable matter called ether, should determine scientific knowledge rather than strict observation.[1]

Pascal continued his thoughts in a later reflection, *Préface sur le traité du vide*. In this work, he challenged the respect for antiquity that, he felt, was hindering the advance of true science. He proceeded to delineate his argument about the spheres of knowledge, each of which has

---

1. Pascal, *Expériences nouvelles*, 198.

its own laws. There was a place for authority and tradition; their rights involved any field that was based on simple fact. Such knowledge could not develop further. Facts are facts and cannot be improved upon, only added to. Other principles were accessible to human senses or to human reason. These principles had nothing to do with authority, and could only be discovered through experimentation and the proper use of reason. Pascal was confident that such an approach rendered the production of knowledge "without end and without interruption."[2]

Pascal considered the advantages and limits of experimentation. He pointed out that the ancients certainly gleaned their knowledge from observation, but that their opportunities were limited. Therefore, it was no disparagement to their authority to go beyond their observations and build on their knowledge. And yet, even so should contemporary scientists recognize their own limitations. When the ancients spoke definitively about a subject, they were implicitly recognizing that their certainty was limited to the few observations and experiments they could actually make. In the same way, scientists must continue to accept the generalization of the laws they deduced. No experiment can cover every possible construct of the hypothesis, and thus every conclusion contains an implicit caveat—that unknown substances or situations may nullify that conclusion. Indefinite factors are set aside in the process of knowledge-production, and yet they remain as silent witnesses to the infinite possibilities and potentialities untapped by human knowledge. No hypothesis is truly verifiable; it remains theory as long as it is based on experimentation and observation. All absolute statements about natural laws derived from inductive reasoning are qualified, and thus every true scientist must cultivate a level of humility. Hence Pascal suggested what Karl Popper would later argue: that falsifiability renders every hypothesis conjectural. "His exacting empirical method, coupled with his penchant for detailed mathematical explanation, helped develop a more mechanical and predictable view of nature that would challenge both Aristotelian/medieval teleology and the Cartesian rationalism concerning supposed natural laws."[3]

Pascal concluded his *Préface sur le traité du vide* by returning to the work of the ancients. He reiterated his confidence in the power of

---

2. Pascal, *Préface sur le traité du vide*, 230. "Sa fécondité inépuisable produit continuellement, et ses inventions peuvent être tout ensemble sans fin et sans interruption."

3. Groothuis, *On Pascal*, 20.

the truth, which would always prevail over the influence of antiquity no matter how "new" such truth appears. For the nature of truth was eternal, greater than authority, and certainly not subsequent to the discovery of it.[4]

Pascal, however, recognized that "démonstrations" may grant a higher level of certainty. Demonstrations are proofs granted through the application of first principles, discernible pieces of knowledge that the mind has natural access to and uses in both daily life (common sense) and in scientific operations that involve deductive reasoning rather than inductive reasoning. In a brief treatise entitled *Réflexions sur la géométrie en general: de l'esprit géométrique et de l'art de persuader* Pascal explored the power of deductive reasoning and its proper use. Geometry perfectly exemplifies this power correctly applied. It makes clear "the art of discovering unknown truths."[5] Such a truth, previously unknown, can only become certain when it is demonstrated. Geometry is the art of such demonstrations; it is the highest process to which human reason can attain.[6]

According to Pascal, the only method more excellent than geometry, superior because it grants absolute certainty, is essentially unattainable, though geometry recognizes this true method and employs its principles to the greatest extent possible. This method, even partially applied, is critical to the production of knowledge. This method has two rules: 1) every term used must be clearly defined and 2) every proposition must be clearly demonstrated. This method, impossible because the requirement of definition pushes back the use of terms *ad infinitum*, always recognizing that even more elemental terms, terms that relate to first principles inaccessible to explication, will proscribe definition. In the same way, the requirement that every proposition be proved will also find itself blocked by the existence of clear, innate propositions that cannot be further analyzed, "and thus it is clear that one never arrives at first principles."[7] Thus, Pascal argued, humans are naturally and unchange-

---

4. Pascal, *Préface sur le traité du vide*, 230–32.

5. Pascal, *Réflexions sur la géométrie en general*, 349. "L'art de découvrir les vérités inconnues."

6. Ibid. "Géométrie, qui est presque la seule des sciences humaines qui en produise d'infaillibilité."

7. Ibid., 349. "Et ainsi il est clair qu'on n'arriverait jamais aux premières."

ably powerless to render definitive, whole, or absolute conclusions in any area of science.

Pascal forged a middle way between skepticism and excessive confidence. True science, he wrote, recognized that some definitions and proofs lie beyond the reach of humanity, i.e., space, time, movement, etc. Such things, subject to futile human analysis, only become increasingly confusing and confused, rendering the thinker paralyzed. However, while the essence of such terms cannot be known, their relationship to known things is clear to everyone, thus making possible common discourse and common working definitions. To attempt any more than this would require propositional proof, which is beyond human reach for such elemental terms. For this reason, nominal definitions must serve in order for science to advance.

Nevertheless, science can focus on what is clear and indisputable. By this means, it attains *a level of certainty* and can proceed with the greater work of discovery that issues out of exploring the relationship between defined knowledge and undefined knowledge. Pascal suggested that three things comprise the entire universe: movement, number, and space. The careful consideration of these elemental attributes of nature opens the human mind to the wonders of a twofold infinity: of the infinitely great and the infinitely small. This greatness and smallness concern size and movement and number. The existence of this quality of infinity, as obvious as it seems, is impossible to prove and inaccessible to human reason; this, however, is not due to obscurity but to perfection.

Pascal recognized that this statement inevitably provokes a disturbance in the human consciousness. Pascal understood that human nature insists on being capable of understanding anything true, and that anything it cannot understand must simply be untrue. Man inevitably uses self—personal experience, understanding, and knowledge—as the measure of truth, an essentially irrational behavior. It is this stubbornness in the face of human reason that diverted Pascal in the second half of this essay to talk about "the art of persuasion." For the human mind, conviction (not necessarily truth) issues from two methods, either that of the will or that of the understanding. While the conviction of the understanding is far preferable, the conviction of the will, known in desire and preference, is far more common.

Pascal's observation of human nature informed his analysis of the human quest for truth. He argued that humans think they "know" certain things to be true because they wish them to be true, even though they may in reality be false. What has no appeal to an individual's beliefs or pleasures is often "false." Thus the art of persuasion is necessary to the pursuit of "true truth." While humans need to be persuaded even in matters of human knowledge, they are in even greater need of persuasion in supernatural matters. Yet human methods of persuasion do not suffice to grant supernatural knowledge. "*Les vérités divines*"—spiritual truths—come by means of divine persuasion alone.

According to Pascal, God alone can introduce such truth into the soul and does so as he pleases. From there, these truths proceed to the mind, and not vice versa, in order that the "great power of reason" be humbled and the weak will healed of all its sinful attachments. "So it appears that God has established the supernatural order, and it is entirely contrary to the order that is natural to men in natural things."[8] God has established a supernatural order that is the opposite of the natural order by which humans delve into the nature of scientific truths.

We shall see how completely contemporary Pascal's arguments seemed to many intellectuals of the *fin-de-siècle* who struggled mightily and, apparently, futilely to assert the power of experimentation and observation to create truth and to generate the certainty demanded of hypotheses. Pascal's insistence on the existence of elemental principles that cannot be demonstrated, *a priori* knowledge, challenged positivist claims regarding the absolute authority of empiricism. Yet this parallel insistence on the inaccessibility of supernatural knowledge by means of natural processes made him incompatible with neo-Thomist claims. Yet Pascal insisted that truth is "out there," waiting to be uncovered by those most diligent. "The secrets of nature are hidden"[9] just as were the secrets of God. The human calling involves discovery, at every level.

## PASCAL ON FAITH AND REASON

For Pascal, the dual purpose of scientific exploration was the discovery of the unknown and the recognition of the unknowable. Scientific knowledge, limited as it is by unfathomable and astonishing mysteries, positions the human being within the matrix of creation, suspended be-

---

8. Ibid., 355. "En quoi il paraît que Dieu a établi cet ordre surnaturel, et tout contraire à l'ordre qui devait être naturel aux hommes dans les choses naturelles."
9. Ibid., 358. "Les secrets de la nature sont cachés."

tween the infinite and the void of nothingness. This suspension cannot but generate spiritual apprehension, an angst that drives the human soul into the arms of God.

According to Pascal, an accurate weighing of this angst, a recognition of the truth about the self—its potential, its condition, its beginning and its end—was critical to the process of all discovery. Without a correct understanding of the constructs of human nature, including both its *intended* status and its *realized* status, the seeker of truth would never be able to penetrate the mysteries of nature, whether of the physical order or of spiritual realities.

In his *Entretien avec M. de Saci*, Pascal described how he found inspiration, though not necessarily truth, in the works of Epictetus (55–135) and Montaigne (1533–1592). From Epictetus and his stoic philosophy, Pascal derived support for his understanding of divine sovereignty and the need for humanity to acquiesce to the will of God. Montaigne, the quintessential Pyrrhonian, provoked Pascal's consideration of the impotence of reason to piece together any kind of solid ground on which faith could stand. Pascal delighted in Montaigne's effective "crushing of the pride of reason ... and by its own weapons."[10]

Pascal made no effort to disguise the fact that he disagreed with Thomistic arguments about the power of human reason to acquire certain truth. Thomas Aquinas had introduced a system of compatibility between an Aristotelian production of certain knowledge through accumulations of observation and inductive reasoning and a Christian worldview of the supernatural role of faith. This synthesis of human ability and divine revelation would grant the neo-Thomists of the late nineteenth century a method by which they could challenge prevailing secular models of knowledge-production.

> It was held together by a metaphysics of being, built around the act of existence, and a metaphysics of man as a dynamic Aristotelian nature, whose knowledge, beginning with sensible singulars, could ascend, by way of the analogy of being, to the infinite existence of God Himself.... Thus, even though man was deprived of a vision of God through Augustinian illumination, the dynamism of his intellect enabled him to abstract universal concepts from singular images, posit the synthesis of universal

---

10. Pascal, "Conversation with Monsieur de Saci," in *The Essential Pascal*, 338.

and singular in the judgment, and mount from the contingent existents of the world of sense to their Infinite Creator.[11]

For Pascal, humans had nothing at their immediate disposal besides "unassisted reason," which is unable to recognize the errors that permeate their world.[12] Montaigne, apart from divine assistance, was right about human reason and human helplessness. Epictetus, arguing in opposition to Montaignesque skepticism about the dignity and power of the human spirit, was right too. Pascal recognized Epictetus's appreciation for the greatness of the human soul, its proper glory, as a true picture of the *imago dei*. Both right, yet both wrong, for neither took into account the position of the other; according to Pascal, both failed because they neglected the synthesizing power of the Christian salvation story to reconcile the reality of the glory of creation with the reality of the "present misery of man."[13] The two positions veritably proved one another. How, Pascal asked, can we explain the human longing for truth and goodness, and consequent despair at our inability to achieve these worthy goals, if we are essentially the desperate creatures that we clearly present to one another? And how can we possibly understand our present misery and despair if we were not inherently created to enjoy something far greater? "It is this imperfect enlightenment which leads both writers into error. The first recognizes the duties of man, but he will not acknowledge man's powerlessness, and he shields himself behind a wall of human pride. The second sees only the helplessness of man, and acknowledges no duty; and he debases himself by falling into laxity."[14]

Thus, faith and reason become mutually contradictory, and yet simultaneously mutually reinforcing. "Neither can stand alone, for each contains a defect; and they cannot unite, because they contain contradictories. Thus they shatter one another, and both come to nothing, so as to make room for the truth of the Gospel."[15] Human nature, Pascal insisted, at its deepest level experienced nothing but contradictions, and those contradictions, allowed to develop to their fullest extent, were the

---

11. McCool, *The Neo-Thomists*, 12–13.
12. Pascal, "Conversation," 339.
13. Ibid., 341.
14. Ibid., 342.
15. Ibid.

path of resolution. For Pascal, this process of reflection, with its resulting paradox, was the first step in gaining supernatural knowledge.

*Pensées,* Pascal's most popular work, is an unfinished collection of disconnected thoughts that explored themes prevalent in the discourses of his day. Pascal intended the book to serve as an apology of the Christian faith for those intellectual contemporaries who found religious faith a meaningless accoutrement to their dilettante lives. The brilliance of this book is not in its synthesis or polish, since he died before he could link his thoughts together into a cohesive argument, but in the dexterity with which he writes and in the enduring relevance of his topics. His ruminations on the origin and destiny of the human individual, the role of reason and the possibility of genuine knowledge, the power of faith, the value of "proof," and the meaning of human suffering resonated with late nineteenth-century discourses.

Pascal's metaphysics cannot be explained without referring to his foundational methodology of self-examination. Pascal rejected the growing rationalism of his day that argued for rigid objectivity. Disinterestedness on the part of the observer made careful observations and well-constructed theories powerful. Reason demanded the removal of the personality from the configuration of truth-seeking. This pursuit of rational objectivity prevailed in late nineteenth century France as well. "The production of truth, so Renan declares, is an objective phenomenon, independent of ourselves, taking place within us, but outside us. The mind in its reflection of reality must be a clear pool unruffled by desire, as passive and impartial as a mirror."[16]

Pascal, on the other hand, began with himself and with the knowledge of human nature afforded by careful observation of the lives of those around him. He started with a recognition of human powerlessness. "Now he wants to be happy and assured of some truth, and yet he is equally incapable of knowing and of not desiring to know" (f. 75).[17] Human nature is caught in its inner hunger to know the meaning of life and its simultaneous inability to attain it. "Imagine a number of men in chains, all under the sentence of death, some of whom are each day butchered in the sight of the others; those remaining see their own

---

16. Eastwood, *Revival of Pascal,* 14.

17. Citations of fragments from Pascal's *Pensées,* here and throughout this work, are from the Lafuma edition. English translations, which also follow the Lafuma edition, are taken from the Krailsheimer translation.

condition in that of their fellows, and looking at each other with grief and despair await their turn. This is an image of the human condition" (f. 434).

This powerlessness stems from the antinomy of the human condition, the disparate experiences of hope and despair, ambition and mediocrity, passion and emptiness. Nothing can reconcile the warring realities of human nature, realities that tear the soul apart in its quest for solid ground. "If he exalts himself, I humble him. If he humbles himself, I exalt him. And I go on contradicting him until he understands that he is a monster that passes all understanding" (f. 130). "What sort of freak then is man! How novel, how monstrous, how chaotic, how paradoxical, how prodigious! Judge of all things, feeble earthworm, repository of truth, sink of doubt and error, glory and refuse of the universe!" (f. 131). No such creature could possibly achieve the glories that reason, soon to be embodied in the Enlightenment, claimed for itself. Until the human spirit can stand on solid ground, it is hopelessly compromised. "Man does not know the place he should occupy. He has obviously gone astray; he has fallen from his true place and cannot find it again. He searches everywhere, anxiously but in vain, in the midst of impenetrable darkness" (f. 400). This state of darkness makes it unavoidable that man must forfeit his claims to certainty. Pascal's most poignant expression of this suspended state is found in his discourse about *l'infini et le rien*, the infinite and the nothing. "For, after all, what is man in nature? A nothing compared to the infinite, a whole compared to the nothing, a middle point between all and nothing, infinitely remote from an understanding of the extremes; the end of things and their principles are unattainably hidden from him in impenetrable secrecy" (f. 199). The recognition of this tension, this place of dangling between two incomprehensible antinomies, is the first step of both reason and faith. Neither can proceed without this elementary acknowledgment.

The acknowledgment is primary, but not terminal, for it leads to hope. "Thus it is wretched to know that one is wretched, but there is greatness in knowing one is wretched" (f. 114). Wretchedness and greatness follow one another "in an endless circle, for it is certain that as man's insight increases so he finds both wretchedness and greatness within himself. In a word man knows he is wretched. Thus he is wretched because he is so, but he is truly great because he knows it" (f. 122). This is the beginning of both faith and reason.

At that point, reason can commence, and because it has issued from its own pit of human degradation, it does so with the readiness to accept its own limitations. "Reason is available but can be bent in any direction" (f. 530). Pascal worked through the fallacy of perfect reason by demonstrating its susceptibility to deception through illness, through custom, through predilection, through distraction, through endless passions. Reason worked best when it brings the soul to the place where it must be left in the hands of God. "Reason would never submit unless it judged that there are occasions when it ought to submit" (f. 174). "Reason's last step is the recognition that there are an infinite number of things which are beyond it" (f. 188). Yet unlike a fideist, Pascal believed strongly that reason has a critical role in the development of faith. Fideism, the advocacy of faith apart from any intellectual foundation, a blind leap across a great chasm, had been condemned by the Church and while Pascal was often misunderstood over the centuries that followed him, he never approached faith as a blind leap. On the contrary, reason was a prerequisite to faith and sometimes even a temporary stand-in until God granted the requisite grace for faith. "That is why those to whom God has given religious faith by moving their hearts are very fortunate, and feel quite legitimately convinced, but to those who do not have it we can only give such faith through reasoning . . ." (f. 110). Such a temporary substitution for faith Pascal called "the Machine," the rational operation of faith in the absence of the supernatural infusion of faith. "Faith is different from proof. One is human and the other a gift of God . . . This is the faith that God himself puts into our hearts, often using proof as the instrument" (f. 7). Thus reason became a tool in the hands of faith, sometimes preparing the heart to receive faith from God and other times acting as the vehicle of divine transmission, but never did reason become a means of faith-production. "There are three ways to believe: reason, habit, inspiration . . . It is not that [Christianity] excludes reason and habit, quite the contrary, but we must open our mind to the proofs, confirm ourselves in it through habit, while offering ourselves through humiliations to inspiration, which alone can produce the real and salutary effect" (f. 808).

The kind of reason that Pascal encouraged came, he believed, from the thinking function of the human soul, the function that defines human identity. "Man is obviously made for thinking. Therein lies all his dignity and his merit; and his whole duty is to think as he ought. Now the order of thought is to begin with ourselves, and with our author and our end" (f. 620). "All our dignity consists in thought. It is on thought that we must depend for our recovery, not on space and time, which we could never fill. Let us then strive to think well; that is the basic principle of morality" (f. 200). Yet even as Pascal encouraged thought, he rejected the subject of thought that intellectuals of his day found most enlightening, that is, the world around them. Because they had become convinced that observation of the natural world was the key to full knowledge, and that proper observation removed their presence from the scene, they had embraced a centripetal concept of true knowledge. Christians considered this natural theology; others simply recognized the power of the natural world to illumine the matters of life; both groups argued that the human being and his place in the world could best be understood if the world around them became more intelligible.

Pascal, however, found this method most unsatisfactory. "Why, do you not say yourself that the sky and the birds prove God?—No.—Does your religion not say so?—No. For though it is true in a sense for some souls whom God has enlightened in this way, yet it is untrue for the majority" (f. 3). Natural theology is fine, he would argue, if you are using nature to speak of the glories of God to a believer, but there is nothing in nature that can enlighten an unbeliever.

> In addressing their arguments to unbelievers, their first chapter is the proof of the existence of God from the works of nature. Their enterprise would cause me no surprise if they were addressing their arguments to the faithful, for those with living faith in their hearts can certainly see at once that everything which exists is entirely the work of the God they worship. But for those in whom this light has gone out and in whom we are trying to rekindle it, people deprived of faith and grace, examining with such light as they have everything they see in nature that might lead them to this knowledge, but finding only obscurity and darkness . . . (f. 781)

There are glimmers of truth, but nothing substantial enough to persuade beyond a shadow of doubt. These glimmers do nothing but disturb the soul and leave it without peace. This restlessness became endemic by the late nineteenth century when it became increasingly obvious that what were before believed to be divine fingerprints could now be seen as the work of evolutionary eons.

> This is what I see and what troubles me. I look around in every direction and all I see is darkness. Nature has nothing to offer me that does not give rise to doubt and anxiety. If I saw no sign there of a Divinity I should decide on a negative solution: if I saw signs of a Creator everywhere I should peacefully settle down in the faith. But, seeing too much to deny and not enough to affirm, I am in a pitiful state, where I have wished a hundred times over that, if there is a God supporting nature, she [sic] should unequivocally proclaim him, and that, if the signs in nature are deceptive, they should be completely erased; that nature should say all or nothing so that I could see what course I ought to follow. (f. 429)

Thus for Pascal, faith became a key to the furtherance of reason and the interpretation of the senses. "Faith certainly tells us what the senses do not, but not the contrary of what they see; it is above, not against them" (f. 185). Reason can only go so far in the pursuit of truth, and then must concede to the power of faith, which can then carry reason into the farthest realms of knowledge. This, Pascal argued, is where Descartes failed. "Descartes useless and uncertain [sic]" (f. 887). For Descartes separated faith from reason, spirit from matter, and thus lost the key to certain knowledge. Descartes pursued both knowledge of a world devoid of spirit—human or divine—and knowledge of God through deduction about that world. Such knowledge, Pascal would argue, was susceptible to the worst kinds of distortions and obscurity. Descartes found his standing ground in thought ("I think, therefore I am"), but Pascal turned instead to the standing ground of the heart. When Pascal spoke of the heart, *le coeur,* he described a heart-intellect, a function that did not involve sentiment or simple feeling; for Pascal, it was an intellectual function that was open to the supernatural in ways that reason and the senses were not. "We know the truth not only through our reason but also through our heart" (f. 110). "The heart has its reasons of which reason knows nothing: we know this in countless ways" (f. 423). "It is the heart which perceives God and not the reason. That is what faith is: God perceived by the heart, not by the reason" (f. 424).

Positioned as he was within the years of the Scientific Revolution and at the cusp of the Enlightenment, Pascal clearly understood the conundrum posed by the demands of faith and reason. The preeminence of reason in the intellectual community tended to extort from faith capitulations that weakened its claims. For this reason, it was much more common to find deists among intellectuals than orthodox Catholics. It was not much different two hundred years later, though the stakes were much higher. Leo XIII's call to a return of a Thomistic system of producing, recognizing, and ordering truth (*Aeterni patris*) was the Roman attempt to regain intellectual credibility. It accepted the demands of reason and empirical observation by superimposing them onto the process of faith, making faith itself a product of reason extended to divine limits. Thomas Aquinas's system served Leo XIII's concerns perfectly.

Aquinas had insisted that his first principles issued from revelation, not from reason. Aristotle had argued that his first principles issued from the intellect's articulation of elementary sense experiences. The combination of Aquinas and Aristotle certainly seemed compelling to many of the nineteenth century who desperately wanted to recapture the imagination of the intellectual community. "Unless they wished to seek refuge in pure fideism, Catholic theologians would have to show how religious faith and human reason, revelation and philosophy, could be reconciled in the believing Christian's intellectual experience."[18] And yet this intellectualism seemed barren to some of those at the *fin-de-siècle* who felt that it catered to a positivist mentality (while certainly rejecting a positivist approach to truth) and failed to attend to the more fundamental matters of faith and human existence. Such intellectualism could only be effectively administered by the authorities of truth, entrenched in theological and ecclesiological bastions of the Church, yet never reach the individual in whose soul alone lay the potential for and call to faith. Pascal offered those most interested in advocating an individual appropriation of the source of faith a metaphysics that explained their methodology and directed them to what seemed more reasonable avenues of knowledge-production.

## PASCAL ON GNOSTICISM AND SKEPTICISM: EPISTEMOLOGY

One of the growing concerns of the late nineteenth century was the elusive quality of truth. While knowledge had seemed increasingly certain throughout the Enlightenment and well into the nineteenth century, by the end of the century, the confidence of some scientists and philosophers (in France, Poincaré, Bergson, Duhem most notably) was being shaken. Absolute knowledge seemed to be slipping away. Theories long held to express reality were becoming structures of knowledge that shifted and

---

18. McCool, *Catholic Theology*, 33.

changed with each addition and with the new perspectives afforded by those additions. The voice of Descartes, long revered, had acclaimed an "ahistorical concept of the status of knowledge," a concept that used reason to prove the existence of God, and the existence of God to provide certain knowledge about the world. For Descartes, the reason and senses could access the physical world and determine certain realities. Pascal believed that only the spiritual realm afforded certain knowledge; the rest was a mental artifact.[19]

This argument about epistemology pervaded French memories of Pascal. Some said he was a skeptic and believed certain knowledge about anything impossible. Jan Miel examines Pascal's theological genealogy and begins with a consideration of a late first-century philosophical/religious movement that stressed the accumulation of secret knowledge given to an elite, insiders who could be trusted to understand and explain truths denied to the common people. "The movement was a kind of intellectual pharisaism in which the key to salvation was not an elaborate set of laws but an elaborate set of beliefs..."[20] This struggle for certain knowledge had pervaded Church structure and, while the Church had formally repudiated such thinking, the persuasion that salvation was linked to perfect or correct knowledge lingered. Ecclesiastical ordination ratified this possession of correct knowledge and, though the absence of such knowledge did not exclude anyone from the process of salvation, the clergy effectively constituted an elite class within the larger Christian body.

Pascal resisted this kind of implicit spiritual elitism and, to combat it, demonstrated the folly of the elite's pursuit of correct knowledge in his critical *Lettres provinciales*. In the *Lettres*, Pascal caricaturized the theological debates between the Jansenists and the Jesuits. He pointed out the ridiculous posture of weighing orthodoxy by word-choice. "What is necessary to be believed in order to be a good Catholic?"[21] Apparently the official answer was the use of the word "proximate" and a proper understanding of the words "efficacious" and "sufficient." Certain knowledge was available, but only to those appointed, through education or privilege, to receive it.

---

19. Phillips, "Pascal's reading and the inheritance of Montaigne and Descartes," 33–34.

20. Miel, *Pascal and Theology*, 10.

21. Pascal, *The Provincial Letters*, 11.

Throughout the *Lettres*, Pascal berated the Jesuits for not deigning to clarify their position, obfuscating instead the issues behind platforms of unreachable authority. The Jesuits' word play, wrote Pascal, effectively manipulated "Scripture, councils, and popes" to achieve their political results. In Letter 18, Pascal charged the pope with fallibility, brought on by deception, the manipulation of others, and sheer distraction.[22] Truth, Pascal insisted, must be accessible to the least educated; this is only possible if the least educated have a spiritual facility for certain knowledge about the God and the self that is equal to the most erudite.

At the other end of the spectrum, the skeptics felt that certain knowledge was impossible, to elites and to the common man. Thomas Huxley coined the term *agnostic* to express this inability to know, though he used it in an exclusively religious sense. Skeptics, fueled by Montaigne's devastating critique in *Apologie de Raymond de Sebond*, had made a position of surety untenable, particularly in areas least accessible to sense experience or simple reason, areas such as faith. "A certain dubious obscurity" (f. 109) rendered the outlines of supernatural truths unintelligible. Fragment 131, one of Pascal's longest ruminations on skepticism, freely admitted the skeptics' position: Natural intuition simply cannot penetrate the darkness. The principles of spirituality may indeed be true; there is no rational evidence to disprove them. "It is not certain that everything is uncertain" (f. 521). Yet they may equally be untrue, and no evidence exists that can substantiate them. There are just enough glimmers of something beyond to make the skeptics' position hard to swallow.

Against the skeptics, Pascal positioned the dogmatists, who asserted the power of sincerity and "good faith" in the pursuit of truth. But there were not enough of those glimmers to convince without doubt. The skeptics had to turn a blind eye to the hints around them; the dogmatist had to turn his back on reason. And yet Pascal agreed with the skeptics: uncertainty about human nature, uncertainty about our origin and our destiny—these unanswered questions make dogmatism completely indefensible. So, Pascal concluded, everyone must choose between the incongruities of the skeptic or the dogmatist. It was for him this very suspension between two contradictory positions that was the key to truth. "Man's condition is dual . . . For who cannot see that unless we

---

22. Ibid., 201–2.

realize the duality of human nature we remain invincibly ignorant of the truth about ourselves?" (f. 131).

Thus it is the heart-intelligence that is the channel of primary truth, for the heart makes sense of the conundrums that face the reason and the senses. The reason cannot grasp the paradox of infinity and nothing; the senses cannot grasp the contradictions of great human aspirations and simultaneous experiences of human degradation and misery. The heart, however, can discern the truth that makes these mysteries meaningful.

Pascal called these different avenues of knowledge "orders." It is imperative for the purposes of this study that we understand the importance Pascal placed on these orders in his epistemological strategy. He spelled out these "principles of knowledge" in Letter 18 of his *Lettres provinciales*. There he listed three sources of knowledge: the senses, reason, and faith, each with their appropriate object of study and method of knowing. Pascal made clear that the confusion of these methodologies and orders would lead to darkness and despair. Maintaining clear and practical boundaries between them released the individual to pursue knowledge of every kind.

Douglas Groothuis points out that Pascal expanded on the three dimensions of geometry—lines, planes, and cubes—to develop his three avenues of knowledge-production. Thus Pascal rejected Cartesian dualism for a triad of human abilities.[23] Senses observe and feed information to the mind. This information may or may not be accurate, since our senses are easily deceived. Illness can generate hallucinations; perspective can dictate a skewed perception. Sense information is valuable, but cannot produce absolute truth. The reason works on principles, developed and innate. Reason operates best in geometric contexts, that is, as a mathematical art working on established truths and applying them to equally structured situations. Faith operates on the unseen (beyond the senses) and the a-rational (beyond the logical, not irrational or against the logical) in order to develop an awareness of the internal and the supernatural.

As we saw earlier, Pascal's *Réflexions sur la géométrie* addressed the roles of logical deduction and careful demonstration and showed both their greatness and their limitations. Desmond Clarke calls this essay "the nearest approximation to an explicit theory of knowledge," and relates the issue of truth to that of certainty. "The scope of human knowl-

---

23. Groothuis, *On Pascal*, 41.

edge is inversely proportional to the certainty required of our beliefs. At the limit, if genuine knowledge requires absolute certainty, then we *know* very little."[24]

It is that "very little" that removed Pascal from the ranks of the skeptics. For Pascal proceeded to develop the third way of knowing, that of the heart. The heart is not merely the source of knowledge about spiritual matters; it also serves as the avenue of knowledge about intuitive principles that operate at the most fundamental level in the methods of senses and reason as well. Innate first principles about space and time, indefinable but essential realities, inform the heart and the heart, then, turns and illumines the reason and the senses. These inconceivable *a priori* propositions can be true without our understanding, and must be operative in all matters scientific and spiritual.[25]

In supernatural matters, according to Pascal, the scripture and the Church interpreted the matters of the heart.[26] Pascal, however, clearly rejected the idea that scripture and the Church supplanted the work of the heart; they merely translated the information that the heart gleans from self-examination, from consideration of the world, and from the interior work of inspiration. This act of internal revelation was a process of intimacy between the soul and God, not an external, intrusive act of exterior authorities. The dual authorities of scripture and Church were secondary and supplemental, though also critical.

Pascal elaborated on this work of the heart in fragment 110. He pointed out that skeptics lean too heavily on reason, which cannot reach the place of first principles. That weakness, they conclude, is symptomatic of reason's complete inability to find truth. Reason, according to Pascal, must depend on the first principles that the heart (which he also refers to as charity, the intuitive mind, or *l'esprit de finesse* in *Discours sur les passions de l'amour*) knows. The senses, the reason, and *le coeur* cooperate, each informing the others. In fragment 933, Pascal called these three orders flesh, mind, and will. The flesh deals with issues of corporeal reality. The mind deals with issues of mental reality. The will deals with issues of moral reality.

Perhaps Pascal's most famous rational argument for the operation of the heart and its connection to the will is the fragment called "the

24. Clarke, "Pascal's philosophy of science," 105.
25. Pascal, *Réflexions*, 306.
26. Pascal, *Provincial Letters*, 204.

wager," which Pascal labeled *l'infini—rien,* fragment 418. In it Pascal addressed the dilettante who could not claim any heart knowledge, who was without inspiration. "Let us then examine this point, and let us say: 'Either God is or he is not.' But to which view shall we be inclined? Reason cannot decide this question. Infinite chaos separates us . . . How will you wager? Reason cannot make you choose either, reason cannot prove either wrong." Pascal employed a method of contradiction, reasonably arguing against the power of reason to discern reality. He began by pointing out that those who demand the all-sufficiency of reason "profess a religion for which they cannot give rational grounds." The decision to believe or not to believe must be made. "You must wager. There is no choice, you are already committed." He then worked out the situation of the man at the gambling table, weighing the chances of winning and losing, measuring risk and gain.

In his argument, Pascal brought the gambler to the point of reasonably accepting the wager. Yet the gambler simply could not bring himself to believe. Pascal concluded his argument by dealing with the gambler's inert desire: "You want to be cured of unbelief and you ask for the remedy . . ." Pascal's remedy? Habit, the Machine. Behave like a man who believes and thus diminish your passions; once the cacophony of concupiscence has dulled, the path to belief will open up. The risk is worth it. As Pascal wrote in the following fragment (f. 419), "Custom is our nature. Anyone who grows accustomed to faith believes it, and can no longer help fearing hell, and believes nothing else." Thus Pascal presented a pragmatic approach that, employing the best abilities of reason, made short work of reason and extended the hope of faith to those who could not find anything but doubts. As Jeff Jordan writes, "The wager is intended to show that unbelief is rationally impermissible."[27] With the wager, Pascal eliminated the claims of both dogmatism/gnosticism (the work of faith as an act of reason based on certain knowledge) and skepticism (the impossibility of faith because of the lack of certain knowledge); neither reason nor doubt could thwart the gambler who weighed the risks.

## PASCAL ON HUMAN FREEDOM AND AUTHORITY

Pascal never aspired to be anything but a good Catholic, in full communion with the Church, the Tradition, and the clergy. He spoke of the

---

27. Jordan, *Gambling on God*, 1.

authority of the Church with deep respect. And yet, Pascal found himself in continual opposition to Church authorities and struggled to find a place to stand that was not compromised by heretical labels, Calvinism being the worst name being bandied about. Pascal was not shy about confrontation and dove into the theological difficulties of his day with a near-suspicious enthusiasm for the fray.

His association with the Port-Royal community and its Jansenist connections may have driven this divisiveness, or Pascal may have found the Jansenist connection appealing because it satisfied his fundamental sense of the antagonism of life. Jansenism incorporated both the affirmation of faith and the negation of sufficient reason. As Eastwood puts this, "Thus the paradoxical and synthetic structure of Pascal's thought, so conceived, suggests the opposing thrusts of an arch with Jansenism as the keystone..."[28]

Jansenism became, in many ways, Pascal's enduring *bête noire*. He entertained a long association with the community of Jansenists, largely through his sister who had joined the Port-Royal order, and throughout his writings expressed a great deal of sympathy for its zeal. Yet Pascal retained a certain distance from the community as well, never properly joining it and frequently denying a Jansenist identity. "You say I am a Jansenist, that Port Royal maintains the Five Propositions, and that I maintain them: three lies" (f. 955). Yet not only did its teachings generate a substantial amount of professional and personal distress in Pascal's life, but they also left a residue of ill repute (for widely divergent reasons) in the minds of later intellectuals.

Jansenists were those who adhered to the teachings of *Augustinus*, Cornelius Jansen's book on Augustinian theology. Jansen revived Augustine's fourth-century emphases on human depravity, the centrality of sin in human choice, and the subsequent doctrines of divine grace and the need for repentance. Faith, then, like grace, was entirely the gift of God, and the human spirit was an earthen vessel waiting to be filled. The Jansenist heresy left an objectionable odor to many of the late nineteenth-century. To churchmen, Jansenism smacked of fideism and a willfulness that challenged authority. To intellectuals, Jansenism with its insistence on human corruption pitched a shadow of skepticism over Pascal's work, a skepticism that was certainly incompatible with the

---

28. Eastwood, *Revival of Pascal*, 8.

mental prowess of the Enlightenment and the positivist optimism of the nineteenth-century.

*Augustinus* had been condemned in 1641, but the controversy about its orthodoxy did not die there. A General Assembly of French clergy had requested papal judgment (from Innocent X) on the five propositions that were supposedly found in *Augustinus*, five propositions that were suspiciously similar to Calvinist teachings: 1) the commandments of God may in fact be impossible to those who lack God's grace; 2) interior grace is irresistible; 3) in fallen nature both merit and fault only exist in situations of external freedom, though interior necessity yet exists; 4) though the semi-Pelagians admitted the necessity of interior grace, they err in teaching that man can resist it if he chooses; 5) it is semi-Pelagian to say that Christ died or shed his blood for all.

These five propositions were condemned by the papal bull, "Cum occasione," in 1653, but Pascal's barbed *Lettres Provinciales,* published in 1657, made clear that the Jansenist devotees retained their commitments to Jansenism by arguing that those five propositions, certainly anathema, were not to be found in *Augustinus*. This argument centralized over the question of right versus the question of fact.[29] In 1661, the papal office issued a Formulary that declared that the five propositions were indeed in *Augustinus;* all suspected Jansenists were required to sign it, renouncing the propositions. Pascal, who had disclaimed any formal membership in the Port-Royal community, broke with the Jansenists over the signing of this Formulary, refusing to admit that political machinations could change the truth. Despite his Catholic loyalties, Pascal was adamant that the Church was infallible, but the pope was not, and that an error was being made.[30] He linked this kind of mistake to that of the Church in the Galileo affair. No matter, he said, what the decrees from Rome declared, they could not change the reality of the planet's revolution around the sun.[31] For Pascal, the Formulary demanded that he declare as a fact what had no reality, i.e., that the five propositions were in *Augustinus*. He insisted that only matters of faith, which have been revealed by God and are contained in tradition, fell within the purview of Church authority. Matters of fact, in this case the truth about *Augustinus's* content, did not fall within that scope of authority. This careful delineation of truth

29. Hubert, *Pascal's Unfinished Apology*, 54.
30. Ibid., 75.
31. Pascal, *Provincial Letters*, 206.

challenged by the power of authority became a model for nineteenth-century Pascalisants.

In the *Pensées*, Pascal made a variety of oblique comments about papal authority. He pointed out that the desire for infallibility was a desire for security (f. 516), and recognized that the centralization of authority in the pope was a dangerous exclusion of "multitude," the opposite error of the Huguenots who excluded "unité" (f. 567). As with so many of his beliefs, the tension between opposites was critical to the place of truth. And while he never hesitated to speak respectfully of the Church, he frequently made carefully crafted remarks that put the pope's exercise of power in some shadow, particularly if it veered in any way from tradition. "Multiplicity which is not reduced to unity is confusion. Unity which does not depend on multiplicity is tyranny. France is now almost the only place left where one is allowed to say that the council is above the Pope" (f. 604). "The Pope hates and fears scholars who are not vowed to his obedience" (f. 677). "*Pope*. There is some contradiction, for, on the one hand, they say that tradition must be followed, and would not dare to disown it, while on the other they say what they like" (f. 714). Pascal felt that the council, the Church body, must undergird papal authority (f. 726), and that all Church authority was vulnerable to corruption. "But when tradition is not listened to any more, when the Pope is the only guide proposed, and he has been taken unawares, and when, with the true source of truth, that is tradition, excluded and the Pope, its trustee, prejudiced, truth is no longer free to appear, then men no longer speak of truth, and truth must itself speak to men" (f. 865).

There are "good" popes and, by implication, not-so-good popes. Fragment 916 treats Pascal's sense of outrage at the persecution he felt for his beliefs from the Inquisition and the Society of Jesus (Jesuits). The theologians argued out of human convictions, not out of holiness. Rome had censured the Jansenists unjustly, and Pascal expressed a longing for a pope who could discern the truth. He cited the apostles' statement, "We ought to obey God rather than men," in defense of his innocence. In fragments 950 and 951, Pascal cited Pope Paul IV's 1558 bull, *Cum ex apostolatus officio*, which imposed draconian measures on those suspected of heresy, including permission to kill excommunicated persons without being guilty of homicide. Pascal reflected on the breach this bull made in the legal authority of the Parlement. Later, Pascal charged the Church with "unjust and tyrannical procedure" in its persecution of the

Jansenists, calling the Jesuits motivated by the sheer political desire to squelch a sect that opposed them (f. 955).

In his *Lettres*, Pascal accused the Jesuits of adopting an approach to spirituality that had as its sole purpose membership retention, "in order to keep on good terms with all the world."[32] According to Pascal, the Church's ambition had led it to reject truth in favor of preeminence. Thus he wrote about the Jesuit mentality, so representative, as Pascal believed, of Rome's priorities:

> Men have arrived at such a pitch of corruption nowadays that, unable to make them come to us, we must e'en go to them, otherwise they would cast us off altogether; and, what is worse, they would become perfect castaways. It is to retain such characters as these that our casuists have taken under consideration the vices to which people of various conditions are most addicted, with the view of laying down maxims which, while they cannot be said to violate the truth, are so gentle that he must be a very impracticable object indeed who is not pleased with them. The grand project of our Society, for the good of religion, is never to repulse any one, let him be what he may, and so avoid driving people to despair.[33]

Clearly, Pascal, a layman, felt qualified to resist the authority of the Church when it came to the discernment of truth and he believed that the individual must be free to exercise reason in the interpretation of authoritative commands. However, as a good Augustinian, Pascal would also be quick to argue that this personal freedom to know and choose the good is not inherent in the individual. It comes from a divine grace and that grace is administered to the individual, even, sometimes, in opposition to the authority that should be defining that good. Pascal effectively circumvented the Church as the sole conduit of grace in his Augustinian resistance to the Jesuits. When the authorities have strayed, the individual can still access this grace, and this confidence in the innate function of the heart as the unmediated receptacle of God's inspiration made Pascal a very suspect Catholic indeed. Yet it is this central position of the individual—lay as well as clerical, ignorant as well as educated—that appealed to our late nineteenth-century intellectuals. They also imbibed his convictions about the relationship between human freedom

---

32. Pascal, *Provincial Letters*, 38.
33. Ibid., 51.

and Church authority, concluding that the latter could not supplant the former.

## PASCAL ON HISTORY AND SCRIPTURE: TELEOLOGY

Perhaps one of the most powerful commentaries of the twentieth century on Pascal was Lucien Goldmann's *The Hidden God* (1964). Goldmann assumes a dialectical interpretation of Pascal's thoughts, a constant movement from parts to a whole and back again. This flux of thought abandons the linear form of analysis, which would involve ideas building on one another and reaching a defined end. According to Goldmann, Pascal introduced the possibilities of dialectic reasoning[34] and he ties Pascal's work to a "tragic world vision."

It is important to take a moment to consider Goldmann's interpretation because a careful reading of Pascal's works cannot but lead us to recognize that Pascal does indeed have a "vision" of the world that differs radically from earlier generations, a vision that infused our nineteenth century Pascalisants' imagination with a sense of destiny. We have noted that Pascal rejected the efficacy of natural theology to enlighten the human soul. This rejection did not become commonplace until late in the nineteenth century, more than two hundred years after Pascal. Pascal also rejected the rationalistic vision of his proto-Enlightenment colleagues. Goldmann tells us that the loss of illumination from the natural world or by means of the functions of reason led Pascal into a consideration of the hiddenness of God, a hiddenness that Goldmann interprets in a Godot-like fashion, an endless waiting for someone to appear who never does.

This leads Goldmann to seek a way out of the conundrum presented by a God who stands in judgment, makes impossible demands, rejects compromise, and yet never grants the revelation needed to sustain hope.[35] The paradox of living a genuine existence in the suspension between all and nothing, the suspension between absolute truth and "extreme realism" is impossible.[36] If the individual embraces the highest values but makes no attempt to attain them, that individual is a Romantic. If the individual embraces these values and feels confident that he can achieve

---

34. Goldmann, *Hidden God*, 5.
35. Ibid., 37.
36. Ibid., 58.

them through his own efforts, that individual is a Thomist. The individual who embraces these values, recognizes the impossibility of wholeness, and yet continues to struggle toward them is tragic, i.e., Pascalian. The key is whether or not the soul believes it can make "progress" in its journey. The tragic man believes that, no matter his efforts or experiences, "he still remains just as *infinitely distant* as ever..."[37]

Goldmann sees Pascal's life as a dialectic between his three recorded experiences of conversion and "the uninterrupted continuity of his quest."[38] Goldmann argues that Pascal believed that man is doomed always to yearn for truth and never be able to attain it.[39] For Pascal, the final synthesis between thesis and antithesis was ever elusive, and thus human existence was inescapably tragic.

Certainly the recognition of opposite truths each demanding reconciliation, an impossible task for humans, generated a deep-seated anxiety in Pascal. We saw this in our consideration of his metaphysics and the powerlessness and wretchedness of the human state. Yet Goldmann neglects or misunderstands Pascal's genuine act of synthesis. For after Pascal described the poignant situation that has left human nature in a posture of hopeless yearning after the good and dread of the nothing, Pascal turned to scripture and its prophetic passages. In his exegesis of scripture, Pascal painted a picture of salvation history and man's place in it. He began with a description of the "Fondements," some of the incomprehensible spiritual truths of Christianity: the strangeness of God's ways, the worthlessness of human attempts at finding God, the uniqueness of Jesus Christ. He then moved into a consideration of the role of the Jewish people, particularly those of the rabbinical tradition, and the proofs of Jesus Christ in the prophecies.

It is easy for contemporary readers to dismiss Pascal's outdated biblical exegesis and development of the prophetic pieces of scripture in light of more than a hundred years of textual and historical criticism. However, the mistake of overlooking Pascal's emphasis on the prophecies is to miss the part they played in his overall vision. Without them, and the conclusions they lead to in Pascal's mind, we do end up with a tragic vision. With them, however, we see that Pascal expressed not a *tragic* vision, but a *dramatic* vision. Pascal interwove his perspective on history

37. Ibid., 63.
38. Ibid., 169.
39. Ibid., 207.

and his biblical exegeses in such a way that he clearly understood the human dilemma, this unbearable prolongation of a dissonance between *ought* and *is*, as a movement of the hand of God. Pascal's analysis was, as Goldmann asserted, not analytically linear, but creatively cultivated. Like Pascal's contemporary, Racine, of whom Goldmann also writes, Pascal viewed the world as a drama, the working out of a story of conflict and resolution.

For Pascal, the point of tension between *l'infini* and *rien* was put to rights with the full recognition of origin and destiny. Teleology was the key to tragedy; it rendered meaning out of apparently meaningless dialogue and actions. For Pascal, prophecy proved the accuracy of the Christian teleological vision. Without the course of salvation history as contained in scripture, Pascal would argue, the skeptics were right, for "uncertainty as to our origin entails uncertainty as to our nature" (f. 131). Thus Pascal equated the story of scripture to the story of history, and thus found a place for himself within the story as it moves to its destined end. "This religion consists in believing that man has fallen from a state of glory and communion with God into a state of gloom, penitence and estrangement from God, but that after this life we shall be restored by a promised Messiah, and it has always existed on earth" (f. 281). He set himself this task: "Read the prophets. See what has been accomplished. Collate what is still to be accomplished" (f. 312).

And yet Pascal was not a literalist about either scripture or history. What were important were not dates and details, but the development of the drama. The outworking of the plot was proof itself of the reality of the story. In fragment 149, Pascal described this drama. The initial creation, perfect in every way, yielded to the fall, where humanity lost its glory. "You are no longer in the state in which I made you. I created man holy, innocent, perfect, I filled him with light and understanding, I showed him my glory and my wondrous works. Man's eye then beheld the majesty of God . . ." The characters—particularly Moses and Jesus Christ—anchor the story in human history, the one pointing to the other. This drama prevents the story from turning tragic, but only for those who interpret it correctly. The audience must realize its role in the story and take it to its place of resolution.

This involvement of the role of the observer echoes Pascal's personal philosophy of understanding truth from the inside out, from the starting place in the human soul. Because it is a drama in which the audience is implicated, it required an element of ambiguity that demanded participation. Dilettantes would not understand, for Pascal firmly agreed with Augustine, "You must believe in order to understand." This ambiguity was expressed in the *Pensées* both in the place of tension and in Pascal's description of the hidden God, *Deus absconditus*. According to Pascal, God chose to disguise himself in order to draw out those who most wished to find him. "Thus wishing to appear openly to those who seek him with all their heart and hidden from those who shun him with all their heart, he has qualified our knowledge of him by giving signs which can be seen by those who seek him and not by those who do not. There is enough light for those who desire only to see, and enough darkness for those of a contrary disposition" (f. 149).

The lack of clarity is intentional, and thus Pascal rebutted the skeptics. In fact, the ambiguity was itself a form of proof, and the prophets cooperated with God's desire to disguise the truth (f. 228). Such a disguise set God free to judge those who reject the quest and enlighten those who take it on. "There is enough light to enlighten the elect and enough obscurity to humiliate them. There is enough obscurity to blind the reprobate and enough light to condemn them and deprive them of excuse" (f. 236).

Fragment 427 worked out this key doctrine in Pascal's dramatic vision. The skeptic complained about the lack of incontrovertible proof, but Pascal said that the obscurity simply reveals the nature within. The purpose of the story was to illumine the nature of each character in the drama. "Thus our chief interest and chief duty is to seek enlightenment on this subject, on which all our conduct depends. And that is why, amongst those who are not convinced, I make an absolute distinction between those who strive with all their might to learn and those who live without troubling themselves or thinking about it."

This hiddenness of God, and subsequent link to the quality of the individual, ran counterintuitive to Thomistic arguments about the human ability to grasp the existence and nature of God by reasoning with and through the general and special revelations given to all humanity. The latter, Pascal believed, led to an intellectualism that failed to generate genuine faith and, even worse, exacerbated the hubris that closed the soul off from God. "If there were no obscurity man would not feel his corruption: if there were no light man could not hope for a cure. Thus it is not only right but useful for us that God should be partly concealed and partly revealed, since it is equally dangerous for man to know God without knowing his own wretchedness as to know his wretchedness without knowing God" (f. 446). Intellectual knowledge alone is futile; only interior, immanent knowledge suffices. As Antony McKenna points out, Pascal's *Pensées* and their insistence on the hiddenness of God and the need for an interior quest troubled his successors. Malebranche's *De la recherche de la vérité* (1674) argued against Pascal's "hidden God" theory; he would insist that God was revealed, not hidden, and that faith can be made certain through reason.[40]

Pascal, according to Goldmann, was convinced that uncertainty and risk played an essential role in human existence, that everything we do is a wager. And yet Goldmann fails to understand that Pascal did *not* believe that faith was a risk; on the contrary, Pascal repeatedly expressed his confidence that faith was the only reasonable conclusion in a world fraught with risks, and that genuine faith opened the curtains to the light of certainty. The wager was merely a first step, and a step that the individual must take, apart from the coercive or authoritarian demands of a corporate structure, whether that structure was society or the Church. The wager was Pascal's parable of the dramatic vision in which each individual plays a vital role, a role that determines for him or her the outcome of the play.

It is not hard, in light of this individualism, to understand the discomfort he produced in the Catholic authorities around him who were dealing with the personal rights and liberties demanded in the wake of the Protestant reformation. Hélène Bouchilloux concurs, arguing that even Pascal's ideas about social and political order stem from his theory of orders. "In usurping the place of God, men have substituted their individual judgment for a knowledge of what is good and true, because a knowledge of what is good and true depends upon a knowledge of God, and a knowledge of God depends upon a love of God."[41] In other words, the corporate authorities, both sociopolitical and, I would submit religious, given Pascal's penetrating critique of hierarchical failures, command compliance not because of their basic corner on truth but because they embody the *image* of what they were created to be. Only the individual's choice makes the system work.

---

40. McKenna, "Reception of Pascal's *Pensées*," 257ff.
41. Bouchilloux, "Pascal and the Social World," 203ff.

## CONCLUSION

As we turn to the *fin-de-siècle*, it will become clear that, while earlier nineteenth-century authors found Pascal's wit and keen turns of expression inspirational, it was the content of his works that infused the Pascalisants' imagination. Pascal's rejection of natural theology as a means to genuine knowledge about God and his careful description of the boundaries of knowledge and the methodologies appropriate to each kind of knowledge informed Duhem's philosophy of science. Pascal's ready willingness to embrace the antinomies of human experience without seeking to eliminate the tension drove Blondel and Laberthonnière to reconsider the paradoxes of their own day and to find within them the intellectual scaffolding they needed to resist easier neo-Thomist solutions. Pascal's resistance to inappropriately exercised papal authority and his advocacy of the individual reinforced the Pascalisants' "method of immanence," a way of returning the act of faith to the experience of the individual rather than deriving it from the mandates of ecclesiastical authority. In every way, Pascal became the guiding light to these writers in their search for an authentic apologetic that was both Catholic and compelling, both orthodox and intelligent, both contemporary and traditional.

# Interlude I

## *Providentissimus Deus* (1893)

Before moving into a closer examination of the works of the Pascalisants, we need to look carefully at the papal encyclical that marked the onset of the most intense years of dialogue regarding the production of knowledge. This interlude provides a brief look at Leo XIII, the author of *Providentissimus Deus*, and at the encyclical in its context. A second interlude examining Pius X and his authorship of *Pascendi* (1907), the encyclical marking the virulent conclusion of dialogue, will follow the chapters on the authors' works.

Gioacchino Vincenzo Pecci had always harbored a deep appreciation for Latin, a flair that lent itself well to a predilection for classical works, classical ideas, and classical values. Upon his ordination in 1837, he entered the papal service without any detours along the way for parish ministry. Administration suited him well, and he served in such a capacity in Italy and, for a time, in Belgium as he rose to episcopal status and then cardinal. As early as the 1850s, he began encouraging the revival of Thomistic thought, considering it an avenue for the reintegration of Catholic thought into modern culture. In the Vatican's search for a moderate leader with a high capacity for intellectual thought, Pecci was elected to be Pope Leo XIII in 1878.

Despite the new pope's interest in *rapprochement* between contemporary and classical Christian thought, he did not deviate far from the course set by his predecessor, Pius IX, who had rejected most political and intellectual trends of the mid-nineteenth century. Pius IX's notable

1864 encyclical, *Quanta cura*, with its accompanying Syllabus of Errors, had condemned many of the liberal ideas coming out of political, economic, and social circles. The Syllabus included a refutation of the idea that "the method and principles by which the old scholastic doctors cultivated theology are no longer suitable to the demands of our times and to the progress of the sciences (Error 13)." Leo XIII certainly embraced scholasticism. The Syllabus also dismissed the notion that the individual human should be granted an individual freedom to choose what he or she believes to be true (Error 15): "Every man is free to embrace and profess that religion which, guided by the light of reason, he shall consider true."[1] The Syllabus reiterated the spiritual and temporal rights of the Church and forthrightly insisted that in no wise should the Roman Pontiff "reconcile himself, and come to terms with progress, liberalism and modern civilization."(Error 80)[2]

Pius IX continued this work of centralizing the rights and privileges of the Church in the person of the Pontiff when he called the first Vatican Council (1869–1870). Just as the Second Empire was collapsing and the Papal States were being lost, Pius IX was defining the papal position of authority in more ultramontane terms than ever before. The constitution *Pastor aeternus*, which issued from the Council, made infallible the pope's definitions of dogma and morals, without needing the consent of the Church, thus overturning earlier conciliar systems of definition. The constitution also enabled the pope to exercise authority in regard to discipline, "a fullness of jurisdiction granting him the right to intervene in any Catholic community, any where, at any time."[3] This suspicion stemmed in large part from a rejection of the immeasurable influence of Cartesian thought, a direction that had located the roots of knowledge in the self.

The Council's dogmatic constitution on faith, *Dei filius*, expressed Pius IX's zeal to eliminate the move toward individualism that had issued out of the Protestant Reformation, its call to personal faith, and its rejection of priestly mediation. *Dei filius* recalled the heresy of rejecting the *magisterium* of the Church and surrendering matters of faith "to the judgment of each individual."[4] The Vatican held the reflections of many

1. *Dogmatic Canons and Decrees*, 190–91.
2. Ibid., 209.
3. O'Connell, *Critics on Trial*, 27.
4. *Dogmatic Canons and Decrees*, 215.

intellectuals in high suspicion, considering them subject to the evils of wayward judgment. O'Connell points out that the Munich Brief of 1863 "laid down the principle that all scientific research carried on by Catholics had to be authenticated by the decisions of the Roman congregations."[5] In response to this unwelcome outbreak of personal judgment, Pius IX reaffirmed the sole authority of the Church and its instructions, focalized in the person of the pope and his understanding of revelation. Pius IX had presided over the loss of much temporal authority throughout Europe, but he left behind a compensatory legacy of enhanced spiritual authority. This legacy empowered Leo XIII in his endeavors to speak a compelling intellectual message to the leading authorities of his day.

Leo XIII continued to build on Pius IX's work by addressing the evils of socialism, communism, freemasonry, and divorce. He interfered with the administrative affairs of national and local bishops and strengthened the role of the nuncio. He closed the door to reconciliation with the Anglican Church by declaring that Anglican holy orders were null and void (1896). He also concerned himself with the teaching institutions of the Church, an area in which most popes had not sought to intervene.

The state of seminary education in the nineteenth century was, in the opinion of many, a dismal matter. Abbé Duchesne (1843–1922, church historian, professor) lamented that in France, "the clergy have read the Bible with about as much attention as they have the Koran." Seminary lectures were "tedious, jejune, and superficial" and authority was given more weight than was reason.[6] Both Ernest Renan and Émile Combes were early seminarians, and both had found the education completely irrelevant to contemporary life.

Early in his pontificate (1879), Leo XIII issued *Aeterni Patris,* an encyclical letter mandating the study of scholastic philosophy according to the "chief and master" of all scholastics, Thomas Aquinas. Leo's great allegiance to the Angelic Doctor, as Aquinas was called, is clear: "With his spirit at once humble and swift, his memory ready and tenacious, his life spotless throughout, a lover of truth for its own sake, richly endowed with human and divine science, like the sun he heated the world with the ardor of his virtues and filled it with the splendor of his teaching."[7] Surely many of the contemporary world's errors derive from false phi-

---

5. O'Connell, *Critics on Trial,* 29.

6. Ibid., 92–102.

7. Leo XIII, *Great Encyclical Letters,* 48.

losophies, a problem that could be amended by a return to the "system of philosophy which Our Fathers so dearly loved ... Let carefully selected teachers endeavor to implant the doctrine of Thomas Aquinas in the minds of students, and set forth clearly his solidity and excellence over others."[8] The scholastic system was set in motion once again.

It is in light of these clear precedents set by Pius IX and adopted by Leo XIII that we turn our attention to another pivotal encyclical, one which addressed the encroachment of liberalism into the most sacred of theological arenas, that of the study of scripture. The Church had always held that the revelation of supernatural knowledge was necessary for human salvation, and that such revelation was contained in both written and unwritten tradition and administered by the Church. If Vatican Council of 1870 had defined the authority of the papacy in the dispensation of unwritten tradition, *Providentissimus Deus* hedged in the management of written tradition.

## *PROVIDENTISSIMUS DEUS* (1893)

The brouhaha began with the increasingly edgy work of Alfred Loisy (1857–1940), priest, biblical scholar, historian, theologian, and professor at the Institut Catholique. Loisy, the most notable French representative of the modernist movement, had imbibed much of the German schools' work on biblical and historical criticism, which introduced the possibility that texts may contain fabrications, and had applied these methods to scripture. Historical criticism invited scholars to reconsider the authorship of historical documents, their relationship to other documents of the same period, and the internal integrity of the documents. He began by suggesting that the scriptures were historical texts and should be treated as such; Loisy introduced the possibility that the Christ worshipped by the Catholic Church was not the same as the first-century person Jesus, and that the dogma regarding the former Christ-figure was a development of spiritual thought and reflection over many years. Loisy's late 1893 article, "La question biblique et l'inspiration des Écritures," printed in *Études bibliques*, triggered his forced resignation from the Institute. Loisy called the ensuing years "a reign of terror which from this time

---

8. Ibid., 56.

on descended upon Catholic intellectual life"⁹ and they culminated in Loisy's excommunication.

The threat that Loisy engendered to one of the two foundations upon which the Church built its authority could not be tolerated. Not only did Loisy's arguments jeopardize the claims to historical veracity made by the Church, but his seemingly ingenuous willingness to adhere to dogma despite the lack of that dogma's rootedness in any factual bases made him seem even more dangerous. His beliefs were freefloating assertions, apparently untethered by any magisterial teaching. Most importantly, the Vatican understood that Loisy's work was more than an objectionable body of material; Loisy had introduced into popular Catholic scholarship an epistemological methodology that subjected Catholic doctrine and tradition to interpretation.

Leo XIII responded immediately with *Providentissimus Deus*. In *Providentissimus*, Leo rehearsed the doctrine of the Church regarding scripture: that it is authored by God, dictated by the Holy Ghost, and reveals God's truths; it must be protected from "fallacious and imprudent novelties."[10] Such deceptions include the broad Protestant one that advocated scripture as the only genuine source of revelation and the highest authority. Along with that argument came the distinctly Reformed one regarding the perspicuity of scripture: scripture was the medium of communication between God and the individual soul, and nothing in scripture was so obscure that it needed a mediator to enlighten the theologically untrained. This, the pope argued, was fundamentally erroneous. "It must be recognized that the sacred writings are wrapped in a certain religious obscurity, and that no one can enter into their interior without a guide."[11] Another deception Leo addressed was that of the rationalists, who rejected the possibility of supernatural revelation altogether. To them, scripture was an anthology of myths and ridiculous legends.

The solution, in the pope's judgment, was a renewed attention to seminaries and their biblical curricula, which should be primarily based on a study of the scripture directed toward devotion rather than academics. Knowledge of scripture should be an aid to faith, not a subject of scientific examination. Unlike other subjects of research, scriptural research is not primarily one of discovery, but one of corroboration and defense.

9. O'Connell, *Critics on Trial*, 139n.
10. Leo XIII, *Great Encyclical Letters*, 272.
11. Ibid., 285.

The first goal of any study of scripture should be "to interpret these passages [which have received an authentic interpretation] in that identical sense [that of the *magisterium*], and to prove by all the resources of science that sound hermeneutical laws admit of no other interpretation."[12] It should be conducted with the Vulgate translation, not in a vernacular, and every interpretation must accord with the teachings of the Church. In fact, scripture could only be safely interpreted "by those who had the apostolic succession." The biblical studies of non-Catholics might yield some interesting fruit, but should never direct Catholic study. Indeed, Catholic scholars should be aware that "the sense of Holy Scripture can nowhere be found incorrupt outside the Church, and cannot be expected to be found in writers who, being without the true faith, only know the bark of sacred Scripture, and never attain its pith."[13]

Leo went on to call for a militant defense against those who attacked the historical validity of scripture. The "trustworthiness of the sacred records" was of vital importance to the authority of the Church, which would always rest on scripture. Leo declaimed the development of "an inept method, dignified by the name of the 'higher criticism,'"[14] which endeavors to establish authorship, dating, and the integrity of a book by its own internal content. Leo rejected this kind of scholarship, and asserted that "internal evidence is seldom of great value, except as confirmation." He also condemned the scholarly work of those who picked apart a scriptural text with an eye to inconsistencies and mistakes, particularly in relation to scientific claims. Leo carefully acknowledged the goal of scripture—to establish faith in the truth of God and not to instruct readers in the truths about the universe. The writers might have voiced opinions about the world of their day, positions now discredited.[15]

Throughout the encyclical, Leo urged a posture of cooperation with the Catholic *magisterium*, a cooperation that would lend itself to enhancing the unwritten traditions and verifying truth as defined by Church dogma. Scientists and philosophers also came within the purview of this encyclical, an indication that the encyclical was about more than the study of the Bible. Leo exhorted such intellectuals to use their studies for

12. Ibid., 287.
13. Ibid., 289.
14. Ibid., 292.
15. Ibid., 295.

the same purposes, to further the reputation of the Church and establish the authority of Church as the moderator of true knowledge. Should Catholic students of other fields of knowledge—physics and philosophy are both named—come to other conclusions about knowledge, they should aim at cooperation rather than criticism.

The study of history also came within the encyclical's purview. The connection between the events recounted in scripture and the Church's dogma—maintained, defended, and interpreted by the *magisterium*—was direct, and those who challenged that link were excoriated. Loisy, a historian, remained unnamed, but his work was addressed thus:

> For the system of those who, in order to rid themselves of those difficulties, do not hesitate to concede that divine inspiration regards the things of faith and morals, and nothing beyond, because (as they wrongly think) in a question of the truth or falsehood of a passage we should consider not so much what God has said as the reason and purpose which He had in mind when saying it—this system cannot be tolerated.[16]

*Providentissimus* is a document about hermeneutics in a much larger sense than merely that of the study of scripture. In it Leo promoted a hermeneutic of concordance, of submission to the definition of knowledge as declared by the *magisterium* of the Holy Roman Catholic Church. Discoveries of science or constructions of knowledge that might invalidate Roman claims must be shown to be erroneous. "Let them loyally hold that . . . nothing can be proved either by physical science or archaeology which can really contradict the Scriptures. If, then, apparent contradiction be met with, every effort should be made to remove it."[17]

*Providentissimus* closed the epistemological circle. Natural sources of knowledge, such as reason and observation, were both inadequate and subsidiary to the greater source of knowledge in revelation, both written in scripture and orally transmitted through tradition. That revelation was organized and administered by the institution of the Church, incarnated in the bishops and supremely defended and maintained by the pontiff.

Pascal would, one suspects, have balked. His way of knowing reversed this epistemological system, culminating, instead of originating, in dogmatic faith. The possibility that the pope could be deceived, that the *magisterium* could be politically manipulated, and that correct doc-

---

16. Ibid., 296.
17. Ibid., 299.

trine could become mere word-play left the earnest seeker far from certainty. There were too many unanswered questions, too much darkness, too little ground to stand on. It is not that Pascal would have disagreed with the definition of scripture as the revelation of God; far from it, for Pascal certainly found scripture to be a valid source of "proof" about the authenticity of the Christian religion. And yet he might have argued that all the dogma in the world, even the truest dogma, cannot persuade, cannot make reasonable the act of faith.

Faith, said the scholastic, is indeed an act of God, not an achievement of the human personality. And yet it is a supernatural shifting of the reason into a higher gear, aided by the proofs of scripture and the authority of the Church, a reason that then must apodictically find the Church to be the foundation of truth. "The Church itself, by reason of its marvelous extension, its eminent holiness and its inexhaustible fruitfulness in every good thing, its Catholic unity and its invincible stability, is a great and perpetual motive of credibility, and an irrefutable witness of its own divine mission."[18] This evidence, like combustible fuel, is ignited by the act of the Holy Spirit and thus becomes faith.

Pascal, on the other hand, might say that all this is to no avail, that faith does not come by contemplating the banquet of revelation and then being given the gift of hunger. Faith, and the knowledge that issues from it, according to Pascal, came first from the pangs of hunger and the emptiness of the individual's belly and the complete dearth of provision. There, in a place of terror at the contemplation of absolute need, comes the spark of faith, and only then is the seeker prepared to recognize both the demands of a hidden God and the consolations of an immanent God.

By the nineteenth century, the great advances of the scientific revolution and the philosophical fruit of the Enlightenment were proving inadequate to the society's "absolute needs," and for many this evoked a sense of distress. The papal solutions to this spiritual malaise consisted of firmer definitions, tighter-drawn boundaries, more clearly cut answers. The Pascalisants, like Pascal, felt such a methodology would only lead to further distress, and in an attempt to restore Pascal's vision of faith, they entered the intellectual discourse.

---

18. "Dogmatic Constitution of the Catholic Faith," *Dogmatic Canons and Decrees*, 226.

# 4

## Knowing and Imagining

IN THE SAME YEAR that Pope Leo XIII issued his encyclical *Providentissimus Deus*, Pierre Duhem issued a critical piece of work illuminating one of the great themes of his scientific endeavors: the distinction between physical and metaphysical arenas of epistemology. "Physique et Métaphysique," published simultaneously in the *Revue des questions scientifiques* (July 1893) and the *Annales de philosophie chrétienne* (August/September 1893), attempted to reply to an earlier article written by Eugène Vicaire, "De la valeur objective des hypothèses physiques" (April 1893). Vicaire's article, in turn, had been written in response to Duhem's provocative article of the previous year, "Quelques réflexions au sujet des théories physiques."[1] This dialogue about the meaning and methodologies of epistemological discovery set the tone for many of Duhem's later articles.

Pierre Duhem, born in 1861, offers a bold vista into the Pascalian revival of the late nineteenth century. Like the other Pascalisants, he focused on the critical role of methodology in the processes of knowing, yet he drew out of Pascal different emphases serving his particular purposes in the study of scientific knowledge. Duhem focused on the role of interpretation in the construction of knowledge, a focus that drew in Pascal's themes of tension and cooperation between different orders of comprehension. Despite being a Catholic *avant tout*, Duhem worked his entire life to keep separate the religious dogma and scientific processes that so threatened to undo each other.

After Duhem's early studies at the Collège Stanislas, he continued at the École Normale Supérieure where focused on thermodynamics. His first doctoral thesis (1884) challenged the work of Marcelin Berthelot,

1. Duhem, "Quelques réflexions au sujet des theories physiques," 139–77.

chemist, ardent republican, member of the Académie des Sciences, and servant of the state (inspector general of public education, senator, minister of public instruction, minister of foreign affairs).[2] This most damaging professional move at the outset of his career tainted his political qualifications in the eyes of his colleagues. In his own headstrong way, Duhem published the thesis anyway. His timing, however, was unlucky, for the year it was released (1886), Berthelot became the Minister of Public Instruction. Duhem then wrote a second doctoral thesis, this time with a mathematical basis, and obtained a doctorate in sciences in 1888.[3]

Duhem's professorships began in Lille and, after a short stint in Rennes, took him to Bordeaux where he spent the remainder of his life as the Professor of Theoretical Physics in the Faculty of Sciences. His 1890 marriage only lasted two years, and his wife's death in childbirth left him a widower with a young daughter to raise. Over the years, Duhem made repeated attempts to gain a Paris position and membership in the Académie des Sciences, but despite reassurances that such honors would be forthcoming, the Paris position was permanently denied him, and he only gained non-resident status at the Académie three years before his death.

Many have suggested that this professional snub was due to Duhem's intransigent political Catholicism, an overt monarchism, and a truculent piety that flouted republican values and the ideals of the Revolution. Leo XIII's attempt at reconciling Church and State was for him a rude and unwelcome development, and he found it hard to embrace the *ralliement*.[4] His unrestrained willingness to collaborate with Catholic scientific communities (for example, speaking at their conferences in defense of Catholic faith) made him, a professor in the state system, "an ideologically unreliable civil servant."[5] Duhem's interest in Édouard Drumont's *La Libre parole*, his early sympathy for the Action française, his monetary support for Colonel Henry's widow during the Dreyfus Affair, his overt support of the Army—all these behaviors, issuing from his Catholic convictions, had political ramifications that did

---

2. Ibid., 96.
3. Martin, *Pierre Duhem*, 6.
4. Jaki, *Uneasy Genius*, 92.
5. Ibid., 103.

not escape the notice of republican authorities.[6] Not that Duhem tried to hide them. Stanley Jaki makes clear that Duhem relished recalcitrance. He was difficult to work with, openly paraded his Catholic alliances, and persistently got on the wrong side of his superiors. His friend Abbé Pautonnier needed to remind him that though "one is willing to recognize that you are basically right, . . . it is bad to be right too often."[7] His early confrontation with Berthelot set the tone for his entire career.

Duhem's increasing interest in the history of physical theories contrasted sharply with positivist constructions, for Duhem argued that medieval Catholic thinkers had laid the foundation for the revolutionary work of Galileo.[8] Toward the end of his life, Duhem worked enthusiastically on a ten-volume history of physical theories, entitled *Le Système du monde*, in which he demonstrated that the Middle Ages had been replete with fertile scientific investigations under the auspices and by means of the largesse of the Roman Catholic Church. Positivist interpretations of scientific history had portrayed a sterile Catholic influence on scientific inquiry, one that had squelched investigation under the name of religion and thrust civilization into the dark ages of ignorance and dogmatic futility.

Positivism, however, had reached a crisis point by the last decades of the nineteenth century. It had held sway in the scientific community largely through its refusal to make a claim about the essences of matter and its insistence that certain knowledge, accessible through empirical observation, was its only concern. It proceeded to make the further claim that the idea of "truth," of an essential reality behind the phenomena, was useless information, that it was, in fact, nonexistent. By the time Duhem had established his place within the scientific discourse of the day, this conviction had begun to fracture. Schools of thought became increasingly divergent from one another in their attempts to create a theoretical handle on the mass of information being generated during

---

6. There is some question about Duhem's anti-semitic sympathies. The record of his relationship with the Action française comes primarily from his daughter's memoirs (Hélène Pierre-Duhem, *Un Savant Français, Pierre Duhem*, 1936). Hélène was herself pro-Action, casting some suspicion on her interpretation of her father's leanings. Duhem also maintained several friendships with Jews, including one with Dreyfus's brother-in-law. When Blondel protested Catholic support of the Action française, Duhem supported that protest. See Martin, *Pierre Duhem*, 23.

7. Ibid., 173.

8. Nye, "Determinism of Nature," 285.

this second scientific revolution. A strictly positivist scientific position gave way to a diversity of scientific theoretical positions, most of which, however, retained a positivist quality in their unqualified grip on certain knowledge.

The majority of scientists (whether atomists, Cartesians, or Newtonians) adhered to a mechanical perspective. This perspective tended to reduce physical qualities to mere figure and movement caused by unobserved contact between minute particles. Duhem rejected this explanation and argued instead for science's restriction to experiential qualities that are assigned symbolic language.[9] He was joined in this rebellion against the status quo by Henri Poincaré[10] and Ernest Mach, both of whom were working under similar principles about the hypothetical status of theories. Mach, along with German chemist Wilhelm Ostwald (1853–1932), began to criticize science's absolute claims, and they were joined by Duhem, who also rejected the certainty of scientific knowledge. He argued that positivism itself, in whatever theoretical school, was hollow; the certain knowledge it claimed to attain eluded its grasp. He charged the positivist mentality with instrumentalism, that is the reduction of scientific inquiry to the realm of active engagement with the phenomena, and called for a renewed realism, that is a correctly structured pursuit of the truth.[11]

Catholics and positivists were equally repulsed by Duhem's argument. He insisted that positivism and religion were on nearly equal ground, for neither of them could find absolute certainty in phenomena; they both required theories/hypotheses that were inaccessible to proof, and these hypotheses came not from the phenomena but from the minds of the physicists. Martin calls this a *"non sequitur"* apologetic, and bases it on "the distinction between authoritarian and non-authoritarian apologetic strategies ... Duhem's arguments did not positively *conduce* to Catholic belief, and to obedience to Catholic ecclesiastical authority."[12] Thus Duhem circumvented the imposition of knowledge from external sources and placed it squarely in the immanent underpinnings of the

---

9. Lowinger, *The Methodology*, 14.

10. Poincaré's cutting edge articles of the last decade of the nineteenth century were published as books, *Science et hypothèse* (1902) and *La Valeur de la science* (1906). See Eastwood, *Revival of Pascal*, 27.

11. Martin, *Pierre Duhem*, 27.

12. Ibid., 35.

physicist's perception. Duhem embraced the concept of an epistemological contingency, though his was not the traditional contingent of knowledge dependent upon some external unknown causation. Duhem, working carefully to position his ideas in scientific terminology, sought to underscore the reality of a contingency that issued from the theorist's own hermeneutical operations. The Pascalian concepts of the theory of orders, the different *esprits*, and the participatory role of the observer came into play to elucidate Duhem's thinking, and Pascal's *Pensées*, a book Duhem had memorized in its entirety, inspired both Duhem's personal life and scientific ambitions.[13]

Duhem was in some ways a Pascalian "evangelist," constantly referring to Pascal, his works, and his ideas. As Fortunat Strowski, one of his colleagues, said: "At Bordeaux I knew well a great scientist who had reflected more than anyone on the history of the sciences, on the methods of science, and on physical theory: Pierre Duhem. He never stopped appealing to the example of Pascal, never gave a lecture, never wrote a chapter, without citing the *Pensées*; he it was who gave me my knowledge of and taste for it."[14] Martin believes the most critical key to understanding Duhem's works lies in his Pascalian orientation.[15]

## DUHEM AND "PHYSIQUE ET MÉTAPHYSIQUE" (1893)

In his 1892 article, "Quelques Réflexions au sujet des théories physiques," Duhem pulled together some of his opening notes for course lectures.[16] He introduced his distinction between physical theory and pure empiricism. According to Duhem, the latter was inadequate for the purposes of science because it failed to grant to theory its proper role. Physical theories organize the empirical evidence into cases that may or may not advance the cause of knowledge. Such theories only need to approximate reality in order to be useful, and their value is not absolute but relative to the use made of it. "All hypotheses are something other than simple translations of an experimental law. They are all the results of a transformation imposed on an experimental law by the mind of a physicist."[17]

---

13. Eastwood, *Revival of Pascal*, 52.
14. Quoted in Martin, *Pierre Duhem*, 59.
15. Ibid., 60.
16. Duhem, *Essays in the History and Philosophy of Science*, 1.
17. Ibid., 11.

Thus it is not the law itself that dictates theory, but the theorist, and each theorist may come up with a different theory based on the same law.

Such a theory differs from mechanical theories, which impose on the scientist an entire system within which the theory must take its place and cooperate. Theories conglomerate under the mechanical umbrella until "physicists are left with no other resource than to complicate the combinations they make with these elements in order to respond to all the demands of experimentation."[18] Kepler had found himself in these straits as he grappled with the evidence of elliptical orbits yet struggled to squeeze that evidence into the Aristotelian theory that required circular orbits. Duhem illustrated the difference between physical theory and mechanical theory by comparing them to two artists, one who had access to a full array of artistic media and one who could use pencils alone.[19]

According to Duhem, mechanical theories retained their grip on the scientific imagination because of their metaphysical claims. "An invincible urge pushes us to seek the nature of the material things that surround us and the basis for the laws that govern the phenomena we observe. This urge covers all human beings from the most superstitious savage to the most curious philosopher."[20] It becomes increasingly clear in Duhem's writings that he was engrossed in this recognition of the human urge to explain experience, to understand the behind-the-scene reality of the sensory input that shapes our lives. This basic human compulsion challenged the positivist's complacent denial of a "realer reality" than the one accessible to phenomenal experience.

Duhem concluded this article by insisting that mechanical theories ultimately obstruct the progress of true science, and that the only course of action to avoid such dead-ends is to recognize the purely symbolic nature of theories. That is, physical theories must avoid metaphysical underpinnings and metaphysical ambitions. He developed his thesis at some length by arguing for a symbiotic relationship between experimental laws and mathematical analysis, the former making available "a confused and inseparable mass" and the latter providing "a thread to

---

18. Ibid., 13.
19. Ibid.
20. Ibid., 15.

guide [the human mind] in this labyrinth."[21] Neither the laws nor the analysis have a place for metaphysical explanations.

Eugène Vicaire, in "De la valeur," had responded to Duhem's thesis by contending that Duhem was himself falling into a positivist trap by relegating certain knowledge to the physical world, robbing the metaphysical world of any true substance, and consigning questions about essence to a netherworld of skepticism. In "Physique et Métaphysique," Duhem argued that metaphysics does offer sure knowledge, but that it was not attained through scientific methods and could not answer scientific questions.

Duhem began by pointing out the purely phenomenological quality of our knowledge. This knowledge is useful, but is neither complete nor completely reliable. Metaphysics takes this knowledge and induces from it the substances that lie behind the phenomena. Duhem was quick to point out that this distinction in knowledge is not inherent in the knowledge itself but in the intellect that tries to discern it. "An angel's intellect," with a full understanding of both the phenomena and the substance, would not differentiate between the two. The human understanding, however, cannot appropriate this level of vision.[22] The human understanding has limitations; these boundaries do not regulate the capacity of knowledge but do relegate orders of knowledge within separate domains that may communicate but cannot interfere with one another.

As soon as Duhem spoke of limitations, he became vulnerable to the charge of skepticism, yet he insisted that it was absurd to think that the tools of science will operate in every field of inquiry. Such a claim demonstrated the preening overextension of dogmatism. "Always it is an illegitimate extension given to a legitimate method of logic. The tool has been prepared for a definite kind of work; the tool user wished to give it another. Manipulating it for a long time, using force, bringing his dexterity to bear, has had no result or no result except drudgery. So, rebuffed, he has thrown the tool away and folded his arms."[23] The result of misapplied dogmatism inevitably led to skepticism when it realized that its claims were empty. Thus Duhem rejected the role of skeptic while simultaneously avoiding the charge of fideism.

21. Ibid., 26.
22. Duhem, "Physique et Métaphysique," 464.
23. Ibid., 474. English translation from Pierre Duhem, *Essays*, 39.

In the eyes of others, Duhem was vulnerable to the charge of positivism, for he denied the ability of phenomenal knowledge to access "real" knowledge. Yet Duhem insisted that positivism was not the simple claim that positive sciences cannot understand causes; positivism "is to assert that there is no logical method other than the method of positive sciences, that anything that cannot be achieved by this method, anything unknowable to positive sciences, is in itself absolutely unknowable."[24] Positivism sought to benefit from the intermingling of positivist methods in realms of metaphysical inquiries. Unable to attain certain results, the positivist could then claim that no genuine knowledge existed beyond the phenomena. As indicated earlier, this argument about the existence of a reality beyond the phenomena and the possibility of knowing that reality was stimulated by the neo-Kantian philosophy so prevalent in the university system at the time. Duhem, however, never embraced neo-Kantian principles primarily because, deriving inspiration from Pascal, he rejected the Kantian idea that the reality beyond the phenomena was essentially unknowable. According to Duhem's belief, such knowledge was accessible, but not through positivist methodologies.

According to Duhem, Descartes was most guilty of mingling the two orders of knowledge.[25] Descartes came out of his plunge into doubt and into the light of physical certainties by deducing from them a metaphysical reality, his consciousness of self. Cartesian metaphysics had ever since wrought havoc in the epistemological world. This does not, however, mean that Descartes's physical theories had not borne fruit, but merely that the careful scientist must discriminate between proper research and metaphysical chimera. "Often illusion inflames human activities more than the clear understanding of the object pursued. Is this a reason for confusing illusion with truth? Admirable geographical discoveries have been made by adventurers seeking the Land of Gold. Does this mean that our maps should include El Dorado?"[26]

Despite the pithy conclusion, Duhem did indeed believe in the Land of Gold. He fended off the role of positivist by reaffirming the reality of

24. Ibid.
25. Ibid., 480.
26. Ibid., 486. "Souvent l'illusion enflamme l'activité humaine plus que la claire connaissance de l'objet à poursuivre: est-ce une raison pour confondre l'illusion avec la vérité? D'admirables découvertes géographiques ont été faites par des aventuriers qui cherchaient le pays de l'or; faut-il, sur nos cartes, figurer l'Eldorado?" English translation, *Essays*, 49.

knowledge outside positive methodologies. He simply wanted to keep such a land—more than mythical, yet less than material—off geographical maps. The Land of Gold might in fact exist, but it would never be found by the positioning of exact latitude and longitude.

In this early article, Duhem laid the foundation for many of the themes he developed in the subsequent decade. His primary concern centered not on the absolute partition between physical and metaphysical fields of knowledge but on their autonomy; he would pursue this line of thought more thoroughly in later articles, holding in constant tension their independence and their concurrent interpenetration as a kind of dialectic.[27] His passing reference to Pascal in this early article as someone who resisted the Cartesian collapse of the two systems grew increasingly frequent in subsequent works, and Pascal's discourse about orders of knowledge and the methodologies appropriate to each order became more and more useful in Duhem's explication of epistemological structure.

Though Duhem used Thomistic thought in "Physique et Métaphysique" to demonstrate the long-established epistemological dichotomy, it was a cursory application of the peripatetic philosophy, and these early efforts to make scholasticism work faded from Duhem's writing until 1905, the year he began collaborating more closely with the *Annales* whose masthead posted a quote from Augustine: "Let us search then like those who must find, and find like those who must continue to search, for it is written: 'the man who has reached the end is only beginning' (Ecclus. 18.7)."[28] Duhem's opinion of Thomistic constructs deteriorated to the point that his daughter's biography recorded his judgment of Aquinas as "a well-meaning philosophical incompetent whose famed 'synthesis' of Christianity and Aristotle was nothing of the sort, merely incoherent!"[29] As the century waned and the new century took root, Duhem's interest in the historical roots of scientific theories and their contribution to human knowledge became more than a hobby or side show to his scientific work. It began to parallel his research in ways that reinforced his thinking about scientific theory as representation rather than explanation.

27. Lowinger, *Methodology of Pierre Duhem*, 1.
28. Martin, *Pierre Duhem*, 51.
29. Ibid., 58.

And finally, the role of the individual scientist in making judgments in ways that lead to "a logical and harmonious order"[30] keys the reader into the stress Duhem would begin to lay on the hermeneutical task of scientific discovery. Duhem granted authority to the inquirer to shape the questions and translate the answers in ways that determine results, and the assignment of this authority challenged both positivists and Catholics by removing the objectivity and certitude of the resulting theories. Instead, Duhem granted the status of certainty squarely in metaphysical claims, which cannot be derived from physical experimentation. Let us examine each of these developments in turn.

### DUHEM AND A DIALECTICAL METHODOLOGY

At the 1894 Third International Congress of Catholics, held in Brussels, Pierre Duhem met Father J. Bulliot, a man who would one day be head of the Department of Philosophy of the Institut Catholique in Paris. In 1911, Duhem wrote a letter to Father Bulliot regarding the relationship between science and religion in which he outlined what he believed to be the proper nature of their association. He expressed concern that scientists and metaphysicists should stay out of one another's business lest religion suffer and positivism, materialism, and agnosticism triumph. Proper method, Duhem insisted, is essential. There are different methods for different sources of knowledge, which have "different principles and different objects ... [requiring] different routes from different points of departure."[31] Harmony is possible, but only if the two orders of knowledge are recognized as separate and sovereign in their own field of inquiry.

He clarified this harmony in his 1904 rebuttal of Abel Rey, "Physique du croyant." Rey had attributed Duhem's epistemological position to that of a physicist whose faith has interpreted his scientific work. Duhem rejected this summary entirely, claiming that if this were so, he would renounce all his work. His goal was to prove that physics issued from an autonomous method independent of all metaphysics and that his theories said nothing about anything except experience. He reasserted that it

---

30. Duhem, "Physique et Métaphysique," 466. "un ordre logique et harmonieux."
31. Duhem, *Essays*, 160.

was impossible to guess the realities that lay behind the sensible, and that therefore his work made no metaphysical claims whatsoever.[32]

Duhem carefully structured his argument to lead the reader into an understanding of the complex but clear-cut nature of the relationship between physical and metaphysical orders of knowledge. His first step was to insist on a positive methodology, by which he meant that his inquiries both came out of and led into a meticulously structured examination of physical observations. Duhem's early training under Jules Moutier, a mechanist in theory, was followed by a period of empirical influence at the École Normale. The professors there were skeptical about mechanistic theories and insisted that the laws of experiment were the only source of truth. Duhem, in trying to blend these two approaches, was faced with trying to construct hypotheses with only the laws that experiment afforded, but with the logical rigor of the mathematical mechanists.[33]

When Duhem began his teaching career, he realized that the combination of these methods was inadequate to explain to his students the process by which science progresses. Both methods aspired to the truth, but neither was capable of attaining it. The mathematical rigor of the mechanists must be completely absorbed and applied to the experimental laws of the empiricists, and the result would be a third thing, a schema of syllogisms that were each subject to rigorous proof and that together constituted a construction of the scientist's own invention. These conclusions, Duhem pointed out, did not come from his personal religious beliefs, but from the hard, cold workshop of the classroom.

He continued to build his case by pointing out that not only was his methodology positive, but the results were positive as well. It is, Duhem argued, a metaphysical claim that everything in the material world can be reduced to matter and movement; it is metaphysics that says that every quality must be reduced to quantitative elements. Duhem believed his work attempted to distinguish between the known and the unknown, but never made a claim about the knowable and the unknowable. In fact, he did not attempt to make any pronouncements regarding the truth or untruth of mechanical theories; he simply attempted to judge the worthiness of such theories by careful analysis, recognizing that none of them was an adequate approximation of the observations granted by experiment.

32. Duhem, "Physique du croyant," 45.
33. Ibid., 48.

Hypotheses were subject to falsification if even one criterion contradicted them, thus the experimental model, applied to mechanistic theories, demonstrated the impossibility of explaining all phenomena. To do the work of constructing a satisfactory theory, the physicist must begin with primary qualities, that is, qualities that cannot be further reduced or broken down. A chemist does not decide that he has discovered a new element until he has done his best to deconstruct that element into more primary elements; he does not make that decision based on metaphysical preconceptions. Nevertheless, Duhem insisted, this does not lead to the logical conclusion that he has in essence discovered a new element, for another scientist on another day may find a way to break that element down further; it only means that in theory, not in certainty, he has discovered a new element.[34]

According to Duhem, it is metaphysical thought that makes absolute claims about unproven qualities possessed by objective realities, for example, the immortality of the soul, the infallibility of the pope, or the freedom of the individual. True science can speak no word about these claims, whether to verify or falsify them. False science, that is scientific theory that finds its source in metaphysical views, makes every attempt to dissect metaphysical claims. For example, Cartesian and atomist theories make similar claims about absolute knowledge as does the Catholic Church; all three schools of thought believe that matter is objectively what they say it is, thus disagreements about conclusions bring the theories into conflict. Cartesian theory is incompatible with transubstantiation; atomism is incompatible with dogma about the soul directing the body. Under Duhem's system, there was no basic conflict because metaphysics made claims about objective reality whereas physical theories "were propositional, relative to mathematical signs divested of objective existence; not having any common ground, the two kinds of judgments can neither agree nor contradict one another." What is physical theory? "It is a mathematical formula used to summarize and classify laws derived from experiment. By itself, this principle is neither true nor false; it simply gives an image more or less satisfying of the laws it attempts to represent."[35]

---

34. Ibid., 56.

35. Ibid., 59. "sont des propositions relatives à certains signes mathématiques dénués de toute existence objective; n'ayant aucun terme commun, ces deux sortes de jugements ne peuvent ni s'accorder, ni se contredire." "C'est une forme mathématique pro-

Such laws can agree or disagree with metaphysical theories, but they cannot make any claims about the truth beyond the theories; they can neither verify nor disqualify them. For example, a question about the compatibility of free will and the conservation of energy makes no sense. The theory about the conservation of energy says nothing about objective reality; it is merely a mathematical formula that is useful to human understanding and that permits certain conclusions that accord with experiment. This does not make the formula or the conclusions either true or false. All that can be concluded is that the theory is good if it corresponds adequately to laws derived from observation and it is bad if it does not. Duhem illustrated this with the image of a shell collector who arranged his shells according to the seven colors of the rainbow, placing each color in a separate drawer. However, when the collector came across a white shell, what did he do? Did he conclude that since he does not have a white drawer, no white shell can exist? In the same way, those who eliminated the possibility of a concept like free will simply because there was not a corresponding drawer in physical theory leaped to absurd conclusions.[36]

Since metaphysical claims about the physical world necessarily rely on past events that cannot be observed and require future events that can never be ascertained, such claims lack substance. They are only the needs of the inquirer imposed on observations. However, Duhem went on to elaborate on the ways a metaphysician should rightly make use of physical theory. Such a natural philosopher must take into account the facts of the senses and observations of the physical world. This is not generally difficult because most observations are common experiences, but it becomes more difficult when the metaphysician must discern between experimental facts and theoretical interpretations.[37]

Duhem illustrated this with a digression into current optical theories. Optical experimentation could speak about light and properties, but it often used language, such as the belief in an ether, that was heavy with metaphysical claims. Thus the metaphysician must thoroughly understand the physical theories and must be able to discern the difference

---

pre à résumer et à classer des lois constatées par l'expérience. Par lui-même, ce principe n'est ni vrai, ni faux; il donne simplement une image plus ou moins satisfaisante des lois qu'il prétend représenter."

36. Ibid., 60ff.
37. Ibid., 134.

between conclusions based on experiment and observation and conclusions derived from preconceived hypotheses. At this point, Duhem drew in Pascal's differentiation between the *esprit géométrique* and the *esprit de finesse* to explain this need for discernment.

> All too often in the accounts of a physical experiment, matter, real and objective, and form, purely theoretical and symbolic, fuse. This synthesis takes place in such a subtle and complex manner that the geometric mind, with its clear, rigorous procedures that are at once too simple and too rigid, cannot separate them. It requires the penetrating and delicate operation of the intuitive mind which alone can slip between matter and form. The intuitive mind alone can discern the artificial construction that is created by the theory and that has no value to the metaphysician. This result of this discernment, rich with objective truth, is appropriate for the cosmologist.[38]

Duhem continued by turning his attention to physical theories, their proper boundaries, and the necessary, but restricted, role of metaphysics. Physical theory must constrain itself to a natural classification of experimental laws. Every physicist, Duhem believed, aspires after "a physical theory that could represent all the experimental laws by means of a system of perfect logical unity."[39] History tells him that this aspiration is as old as science itself, and that the tendencies that direct this development are not intelligible to the physicist unless he is more than a physicist. If a physicist remains an intransigent positivist, believing that anything unsusceptible to scientific method cannot ever be known, he will take that tendency into his work and will thus ignore its real progress. If, however, he is open to the human spirit, which rejects such positivistic arguments, he will be able to leap over the wall of ignorance and explore the possibilities of a united theory.

38. Ibid., 135. "Bien souvent, dans le récit d'une expérience de physique la matière, réelle et objective, et la forme, purement théorique et symbolique, se compenètrent d'une manière si intime et si compliquée que l'esprit géométrique, avec ses procédés clairs, rigoureux, mais trop simples et trop peu souples pour être fort pénétrants, ne peut suffire à les séparer; il y faut les démarches insinuantes et déliées de l'esprit de finesse; lui seul, se glissant entre cette matière et cette forme, les peut distinguer; lui seul peut deviner que ceci est construction artificielle, créée de toutes pièces par la théorie et sans usage pour le métaphysicien, tandis que cela, riche de vérité objective, est propre à renseigner la cosmologiste."

39. Ibid., 140. "une théorie physique qui représenterait toutes les lois expérimentales au moyen d'un système d'une parfaite unité logique."

> He will affirm that, beneath the observations of the senses, only accessible to certain methodological procedures, are hidden realities, the essence of which is inaccessible by those same procedures; that these realities are arranged in a certain order that physical science will never be able to observe; but that physical theory, by its successive developments, tends to arrange experimental laws in an order more and more analogous to that transcendent order by which the realities are arranged; that thereby physical theory gradually moves toward a form that is in fact a natural classification; finally, that the logical unity has a character without which physical theory can never hope to attain the status of a natural classification.[40]

The physicist is suspended between the necessary indifference regarding the outcome of experimental laws in according with his theory, yet the necessary hope that such an outcome is probable. So what is the difference between the physicist predicting the existence of a law and the shell collector predicting the existence of a blue shell just because he has a blue box? The difference, Duhem argued, is that the classification system of the collector is a purely arbitrary system—the colors of the rainbow—whereas the theories of a physicist must reflect an ontological order. The physicist must make theoretical claims that cannot be proven, but this vision of an ontological ideal is essential to the proper development of a comprehensible physical theory. "Thus, in order to find the headings that establish its legitimacy, physical theory must draw them from Metaphysics."[41]

By this point in his article, Duhem had clarified the absolute autonomy of the two different sources of knowledge. He had explained the way that the metaphysical order must understand and use physical knowledge and he had demonstrated that the physical order must find inspiration and a teleological purpose from metaphysical knowledge.

---

40. Ibid., 141. "Il affirmera que sous les données sensibles, seules accessibles à ses procédés d'étude, se cachent des réalités dont l'essence est insaisissable à ces mêmes procédés; que ces réalités se rangent dans un certain ordre dont la science physique ne saurait avoir la contemplation directe; mais que la théorie physique, par ses perfectionnements successifs, tend à ranger les lois expérimentales en un ordre de plus en plus analogue à l'ordre transcendant selon lequel se classent les réalités; que, par là, la théorie physique s'achemine graduellement vers sa forme limité qui est celle d'une *classification naturelle*; enfin, que l'unité logique est un caractère hors duquel la théorie physique ne saurait prétendre à ce rang de classification naturelle."

41. Ibid., 142–43. "Ainsi, pour trouver les titres qui établissent sa légitimité, la théorie physique les doit réclamer de la Métaphysique."

This reciprocal service is possible because of the analogical relationship between physical theory and cosmological theory. Duhem used a Platonic image of shadows cast on a wall in combination with an Aristotelian method of sensory analysis to affirm the real existence of solid figures that cast the shadows. In the same way, the mathematical symbols of a physicist's theories are the shadows behind which lie the ontological realities.

According to Duhem, the reflections of a cosmologist (one who studies the origins and essences of reality rather than the appearances and mechanisms of reality) and a physicist have a common point of departure. They must both begin with the experimental laws derived from observation. It is the direction that each reflection takes that distinguishes the two modes of inquiry. The physicist wishes, with the help of discovered laws, to acquire an increasingly precise knowledge; the cosmologist analyzes those same laws to uncover, if possible, the essential relationships accessible to human reason. For example, the physicist and cosmologist both study the laws of chemical combustion, but the physicist wants to know exactly about conditions of temperature, pressure, and the like whereas the cosmologist wants to know the reasons why certain elements cease to appear while a third element appears. The cosmologist applies this to a speculation about the change of existence versus permanence under different appearances.[42]

The physicist observes matter; the cosmologist defines form. They speak to one another, encourage each form of inquiry, and then retire to their own corners. This dialectical relationship is not Hegelian because the thesis and the antithesis cooperate but do not blend to form a third alternative, a synthesis. They remain theses in their own rights, each serving as the antithesis to the other. This antimony is itself a Pascalian theme, central to Pascal's understanding of the great gap that lies between the understanding of what the human is or experiences and what the human is meant to be, between what the reason can discern and what the will can choose.[43] Duhem maintained a "perpetual tension between intuitive and deductive factors" and did not seek to resolve the tension but, on the contrary, found the place of antimony the only fruitful ground to stand on.[44] Duhem believed that there was a reciprocal and interactive relationship between induction and deduction. The mathematician can-

---

42. Ibid., 145.
43. Eastwood, *Revival of Pascal*, 8.
44. Martin, *Pierre Duhem*, 115.

not perfectly follow the deductive method because, as Pascal showed, it is impossible to define properly and demonstrate perfectly every principle.[45] And yet inductive methodologies do not belong at all in the theoretical stage of physics for they lead to presuppositions (fictitious or absurd experiments) that mislead and create imaginary results.[46]

Pascal was not ultimately interested in a unified system of knowledge. The scholastic method was a nested-cup approach, wherein inferior sciences were subsets of superior sciences and the principles of the latter trickled down to those of the former. Pascal kept the sciences discrete, and believed that the different ways of knowing were not for the purpose of synthesis but for illumination.[47] Duhem clearly agreed with Pascal, and thus, deprived of an interpretive grid, must of necessity introduce a system of hermeneutics by which the physicist draws meaning out of the natural classification of laws.

## DUHEM AND PHYSICAL HERMENEUTICS

Duhem elaborated on these ideas in his fourteen-article series, "La Théorie physique: son objet, sa structure," published in *Revue de philosophie* between 1904 and 1905. In this lengthy work, Duhem reiterated his "positivist and pragmatic" view of nature. He declared himself to be neither an idealist nor a phenomenalist, for he believed there was an essential reality beyond the sensible yet did not believe it was accessible through means of physical experimentation. Physical theory can either attempt to explain the laws discovered through experiment, or it can be satisfied with the construction of an abstract system that summarizes and classifies these laws in logical, rational ways. Explanation seeks to *translate* these laws into substance; an abstract system seeks to *interpret* these laws and create a meaningful schema. The translation will always fail to reach the unexplained and inexplicable; the interpretation deals

---

45. This recalls Pascal's theory of "infinite regress," the inability to ever define and prove every portion of an experiment or hypothesis. Pascal believed that there are some things that do not need proof, that are accessible to common sense. See Martin, *Pierre Duhem*, 60.

46. Duhem, *Aim and Structure of Physical Theory*, 202. This English translation of the original fourteen-article series is faithful to the first edition. The author introduces it with the reassurance that no substantive changes were made between the original 1906 publication and the subsequent 1914 publication of the articles in book format.

47. Martin, *Pierre Duhem*, 99.

only with the data at hand and its analysis so that the inquirer can make use of the information.

In "La Théorie physique," Duhem outlined the steps to forming an interpretive theory: 1) the selection of simple properties and the assignment to them of mathematical symbols of measurement; 2) the generation of principles that logically group together these properties; 3) the construction of hypotheses that can be employed in the effort to measure and calculate (with the caveat that these hypotheses are not stating "real relations among those realities"); and 4) the drawing of conclusions that are then compared to the experimental laws in search of the "degree of approximation."[48]

Duhem believed that theory should be considered as merely an economy of thought (and supported this by citing Mach). Theories are mere classifications, organizing arrangements facilitating the use of knowledge. The art of a genuine physical theory is to bring together the laws supplied by experiment into groups that facilitate their management and application. The true physicist works with theories while always understanding them to be representations, not explanations. Though he will be constantly tempted to believe that the relations a theory perceives correspond to reality, the physicist must always set aside these suspicions and hopes in order to focus on data observation.[49]

At this point, Duhem recognized the value of this inducement to believe in the reality of the theory rather than its purely conjectural status. This conviction, that a reality lies behind the sensory and that his theory may approximate that reality rather more than other theories, was useful in its verification of the intuition, the knowledge of the *coeur*, "his faith in a real order reflected in his theories more clearly and more faithfully as time goes on." Thus, this intuition made clear that these theories were not explanations but neither were they mere artificial concoctions. Duhem quoted Pascal: "We have an impotence to prove, which cannot be conquered by any dogmatism; we have an idea of truth which cannot be conquered by any Pyrrhonian skepticism."[50] The ambiguity of theory was something neither the positivists nor the neo-Thomists could abide.

48. Duhem, *Aim and Structure*, 20.
49. Ibid., 23ff.
50. Ibid., 27.

Duhem also recovered the wager illustration, and discussed the ways that good theories, which are based on natural classifications, merit a bet on their success whereas theories that issue from artificial explanations make foolish bets. This idea of a wager was Duhem's way of talking about that foundational principle of experimentation: prediction. The ability of a good theory to suggest possible outcomes stems from its proximity to the classification of laws derived from observation. This is how Duhem explained the relationship between induction and deduction. Experimental laws must be built on observation, an inductive procedure, whereas the construction of a theory that can point the way to new inquiries is a deductive procedure. To apply deduction to the experimentation step is to become lost in the mire of explanation; to apply induction to the hypothesis-construction step is to fail to make good use of the scientist's interpretive powers.

Duhem described these interpretive powers using Pascal's distinction between exact minds and geometrical minds (f. 511). Duhem understood this to imply that there were two sorts of scientific mindsets: abstract, which "attract strong but narrow minds" and ample, which appeal to "broad and weak minds."[51] An ample mind (which Duhem illustrated by recalling Napoleon, Frenchman though he was) can manage extraordinary amounts of information but cannot make good abstractions and generalizations. This mind was more attuned to Pascal's *esprit de finesse*. The ample mind is often found in the English world, and Duhem referred to novelists (Charles Dickens, George Eliot), vocations (chess players, military heads of state), playwrights (William Shakespeare), and scientists/natural philosophers (Francis Bacon, John Locke, and David Hume) to demonstrate the ample mind. The narrow mind was more tied to Pascal's *esprit géométrique*, and was, according to Duhem, best represented in the French world (Pierre Corneille, René Descartes, Honoré de Balzac).[52]

Both mindsets must share a universal trait in order to best work out their vocations in productive ways. Duhem here introduced the role of common sense in physics. Common sense insists on the laws of logical non-contradiction in generating hypotheses. Common sense resolves the "confused collection of tendencies, aspirations, and intuitions" that often assail the physicist in his search for truth. "No language is precise

51. Ibid., 57.
52. Ibid., 64.

enough and flexible enough to define and formulate [the requirements of reason and the needs of the imagination]; and yet, the truths which this common sense reveals are so clear and so certain that we cannot either mistake them or cast doubt on them; furthermore, all scientific clarity and certainty are a reflection of the clarity and an extension of the certainty of these common-sense truths." He reinforced this assertion by citing Pascal: "nature supports reason when impotent and prevents it from talking nonsense even at that point."[53]

Duhem carefully explained the interpretive stage, the transition between concrete observations and symbolic language. He pointed out how dangerous this step is (*traduttore, traditore,* "to translate is to betray") because of the impossibility of attaining a complete equivalence.[54] "An experiment in physics is not simply the observation of a phenomenon; it is, besides, the theoretical interpretation of this phenomenon."[55] Good experiments go beyond the accurate recording of observations into the interpretation of those observations into abstract symbols of representation; this interpretation is a judgment on the part of the physicist and therefore can itself be interpreted in various manners.

This delicate operation of interpretation means that certainty and precision are related in inverse proportions. An experimental observation is always less certain but more precise than a non-scientific observation because of the interpretive role. Duhem used the example of someone testifying to the fact that he saw a white horse at a certain time and place. Such an observation has a high certainty, but low precision; while it tells you broadly where and when, it cannot tell you anything about the age of the horse, the breed of the horse, the exact time or the placement of the horse's hooves. A scientific observation can offer extreme detail, but those details are subject to the observer's interpretive grid, lending less certainty.[56] Unlike common-sense laws whose truth can be asserted or denied, a law of physics "can acquire this minuteness of detail only by sacrificing something of the fixed and absolute certainty of common-sense laws. There is a sort of balance between precision and certainty: one cannot be increased except to the detriment of the other . . . A man

53. Ibid., 104.
54. Ibid., 133.
55. Ibid., 144.
56. Ibid., 163. Also see Duhem's arguments in "Quelques réflexions au sujet de la physique expérimentale," ibid., 211f.

may swear to tell the truth, but it is not in his power to tell the whole truth and nothing but the truth. 'Truth [citing Pascal again] is so subtle a point that our instruments are too blunt to touch it exactly. When they do reach it, they crush the point and bear down around it, more on the false than on the true.'"[57]

The result is the progress of physical theory that involves creativity and imagination, that involves the scientist as an artist working on "a symbolic painting in which continual retouching gives greater comprehensiveness and unity, and the *whole* of which gives a picture resembling more and more the *whole* of the experimental facts, whereas each detail of this picture cut off and isolated from the whole loses all meaning and no longer represents anything."[58] Common sense begins with observation, an inductive procedure, which yields to schematic representation, a deductive procedure. "But between the two domains there is established a continual circulation and exchange of propositions and ideas."[59]

That exchange becomes valuable when it is properly applied in the construction of hypotheses, hypotheses that must change (unlike absolute truth) relative to the influx of new information. "All hypotheses are something other than simple translations of an experimental law. They are all the results of a transformation imposed on an experimental law by the mind of a physicist."[60]

Duhem's 1894 article, "Quelques Réflexions au sujet de la physique expérimentale," elucidated this hermeneutical task. Interpretation makes a substitute of symbolic representation for the concrete data. That symbolic representation, Duhem suggested, is like a language: "Just as French speakers, accustomed to their native language, cannot conceive a thought without at the same time stating it in French, so also physicists no longer conceive an experimental fact without simultaneously making it correspond to the abstract and schematic expression that theory gives it."[61] Interpretation is the critical method, which explains why so many scientific observations throughout history have been lost to contempo-

---

57. Ibid., 179.
58. Ibid., 204.
59. Ibid., 266.
60. Duhem, *Essays*, 11.
61. Duhem, "Quelques réflexions au sujet de la physique expérimentale," 185. See also Duhem's metaphors of language on pages 200 and 208. English translation from Pierre Duhem, *Essays*, 80.

rary scientists who lacked the interpretive matrix. "They have sealed in their ideas in signs for which we lack the keys."[62]

Hermeneutical methodology demands a delicate sense of reasoning, "that rare subtle quality, that sort of flair which is called experimental sense—an endowment of the subtle mind (*esprit de finesse*) more than of the geometrical mind (*esprit géométrique*)."[63] Even so, the best physical theory can never prove or disprove a cosmological doctrine. One thinker may see an analogy where another sees nothing. The two can compare and contrast their reflections, but they cannot convince or convict. "All that [the theorist—physicist or cosmologist] can do is, by his discourse, direct the attention of his adversary to the similarities he thinks are important, and to divert his attention from the discrepancies that he thinks are negligible; he can only hope to persuade; he can never claim to prove."[64] A physicist chooses his interpretation based on elegance, simplicity, and convenience—all reasons that are subjective; contingent; and variable with time, schools of thought, and persons. A physicist finds a resonance between a theory and his own predilections. The contingency is within. Duhem proceeded to illustrate this process through an examination of historical theories and their fruitfulness for the progress of science.

## DUHEM AND HISTORY

Duhem's 1894 article, "Les Théories de l'optique," used a study of the history of optical theories to examine the lasting value that antiquated theory has had in contemporary science.[65] Duhem traced the progress

---

62. Ibid., 209. English translation from *Essays*, 97.

63. Ibid., 211. "cette qualité rare, subtile, à cette sorte de flair qui se nomme le sens expérimental—apanage de l'esprit de finesse plutôt que de l'esprit géométrique." English translation from *Essays*, 98.

64. Duhem, "Physique du croyant," 147. "Tout ce qu'il peut faire, c'est, par ses discours, d'attirer l'attention de son adversaire sur les similitudes qu'il juge importantes, de la détourner des divergences qu'il croit négligeables; il peut souhaiter de persuader celui avec qu'il discute; il ne saurait prétendre à le convaincre."

65. Later, in "La Théorie physique" (p. 33), Duhem will illustrate these thoughts with the image of a relay runner passing on a lighted torch, concluding with these remarks: "The same is true of most physical doctrines; what is lasting and fruitful in these is the logical work through which they have succeeded in classifying naturally a great number of laws by deducing them from a few principles; what is perishable and sterile is the labor undertaken to explain these principles in order to attach them to assumptions concerning the realities hiding underneath sensible appearances."

of optical science beginning with Descartes's mistake about the instantaneous transmission of light. Duhem's point was that despite Descartes's metaphysical muddle, he still produced valuable work.[66] Duhem pushed on with the work of Christian Huygens (1629–95), Isaac Newton (1642–1727), Thomas Young (1773–1829), and Augustin Fresnel (1788–1827), demonstrating in each case that the individual metaphysical assumptions (for example, the existence of the ether as a transmission matrix for either light waves or particles) were elaborate constructions made in a desperate attempt to fit the realities observed.

More contemporary work in the area of electromagnetics (Henry Cavendish [1731–1810], Charles Augustin de Coulomb [1736–1806], Michael Faraday [1791–1867], Antoine Henri Becquerel [1852–1908], James Maxwell [1831–79]) was also, Duhem insisted, rife with contradictions largely because of the discrepancies between the theories and the experimental observations. Many wished to overlook such incongruities, a development in the scientific world that made Duhem echo Pascal: "We must speak in broad terms of figure and movement, because these are true. But to speak of what the machine is actually composed of is ridiculous; such statements are useless, uncertain, and tiresome."[67]

Duhem concluded by philosophizing about this history of optical theories, insisting that just as the work of one generation becomes the mockery of a later generation, so today's theories will have to give way to the thinking of the next generation. Ergo, the knowledge that these theories generate is temporary, not absolute.[68] Nevertheless, Duhem perceived in the historical construction and deconstruction of theories lasting value. He rejected skepticism in light of the experience of those who perceive "the thread of a tradition, a slow but uninterrupted progress; they are not slow to see that a theory never disappears entirely; that one part of their accomplishments, sometimes great, sometimes small but never nothing, remains a part of science."[69] Even when a theory proves

---

66. Duhem, "Les Théories de l'optique," 98.

67. Ibid., 122. "Il faut dire en gros cela se fait par figure et mouvement, car cela est vrai. Mais de dire quels, et composer la machine, cela est ridicule; car cela est inutile, et incertain, et pénible."

68. Ibid.

69. Ibid., 123, "le fil d'une tradition, d'un progrès lent, mais ininterrompu; ils ne tardent pas à voir qu'une théorie qui disparaît jamais tout entière; qu'une part de ses conquêtes, part quelquefois très grande, souvent petite, jamais nulle, demeure acquise à la science."

untrue, it leaves a residue of truth that contains experimental laws which have been discovered to the benefit of future theories. It is, Duhem explained, like the waves beating the shore, rising and falling with the tide. It may seem to the casual observer to be a vain effort, with much foam and little noise, but little true progress. Nevertheless, over the span of time, the ocean continues its relentless conquering of the shores.

This gradual evolving of history, inaccessible to superficial observation, is echoed in the physicist's internal evolution as well. Duhem believed that the interpretive grid of the physicist, the matrix that leads to new hypotheses, "germinate in him without him."[70] History, whether external or internal, is not tangential to the process of physics because history alone can trace the progress, understand the errors, and build on the successes.

## CONCLUSION

We can see that Duhem found in Pascal the guiding light to his physical theory of the distinction between physics and metaphysics. The contingency is interior; the gap is within, and must remain an abyss. That, according to Duhem, was not the disaster that positivists nor neo-Thomist Catholics would believe, for that abyss made possible the explorations and reflections that provided the inquirer with enough light to make an interpretation. That interpretation, an individual act, either granted or denied faith. Duhem refused to relinquish unquestioned authority to any scientific tradition or theory and consistently redirected the theorist's attention to the careful methodology that involved an interplay between observation and imagination; both operations required the hermeneutic of the individual.

---

70. Duhem, *Aim and Structure*, 252.

# 5

## Reversing Epistemological Methodologies

THE SAME YEAR THAT Leo XIII issued *Providentissimus Deus* and Duhem published "Physique et Métaphysique" (1893), Maurice Blondel published his doctoral thesis *L'Action: Essai d'une critique de la vie et d'une science de la pratique*.[1] In it he, like Leo XIII with *Providentissimus*, responded to the issues of *fin-de-siècle* Catholic French thought. He, too, was interested in defending the integrity of Catholic faith and dogma, though, as we shall see, his apologetic had a far different flavor that that of the pope. This foundational work was followed up with numerous philosophical articles that addressed the unsettling developments in Catholic discourse. While Duhem spoke most directly to the scientific world and, as we shall see, Laberthonnière spoke most forcefully to the Catholic community, Blondel worked harder to bridge the gap between the secular, professional philosophical community and the religious community.

In this chapter, we will consider two of Blondel's primary works: his doctoral thesis, *L'Action*, and a subsequent five-article work on apologetics. In these two works, Blondel laid the foundation for his method of immanence, his philosophical argument for the primacy of process over substance in the apologetic endeavor and of the teleological hermeneutic as an epistemological principle. Blondel built on Pascalian ideas about the nature of the individual human experience and its centrality in the process of faith. Blondel also incorporated Pascal's strong emphasis on human dignity and the destiny of each individual, countered by the present experiences of dissatisfaction or suffering. In his focus on the in-

---

1. More than forty years later, Blondel published a trilogy of philosophical works that included a revised version of the original *L'Action*. The concerns of this book revolve around the original work.

ternal act of the will, Blondel reiterated Pascalian ideas about the source of spiritual authenticity, the inadequacy of scientific knowledge, and the limited role of reason.

Like Duhem, Blondel was born in the last decade of the Second Empire (1861), and then grew up in a pious, land-holding Catholic family in Dijon. Blondel's decision in November 1881 to leave his sequestered family background for Paris, the big city, and for the École Normale Supérieure came as a surprise to his family, whose impression was that Blondel's timid personality would not be able to take on the challenge. Yet, private reflections from Blondel's journal reveal that his personal philosophical ambitions display an intellectual strength that belied any weakness:

> Without perceiving the strangeness of the means, it seemed to me that the École (I only knew of it by name), which inspired awe in all those around me and in myself, was the path which I should have to take in order to attain my end, to arm myself against those whom I longed to make hear the truth, to acquire a more direct and profound knowledge of those who were mistaken, sincere unbelievers whose prejudice it was the dream of my youth to dissipate by talking to them in their language.[2]

Despite the disparities between his former secluded life and his new life in an academic community, Blondel found two mentors at the ENS who fostered his personal and philosophical aspiration: Émile Boutroux, Professor of Philosophy and Blondel's advisor; and philosopher Léon Ollé-Laprune, who served as his Director of Studies.[3] Robert Smith describes both of these professors as highly influential in shaping the philosophical spirit of the ENS. They, along with Lucien Herr, the École's librarian from 1888 to 1926, encouraged a broad liberalism of thought and curriculum, one that encouraged the incorporation of German scholarship and the engagement with scientific philosophies, including positivism, but preferred an expansive humanitarian eclecticism of thought and attitude.[4]

2. Quoted in Blondel, *The Letter on Apologetics*, 35.

3. Ibid.

4. The larger university establishment, much more given over to the scientific method in every area of study, opposed the ENS's philosophical freedom. Ernest Lavisse, along with many others in the university, felt that the École's elite status and lack of philosophical constancy weakened the university system. The final solution was to eliminate its separate status and, with the other *grandes écoles*, bring it under the Sorbonne. See Smith, *École Normale*, 70; and Weisz, *Emergence of Modern Universities in France*, 290.

Ollé-Laprune injected a broad Catholic spirituality into his lectures, well tolerated despite the prevailing materialism of the academy at large. The ENS had always maintained a high regard for individual freedom, and this underpinning made room for a greater degree of tolerance regarding all kinds of spiritualities, including the nebulous ones introduced by Victor Cousin, the École's Director from 1835 to 1840. Émile Boutroux, also a devout Catholic, reintroduced Kantian ideas and broader German philosophy.[5] While neo-Kantianism proliferated in many of the intellectual discourses within the ENS and the larger university community, it does not seem to have been a philosophical position *de rigeur*. On the contrary, the Kantian idealism mitigated the influence of the empiricism of the scientific philosophies.[6]

Within their own philosophical predilections, both Boutroux and Ollé-Laprune made room for Pascalian thought, and under their tutelage Blondel found a philosophical home. Nevertheless, the rigid scholastic training he had received as an undergraduate came back to haunt him, making his work at the École an at-times frustrating encounter with an intellectual freedom that was new to him.[7] The private commitment to contribute to the philosophical world in such a way that dormant Catholic roots might be reinvigorated led him to focus on the subject of *action*, the movement of the human will toward choices that shape life.

*L'Action*, Blondel's opening salvo, had simmered in his mind for nearly a decade before it was released in its final form. In the fall of 1883, while Blondel was enrolled at the ENS and studying under Boutroux and Ollé-Laprune, he began a lifelong friendship with Pierre Duhem who, as we have seen, also prized Pascalian thought. According to his private journals, however, Blondel's interest in Pascal predated his time as a *normalien*. An 1881 entry shows an aspiring nineteen-year-old whose inspiration was Pascal: "I have been enthralled all over again, despite having encountered him many times. I admit, my greatest desire is to emulate him."[8]

In early 1884, Blondel reflected on Maine de Biran's "théorie de l'Effort," effort being a trigger to his ideas of action. In the same entry,

---

5. Smith, *École Normale*, 63–64.

6. See Keylor, *Academy*, 184.

7. Blondel, *The Letter on Apologetics*, 36.

8. Blondel, *Carnets Intimes (1883–1894)*, 11. "J'avais été ravi tout à la fois et dépité de m'être rencontré quelquesfois avec lui. L'avouerai-je, je me piquai d'émulation."

Blondel again recalled Pascal: "Our destiny, according to Pascal, is within us and outside of us; in us, by effort; outside of us, because you [God] are the beginning and end of our existence."[9] By early 1886, these ideas were beginning to take firmer shape. On 25 February, he wrote: "Pascal and the wager: theory of action. Action incorporates the mysterious infinite, and one has, by pleasure, by moral satisfaction, the inexplicable feeling that by it we succeed."[10] Action, as a philosophical point of inquiry, was becoming central to Blondel's thoughts; it served as an entry point for what he perceived to be the crux of the matter for his generation, that is, the purpose of inquiry, the goal, the destiny of the human quest.

Blondel recognized and regretted that his contemporaries were dilettantes and skeptics, content to observe the world in a spirit of tolerance and neutrality without making any commitments. Reason and science had posed a multitude of questions, but had, he feared, answered nothing. "Science multiplies the mysteries and resolves none of them."[11] His mid-October 1886 reflection on "the state of the contemporary mind" lamented the intellectual waywardness of his generation that had lost the "secret of the heart" and had abandoned the Church.[12] People had abandoned faith for the false promises of science but were left with nothing but more confusion. This disorientation, Blondel believed, came from a misplaced conviction, that of the absolute rewards of science.

> March 1889: "Poor idol of human Science, how you are abused by those who do not understand that there is no science that is not surrounded by vast ignorance out of which only small rays of knowledge like light escape! And it is clear that the human problem does not depend on the understanding alone because, amidst the greatest minds and the wisest people one finds the same disagreements that exist between the smallest and the simplest ... No, the question of human destiny is not at all a scientific one, since science is infinitely small within the immensity of the knowable unknown; and since there are altars elevated to God that ignore the limitations of our minds; and since both fools

---

9. Ibid., 44. "Notre fin, dit Pascal, est en nous et hors de nous; in nous, par l'effort; hors de nous, parce que vous en êtes le principe métaphysique et la fin morale."

10. Ibid., 78. "Pascal et le pari: théorie de l'action. L'action envelope mystérieusement l'infini, et on a, par le plaisir, par la satisfaction morale, l'inexplicable sentiment qu'elle réussit."

11. Ibid., 82. "La science multiplie les mystères, ne les résout pas."

12. Ibid., 85.

and intellectuals, great and small, all have the same aptitudes, the same difficulties, the same ability to resolve the enigma..."[13]

Blondel pushed past inquiry for inquiry's sake and touched at the heart of what would become *L'Action*: "What is conversion? How was Pascal converted?... Nothing is accomplished in the mind. But everything in the heart. His faith always supernatural. The reason never interferes."[14] Blondel's *L'Action* was not an evangelistic work, but it did address what Blondel believed to be the crisis of his day: Why doesn't the Catholic faith appeal to this generation? In what ways has it failed to communicate effectively and persuasively? And how could he contribute to a new enlightenment, one that both embraced the great achievements of science and philosophy and integrated them with religious faith?

For Blondel, the solution lay not in abandoning his generation's preoccupations with science, nor in ignoring the powers of human reason, but in harnessing them both to the purposes of faith: "science by action. There is a train of thought that one cannot enter without the grinding of the active life. God is an act. The truth is an act. To be like God, to know him and to love him, is to act. One should not fret over feelings, but over what one does."[15] Action is the only meeting place of contradiction, the fusion of antinomies that can result in the ignition of faith. "Action, source of internal contradictions, of heartbreak even: fertile."[16] And faith alone, according to Blondel, could assuage the human craving for cer-

---

13. Ibid., 180. "Pauvre idole de la Science humaine, comme on abuse de toi, sans voir qu'il n'y a science que par l'ignorance immense qui enveloppe et fait ressortir la petite lumière du connu! Et la prévue que le problème humain ne dépend pas de l'entendement seul, c'est que, parmi les plus hauts esprits et les plus savants, l'on rencontre la même opposition qu'entre les petits et les simples... Non, la destine humaine n'est point une question scientifique, tant la science est infiniment petite dans l'immensité du connaissable inconnu, tant il y a d'autels élevés au Dieu ignore sur tous les confines de notre esprit, tant il importe que sots et intelligents, humbles et grands, que tous aient même facilité, même difficulté, même mérite à résoudre l'énigme..."

14. Ibid., 79. "Qu'est-ce que conversion? Comment Pascal s'est-il converti?... Rien ne s'est fait dans l'esprit. Mais tout dans le coeur. Sa foi toujours surnaturelle. Jamais la raison n'est intervenue."

15. Ibid., 211. "la science par l'action. Il y a tout un enchaînement de pensées qu'on ne peut devoir qu'à la trituration de la vie active. Dieu est un acte. La vérité est un acte. Être semblable à Dieu, le connaître et l'aimer, c'est agir. Ne pas se préoccuper de ce qu'on sent, mais de ce qu'on fait."

16. Ibid., 278. "L'action, source de contradictions intérieures, de déchirements: fécondante."

tainty, a craving that found the claims of science empty. "When one casts one's eyes on the new horizons of science and our glance lands on the impenetrable depths [of what is not known], a great and inconsolable sadness invades our soul, inconsolable if we do not have, my God, the absolute truth of your holy word to assuage the desperate need to know, to know absolutely."[17]

The year before he finished his thesis, Blondel recorded in his journal a prayer that reiterated his personal goal: to offer something to his contemporaries that could help them, "to clarify and strengthen those poor minds so full of vain science, so empty of the only reality."[18] Thus it can be argued that Blondel's purpose in *L'Action* was to prove philosophically that no morality or ethical foundation—one key battleground between the Catholic Church and the Third Republic—could be sustained apart from a position of faith.[19] Blondel was convinced that the supernatural had been exorcised from the vision and imagination of his generation, leaving an intellectual posture consumed by rationalism and naturalism, and that access to the supernatural could not come about through standard Thomistic avenues of intellectual argument. The recovery of the supernatural, and the consequent appropriation of the source of true knowledge about the meaning of life and human destiny, could come about only through a rediscovery of the one genuine link between existence and essence, that is, action.

## BLONDEL AND *L'ACTION* (1893)

The first sentence of Blondel's *L'Action* faces the dilemma: "Yes or no, does human life make sense, and does man have a destiny?" For Blondel, this was the fundamental *fin-de-siècle* question: What are we and where are we going? While the question itself is timeless, the answers offered at the end of the nineteenth century were new. Darwinism had wrought two vital changes in this question of destiny: First, it had eroded the idea that

---

17. Ibid., 291. "Quand on jette les yeux sur les nouveaux horizons de la science et que notre regard y découvre des profondeurs toujours fuyantes, c'est une grande et inconsolable tristesse qui envahit l'âme, inconsolable si nous n'avions pas, mon Dieu, l'absolu de votre sainte parole, pour contenter notre impérieux besoin de connaître, de connaître absolument."

18. Ibid., 453. "pour éclairer et fortifier quelques-uns des pauvres esprits contemporains si pleins de vaine science, si vides de la seule solide."

19. Blanchette, trans., *L'Action*, xv.

human destiny has any nonmaterial meaning. Human destiny was tied to an evolutionary process, and no defined end could exist. Humanity was not working toward anything; its random progress, an oxymoron evident in the works of Herbert Spencer, made the idea of purpose or destiny meaningless. A second, ironic, result of Darwinian thought tied human destiny to its own will. No longer did suffering humanity need to look forward to the promises of heaven in order to endure the pains of earthly life. Progress, and its handmaiden, Science, involved making this world better now.[20] Neither the evolutionary process nor material progress could assuage the questions Blondel was asking, questions he believed lay beneath the angst of his generation.

Positivism had rejected this question altogether, and rationalists and naturalists persisted in the exclusion of any questions of essence, of cause, of teleological import. And yet, as Blondel saw it, the elimination of the question had not abated the keenness of the human longing. Darwinism had eviscerated the anthropological focus and had stranded humanity on a deserted floating island-planet in a closed universe, without either a source or a destiny. Yet Blondel offered a new vision, a new hermeneutic, one which could reinterpret the vicissitudes of experience and glean from them the clues to a meaningful life.

Blondel's argument began with a rejection of the late nineteenth-century obsession with positive evidence. Amidst the plethora of facts that assault the senses, there are multiple opportunities of assimilation; the individual must choose a course of action, and that choice will not depend on the perfect accumulation of information but on choice alone. Blondel pointed out that in every normal life, choices are made without sufficient evidence, and such choices define the courses of life.

We all act in darkness, even, Blondel insisted, the scientists. "The scientist, too, is often forced to be daring and to risk the possibly precious material he has in hand. He does not know in advance what he is looking for, and yet he looks for it. It is by anticipating the facts that he reaches them and discovers them. What he finds, he did not always foresee, nor does he ever entirely explain it to himself, because he never goes into the workshops of nature down to their last depth—This precious material I have to expose is myself."[21]

20. Wilson, *God's Funeral*, 158.
21. Blondel, *L'Action*, 7.

At this point in his argument, Blondel positioned his line of reasoning before the methodologies of Cartesian doubt, before the categorical imperative of Kant, and even before Pascal's wager. Before action comes the clarity of recognition and definition. "The whole nature of things and the chain of necessities that weigh on my life is [sic] only the series of means I have to will, that I do will in effect, to accomplish my destiny."[22] Thus Blondel named the dilettantism and essayism (an attitude of life that is interested in sampling experiences without giving any weight to any of them) of his contemporaries, and exposed them as actions in themselves, subconscious choices to will nothingness. Like Pascal, Blondel argued that not choosing is impossible; the choice not to choose is itself an act of the will. No matter what we may wish, we are engaged.

Nihilism, the conscious embrace of nothingness, also came under Blondel's attack. This sense of nothingness stemmed from the obsession with the senses, the knowledge produced by scientific analysis bereft of mystery. And yet this deprivation of the unknown is false, and the human being flounders in a sea of information without any solid ground. Knowledge, produced scientifically, is ephemeral and offered nothing in the way of sustenance.

> The progress of knowledge analyses and reduces its object to an abstraction, because reflexion destroys instincts and natural inclinations, because it creates new needs faster than it can satisfy them. If the life of the senses leaves us with an infinite lassitude, scientific research leads to a more profound emptiness, to a collapse without remedy. To know is vain, is painful, because the knowledge brings to light an unsatisfied and inexplicable desire, the unknowable and the vanity in human being. Through its very development, science multiplies our contacts with the mystery as an expanding sphere touches at more and more points the void into which it is plunging. What is even a simple fact? Can we place ourselves in the presence of any positive, palpable, complete fact? No, every fact is already a complex fiction, an organic integration, a mental construction ... Science leaves an enormous amount unknown in the world; in vain do we seek from it reasons for acting ... It cannot furnish us with a single motive for action, nor render an account for any one of them; it could not even justify itself, nor posit itself as real and necessary.[23]

22. Ibid., 14.
23. Ibid., 38.

Despite this declamation against science's all-sufficiency, Blondel did not pursue a fideist course. He held on to science as an avenue of revelation—not a supernatural revelation nor even an adequate natural revelation, but a critical one nonetheless. "Science knows what it knows and does not know what it does not know ... [W]e must, on the contrary, exalt science because it demonstrates to man that nothingness is the end of what he calls his person, his life, his acts and his destiny."[24] Blondel dispelled the nihilist vision by pointing out its inconsistencies. The nihilist is recognized by his relentless pursuit of the phenomenal (the external appearance rather than the essential meaning), leading to a life of decadence and indulgence. Thus the nihilist betrays his hope of satiating his need. Even the suicide's act of death, in Blondel's judgment, is a cry for the fullness of being, a fullness denied him and leaving him in despair. "We can goad thought and desire as much as we like: in *willing-to-be*, in *willing-not-to-be*, in *willing-not-to-will*, there subsists always that common term, *willing*, which dominates with its inevitable presence all the forms of existence or of annihilation and sovereignly disposes of the contraries."[25]

So Blondel moved to the examination of the will, its powers and frailties. Blondel insisted from the beginning that the will in itself has no power. It cannot create what it imagines; it cannot generate what it desires; it cannot bring into being the thing that can satisfy its needs. It is, in its aching emptiness, futile. Its purpose is simply to betray the gulf between "what we are and what we will to be."[26] Yet science claimed that the human will can synthesize knowledge, integrate all knowledge according to its analytical organization. Science tries to tell us what we are: "In [science's] desire for universal conquest, it wants the phenomenon to be, and to be as it knows it and disposes it; it admits that observing facts and their interconnection is to explain them completely." The scientific

---

24. Ibid., 39. This nothingness, undiluted by Blondel's philosophical solution, becomes the absurdity so celebrated in the writings of early to mid-twentieth-century French works, such as Jarry's *Ubu Roi*, Sartre's *La Nausée*, and Camus's *L'Étranger*. Blondel foresees this course of intellectualism: "For we live and are only through an illusion, we want to be whereas we cannot be; and that is the evil, the inexplicable pain, the pure absurdity we must be cured of." *L'Action*, 41.

25. Ibid., 48.

26. Ibid., 54 n. 1.

method that observes and explains should be adequate to dispel any deeper quest.[27]

At this point in his essay, Blondel drew on one of Pascal's childhood experiences, a time when he struggled to understand a sound and the confusing feeling he had of the sound being his and not his. Blondel used this account to illustrate the underlying reality of the duality of knowledge, that humans have internal experiences which come from something external. There is a fundamental lack of cohesion between the internal experience and the external reality. Blondel proceeded to examine the scientific discourse that breaks down when it faces the phenomenal and the noumenal, the objective reality and the subjective experience of that reality. Thus science is marred with a "triple stigma": the inability to bridge the gap between reality and the knowledge of it; the inability to explain reality as it is in itself; and the scientist's reliance on the definitions of form without any recognition of his own ignorance.[28] Science is permeated with a ready acceptance of convention, of useful hypotheses that approach the appearance of reality but never do more than offer a pleasing fiction. Agreeing with Poincaré and Duhem, Blondel insisted that "physical and chemical laws are symbols that have neither more nor less subsistence than geometrical formulas." Science involved the imaginative creation of coherence, useful for providing answers for the phenomena but never addressing the essence.[29]

The practical solutions of science, successful as they have been, mask the antinomies that reveal their illusive qualities. Its power probes one order and is blind to the other, leaving a critical conflict at the very heart of epistemological inquiry. Blondel concluded this section with twelve conclusions about the inefficacies of science. These conclusions focus on the fallibility of scientific knowledge, its basic symbolic character and its inability to produce certainty. Science concerns itself with relations; a scientific fact merely defines itself over and against another scientific fact and never offers definitions of things in themselves. The true value of science is not in what positivists would claim for it, but in what these claims reveal about the human mind and the quests it gives itself to. Science gives true knowledge only when it turns itself to an

27. Ibid., 54–55.
28. Ibid., 70–71.
29. Ibid., 78.

examination of the human act that has shaped it.[30] Only thereby can science reach the end of its inquiry and know itself to be inadequate. "The sciences have before them an immense but restrained career; and it is in what they know that, without recourse to any metaphysical critique, is to be found the certitude of what they will never be able to know. They will grow indefinitely without encroaching one bit on the mystery they bear within them." Blondel reflected the ebbing confidence in science, which would be argued provokingly by Ferdinand Brunetière's reflections on the "bankruptcy of science," by Pierre Duhem's "Physique et Métaphysique"(1893), and by Henri Poincaré's *Science and Hypothesis* (1903). Blondel saw that "the split [between the knowledge afforded by science and the knowledge pursued by philosophy or metaphysical inquiry] is accomplished for good, an era of thought is closed."[31]

Blondel's conclusions about the true value of science led him to claim that genuine epistemological inquiry, a quest that goes to the heart of what it means to be human, cannot be reserved to the intelligentsia alone. The specializations of scientific inquiry, incomprehensible to most common people, are by their very impenetrability symptomatic of superficial knowledge. "Thus falls, along with the superstition of *Science*, the unworthy presumption of whoever abuses of the prestige of a magic word before simple folk and makes himself their guide, as if the scientist knew more about the secret of life than the least of the humble."[32] Blondel thus turned from the superiority of the educated elite—scientific or, we shall see, theological—to what he believed to be the source of true knowledge, the interior of every individual.

This interior is the source of knowledge, but not the producer of it. The inquirer must embrace the dichotomy between what he wills and what he does—there alone is the void into which revelation penetrates. These inner conflicts "tell us about ourselves the secrets we would perhaps like to keep from ourselves . . . It is this domain of the oppositions, the passions, the rebellions in action that we must explore, in order to follow therein the very growth of the will."[33] Blondel was putting into psychological language Pascal's argument about the *infini-rien*, the painful suspension between all we are and all we feel we are meant to be. That

30. Ibid., 91–92.
31. Ibid., 92.
32. Ibid.
33. Ibid., 161.

very wretchedness creates the disequilibrium that thrusts the inquirer in the right direction. Only by examining the soul, by a careful probing of the true self, can the searcher for truth find a solid place to stand. "It is a strange ignorance, this blindness each one remains in regarding himself; and the beginning of philosophy is to have noticed this."[34]

Blondel rejected the bifurcation between philosophy and theology, arguing that the latter must penetrate the former in tangential ways rather than merely through superimposition. In a later article, "Le Point de départ de la recherche philosophique," Blondel examined different ways of knowing, insisting that external realities—whether natural or supernatural—could only ever be "a mystery of initiates and specialists."[35] He carefully considered, and then dismissed, the methodologies of direct knowledge, intuitive knowledge, and logical knowledge as proper sources of philosophical knowledge. All the reflection in the world, he believed, could not give full knowledge about the whole picture. There was no end to possible avenues of exploration, and the thinker would inevitably end up in a morass of "contradictions and impossibilities."[36] Blondel called these reflective forms of knowing,[37] and believed that the one who advocated their use alone would of necessity become a fideist, for such a person would never be able to reach the end of reflection and would finally need to make a blind leap.

Blondel also repudiated psychological intuition as a genuine means of philosophical knowledge, particularly rejecting Bergsonian intuition as a chimeric intellectualism that left the seeker wallowing in thought and never moving forward in authentic living. It is not memory that draws us on, Blondel argued, but anticipation. Here again, Blondel introduced the role of internal desire and the actions that issue from it. Choice alone, built on the hope of a divine destiny, has the power to illuminate.

By turning his examination away from the external, natural world and the work of science to the inner life, Blondel dissected the impotence of reason. Reason, he argued, is powerless to govern our moral

---

34. Ibid., 166.

35. Blondel, "Le Point de Départ," 338: "un mystère d'initiés et de spécialistes."

36. Ibid., 349.

37. The problems associated with reflective knowledge, especially the inability to find a solid starting point since there are always other angles that need definition, echo Pascal's arguments in "Réflexions sur la géométrie en general de l'esprit géométrique et de l'art de persuader."

lives (hence rejecting Kantian ethics); our very absurdities trigger our own irritation and exasperation, which simply serve to throw us into new frenzies of foolish behavior. Reason merely serves to make our behavior look reasonable; it serves the needs of the ego rather than serving reality. The knowledge of the world around us does nothing to explain to us our irrational choices, therefore, Blondel concluded, there must be something above or beyond, an ideal that renders a soothing order to the experience of chaos.

The recognition of an ideal is not faith, however; it merely becomes another method of self-deception. By imagining a divine that satisfies the desires of the ego, the human individual can create a god that he can also master. Idolatry is easy, and man-made idols—science, the State, reason, new forms of mysticism—can anesthetize human suffering.[38] These efforts inevitably fail, yet in their failure they preach the message: "All attempts to bring human action to completion fail; and it is impossible for human action not to seek to complete itself and to be self-sufficient. It has to, it cannot."[39] This is the ultimate human paradox. The great gaps in knowledge that once seemed insurmountable in the natural world, gaps that made the God-hypothesis necessary, had seemingly disappeared. Yet the idea of contingency (the suggestion that reality is neither logically necessary nor logically impossible), which makes reality dependent on the decisive action of an external factor, such as a divine being, persisted in the chasm of the human psyche. The contingencies that make God a vital component of human existence exist in the antinomies of paralyzed freedom, of ignorant reason, of emptiness crying out for fullness. "All the beautiful order of phenomena where science ranges at ease, we have not found to be too much; we find that it is too little."[40]

That singular contingency led Blondel to identify the "l'unique nécessaire," the one thing necessary. "Instead of proving simply the impossibility of affirming the contingent alone, it proves the impossibility of denying the necessary that grounds it ... Hence the entire order of nature is inevitably a guaranty of what surpasses it. The relative necessity of the

---

38. Early in the twentieth century, Blondel became involved with the Semaines Sociales and the Christian Democratic movement. He also challenged, despite an early friendship with Charles Maurras, Maurras's growing nationalist movement, the Action française.

39. Ibid., 302.

40. Ibid., 311.

contingent reveals the absolute necessity of the necessary."[41] Discovering this necessary thing, we must, according to Blondel, begin within. The necessary does not reside there, but we conceive it by understanding its surpassing presence within our own consciousness. The perfection that we dimly perceive and grasp for in every action is the divine. "At the end, quickly reached, of what is finite, from the very first reflexion, we find ourselves in the presence of what the phenomenon and nothingness equally hid and manifest, in the face of one we can never speak of from memory as though of a stranger or of one who is absent, before the one from whom in all languages and in all consciousnesses there is a word and a feeling to recognize him by, God."[42]

Action is a path, and as such it implies constant movement. That movement, when it corresponds to the action of God within us, Blondel called "theergy," an integration of divine and human action. This collaboration takes place not in the head, but in the heart, echoing Pascal's iteration of the role of the *coeur*.[43] But like Pascalian thought, this operation of the heart is not one of sentiment or of mere feeling; it is an intellectual process, but originates not from reason but from a deep discernment akin to intuition. It is not a flash of insight nor a divine imparting of special knowledge, not a *gnosis* in the sense of the Greek mystical religions, but a decisive choice of the will to move past external certainties into a darkness that, Blondel reassured his contemporaries, will lead to internal certainties. "The act is like the tollhouse and the gateway of faith: it supposes a total abdication of one's sense of oneself; it means the humble expectation of a truth that does not come from thought alone; it places into us a spirit other than our own. *Fac et videbis* (do and you will see). Hence (however strange this rule of conduct may seem), whoever has understood the necessity, whoever has felt the need of faith, must, without having it, act as if he already had it ... For it is not from thought that faith passes over into the heart, it is from practice that it draws down a divine light for the spirit."[44] Here is Blondel's recovery of Pascal's advice to "abêtir la raison" (suppress reason), to silence the arguments of doubt and act as a believer, "taking holy water, having masses said" (f. 418), kneeling in the motions of faith. Here, too, is Augustine's conviction

41. Ibid., 318.
42. Ibid., 324.
43. Ibid., 345.
44. Ibid., 371.

that you must believe in order to see, rather than see in order to believe. Revelation, then, comes to the individual not through any natural powers, which may be unequally distributed among men; action replaces reason as the avenue of divine revelation. Dogmas, then, can only be meaningful in light of the primary action that makes the individual able to internalize them.

All external sources of knowledge, whether scientific or theological, have no footing in the human psyche; they cannot impart the supernatural. The individual alone has the opportunity and the power to step into the realities of the supernatural and to ascertain its certainties. As Blondel concluded that the supernatural cannot be proved, either through "the development of its consequences or through its internal appropriatenesses," he threw down a gauntlet to the neo-Thomists who so vociferously, and tautologically, argued for the accessibility of the supernatural through the workings of a reason illuminated by the supernatural.

Even before *L'Action* was published, Blondel was aware of the hostilities it could generate. Boutroux encouraged him to meet separately with his examiners, including Jules Lachelier and Paul Janet, in order to reduce antagonisms and gently introduce his arguments.[45] But Blondel could make no one happy. His university examiners, who took offence at the introduction of the supernatural and found his style impenetrable, passed him only with some reluctance. After his thesis was published, Blondel then faced criticism from the Catholic community. Blondel's reorientation of the point of revelation to the inner soul, a place of profound inaccessibility to the authoritative claims of the Church, to the mediation of the hierarchy, and to the workings of the intellect horrified his religious audience. "Blondel was consistently referred to as a Kantian, an immanentist, a subjectivist, was denounced to Rome, and, as soon as the word gained currency, labeled a Modernist."[46] From Blondel's arguments, it could only be concluded that individual human freedom, so anathema to nineteenth-century papal authority, was essential to human existence.

Few grasped the import of Blondel's argument, and even fewer admired it. In 1895, Abbé Charles Denis, then editor of *Annales de philosophie chrétienne (APC)*, published a review of *L'Action* in which he

---

45. Blondel, *The Letter on Apologetics*, 40.
46. Dru, introduction to *The Letter on Apologetics*, 56.

argued that Blondel was introducing a psychological apologetic, that is, an apologetic that justified faith by focusing on personal feelings or aspirations. Blondel was profoundly disturbed by this reduction of his argument and, in rebuttal, composed a series of five articles, published in *APC* between January and July of 1896, entitled "A Letter on the Requirements of Contemporary Thought and on Philosophical method in the study of the Religious Problem," commonly referred to as *The Letter on Apologetics*.[47]

## BLONDEL AND "LETTRE" (1896)

Blondel's first concern in rebutting Denis's interpretation of *L'Action* was to resist the notion that the philosophy of action was a psychological apologetic. He focused, then, at the beginning on a consideration of traditional apologetic methodologies, and claimed that what made them ineffective in the contemporary age was their inability to communicate with those who did not believe. Traditional apologetics aimed at justifying the faith of those who already believe; they were written for a theological audience. Blondel wished to say something to a different audience and to demonstrate to them that faith is not merely reasonable, but "technically rational."[48]

For Blondel, methodology was critical, not extraneous to the argument, but integral to its message. He wrote at some length about the dangers of trying to convince or convict using evidence that might one day be refuted and the faith then lost. He admitted that most apologists had such an arrogant spirit that their smug certainty drove honest seekers away. Many of these apologists tried to use science to testify to spiritual realities, and this astonished Blondel. "There is no more continuity between scientific symbols and philosophical ideas than there is between the qualities perceived by the senses and the calculation based on these same data of intuition." The purpose of the sciences is not to penetrate the essence of anything but to create a system of coherent relations between things.[49]

---

47. "Lettre sur les exigences de la pensée contemporaine en matière d'apologétique et sur le méthode de la philosophie dans l'étude du problème religieux."

48. Blondel, "Lettre," 339.

49. Ibid., 342. "Pas plus qu'il n'y a resemblance entre les qualités perçues par les sens et les calculs du savant sur ces mêmes données de l'intuition, il n'y a continuité entre les symbols scientifiques et les conceptions d'ordre philosophique." English translation, *Letter on Apologetics*, 131.

Neither did Blondel find it helpful to use the Christian stories as historical proof. As accounts of human happenings, interesting as they were, they remained facts that the unbeliever may or may not have found engaging and pertinent. As accounts of supernatural intervention into the natural world, they were revelation, and as such could not be digested without faith. No argument—theological, philosophical, rational, dogmatic, or historical—could generate faith, a possession that Blondel believed was both necessary to the fullness of human existence and simultaneously unattainable. Even miracles were useless as apologetic tools, for they were subject to interpretation and became miracles only to those who perceived them as such. "[Miracles] are a witness written in a language other than that of which [philosophy] is the judge."[50] Philosophy, according to Blondel, was powerless to ratify the meaning of the historical facts of Christianity, but this did not throw philosophy out of the discussion.

Blondel then considered the possibility that Christianity was valid because it delivered a moral order and intellectual integrity. This, Blondel insisted, was a vacuous argument, for the moral imperatives of Christianity issued from its supernatural authority, and could neither persuade nor compel. It was nothing more than using the supernatural as the starting point, which clearly defeats a careful reasoning geared toward embracing the supernatural. The effective apologist must begin with the absence of the supernatural and with a simple recognition of the role of human reason, a role that will change as faith becomes active.

> Our reason has not the same lights or the same duties *before* the decisive act of faith and *after* it, but it remains true that the alternatives between which we must choose are bound up with one another. *After* the act of faith, human co-operation remains coextensive with the primary and gratuitous activity of God; thus there is still a natural life to be found even in the supernatural life. *Before* the act of faith, God's secret summons does not leave man's reason and will in a state of legitimate indifference or innocent and definitive neutrality; we must therefore necessarily take account of what might be called the supernatural insufficiency of human nature.[51]

---

50. Ibid., 346. "sont un témoignage écrit dans une autre langue que celle dont elle est juge." English translation, *The Letter*, 135.

51. Ibid., 472. "S'il est vrai que, selon qu'on se place *avant* ou *après* l'acte pratique de foi, la raison a des lumières inégales et des devoirs différents, cette distinction toutefois

Reason must lead the seeker to the precipice and there, before the abyss, the seeker must recognize the "supernatural inadequacy" that makes further progress impossible. Yet progress is exactly what is demanded, expected, needed of human nature. This radical breach between what is essential to human existence and what is possible for human existence becomes the point where true apologetics must begin.

Blondel reviewed doctrinal apologetics that merely leapt from reason's proof of God's existence to the historical accounts of God's intervention to the authority of the Church. He admitted that these arguments may have worked when metaphysics and theology ruled over people's minds, but that contemporary thinkers had no way of entering that cycle. This line of thought, a standard Thomistic one, is static and involves the simple and external construction of ideas into a scaffolding that, for the modern mind, remains void of any internal reality. It is a worthy "donjon," and those who can occupy it are immune from harm, but the problem is entry. Of Thomism, Blondel insisted: "Since the Thomist starts from principles which, for the most part, are disputed in our time; since he does not offer the means of restoring them by his method; since he presupposes a host of assertions which are just those which are nowadays called into question; since he cannot provide, in his system, for the new requirements of minds which must be approached on their own ground, one must not tend to treat this triumphant exposition as the last word ... We must not exhaust ourselves refurbishing old arguments and presenting an *object* for acceptance while the *subject* is not disposed to listen." Unlike Loisy, Blondel was never interested in changing the content of the doctrine, only in the manner of its presentation.[52]

---

n'empêche pas la solidarité des deux alternatives entre lesquelles il faut nécessairement opter. *Après*, la coopération humaine reste coextensive à l'opération première et gratuite de Dieu: il y a donc une part de vie naturelle à retrouver dans la vie surnaturelle elle-même. *Avant*, la sollicitation secrète de Dieu ne laisse point la raison et la volonté de l'homme dans un état de légitime indifférence ou de neutralité innocente et définitive: il y a donc à tenir nécessairement compte de ce qu'on appellerait bien l'insuffisance surnaturelle de la nature humaine." English translation, *The Letter*, 141.

52. Ibid., 478. "Comme il part de principes qui, pour la plupart, sont contestés aujourd'hui; comme il n'offre pas la possibilité de les restaurer par sa méthode; comme il suppose une foule d'assertions qui sont précisément mises en doute; comme il ne peut se prêter, sous sa forme systématique, aux exigences nouvelles des esprits qu'il s'agit d'atteindre tels qu'ils sont, on ne peut, on ne doit pas tender à se contenter de cette exposition triomphante ... Ne nous épuisons pas à ressasser des arguments connus, à offrir un *objet*, alors que c'est le *sujet* qui n'est pas dispose." English translation, *The Letter*, 146.

Scholasticism, Blondel explained, had always approached the two orders, natural and supernatural, as a hierarchical structure, much like a collapsing telescope, the inferior, lower order of nature subsumed under the superior order of the supernatural. A continuum of knowledge, beginning with reason and ending with faith, spanned this epistemological conduit, and in the middle reason and faith overlapped, "where reason discovered in an incomplete way the more important of natural truths, and these were confirmed and further explained by faith." Though this worked temporarily, it generated further problems, particularly seen in the Protestant rejection of the rational undergirdings of faith. This led to a side-by-side arrangement of reason and faith, reason taking the natural order and faith the supernatural order. When, however, reason had so successfully answered questions of knowledge through its own efforts, it dismissed the entire arena of the supernatural, and faith along with it. The symmetry of the scholastic age no longer existed.[53]

Blondel's solution was methodological. He maintained the Christian recognition of the supernatural, and was careful to reiterate that he was not attempting to collapse the supernatural into the natural. The division between the two was critical to theistic thought. Yet Blondel offered a method of immanence, a method that drew distinctly on Pascal's bleak assessment of human wretchedness. "For if [men] are 'sick' it is the great and inevitable sickness of man before God from which they suffer, the supreme human sickness."[54]

Contemporary measures, such as a dichotomous management of the demands of reason and faith, which never lets the two engage, or a sentimental yearning for the ideal, which never incarnates the supernatural in a flesh-and-blood existence, were quite inadequate to the task of faith, for they never penetrated the core of the dilemma. The dilemma, according to Blondel, was that human nature has suffered a wound, a scandal, and without a full examination of the condition the cure can never be prescribed. Like Pascal, Blondel recommended a thorough probing of the conscience and the will and the desire, "so that behind factitious negations and ends which are not genuinely willed may be

---

53. Ibid., 481. "la raison découvrant imparfaitement ce que la foi éclaire et confirme des vérités naturelles les plus importantes." English translation, *The Letter*, 148.

54. Ibid., 603. "Car, s'ils sont maladies, on peut bien dire que c'est du grand et inévitable mal de l'homme en face du divin, du mal humain par excellence." English translation, *The Letter*, 154.

discovered our innermost affirmations and the implacable needs which they imply."[55] The method of immanence simultaneously embraced the existence and absolute need of the transcendent while recognizing that the attainment of it is impossible.

Blondel then drew on Pascal's perception of the limited, but critical, use of reason—that reason does its job best when it stretches to its utter limits, reaches the end, and then reasonably bows before the greater requirement. Pascal: "Reason's last step is the recognition that there are an infinite number of things which are beyond it" (f. 188). Blondel: "And this movement of free thought and exclusive rationalism, becoming fully conscious of itself and reaching, so to speak, the very end of its course, was precisely what was required so that there should arise as a philosophical hypothesis the religious thesis on which this whole movement logically depends, so that one may see clearly what its very existence implies."[56]

Blondel's apologetic was not one of psychology, but one of methodology. His method called for personal conversion via the removal of external authority and the generation of an internal authority. It put epistemological certainty within reach of the individual human being by granting that human being the dignity of naming his reality and choosing his destiny. That reality was accessed through reason, but that destiny lay hidden—implied, suggested, intimated, but hidden, like Pascal's *Deus absconditus*: "Thus wishing to appear openly to those who seek him with all their heart and hidden from those who shun him with all their heart, he has qualified our knowledge of him by giving signs which can be seen by those who seek him and not by those who do not. There is enough light for those who desire only to see, and enough darkness for those of a contrary disposition" (f. 149). Blondel agreed: "we must reach implicitly the point at which the option becomes possible (at which, in default of any other enlightenment, it becomes necessary and decisive) between the solicitations of the hidden God and those of an egoism which is al-

---

55. Ibid., 605. "de telle sorte que dans les négations factices ou les fins artificiellement voulues se retrouveront encore les affirmations profondes et les besoins incoercibles qu'elles impliquent." English translation, *The Letter*, 157.

56. Ibid., 607. "Et il fallait précisément que le mouvement de la pensée libre et du rationalisme exclusif, prenant pleine conscience de lui-même, atteignît pour ainsi dire son extrémité, avant que surgît comme hypothèse philosophique la thèse religieuse dont il dépend logiquement, et afin qu'on vît clairement ce qu'implique sa propre existence." English translation, *The Letter*, 159.

ways evident enough."[57] Each individual must choose; "Here, then, as in all cases where our method requires scientific necessity, the reality or rather the realization of what is proposed as necessary is subordinate to another factor which is alien to science: only practical action, the effective action of our lives, will settle for each one of us, in secret, the question of the relations between the soul and God."[58]

Blondel decried the practice of bringing in the semantic weapons of theological language, doctrinal formulae, or philosophical arguments in order to coerce reason. The freedom of choice, he argued, belongs to the least educated and cannot be induced or manipulated. "It is the merit and the beauty of the philosophical method of immanence that it establishes, in each one of us, that which judges each one of us."[59] Theological systems are valid, but abstract, and the application of their implications must lie in the hands of the individual, not in the hands of professionals who dictate faith. It is the "conversion intérieure" that matters.[60] The new apologetic must be one of persuasion rather than justification. Genuine knowledge of the deepest matters of the human experience required an inductive methodology. Scholasticism insisted on a deductive epistemology. We have seen how Blondel's insistence on the abandonment of a deductive theological structure in favor of an inductive one was echoed in Pierre Duhem's challenge to the scientific community in which he rejected the prevailing inductive empiricism in favor of a deductive scientific base.

## CONCLUSION

Blondel was facing a new world of evangelization, something that had been unknown and unnecessary in earlier French culture. Even under the Reformation, the process of conversion had been primarily a process of turning away from Protestant heresies and back to Catholic Christian

---

57. Ibid., 610. "il faut implicitement passer par le point où l'option devient possible, et où, faute d'autres lumières, elle devient nécessaire et décisive entre les sollicitations du Dieu caché et celles de l'égoïsme toujours évident." English translation, *The Letter,* 162.

58. Ibid., 612. "pour chacun dans le secret, la question des rapports de l'âme et de Dieu." English translation, *The Letter,* 163.

59. Blondel, "Lettre," 266. "C'est le mérite, c'est la beauté de la méthode philosophique d'immanence de placer en chacun ce qui juge chacun." English translation, *The Letter,* 194.

60. Ibid., 339.

belief. Blondel recognized that the Catholic Church needed to find ways to communicate to a non-Christian mind. Scholasticism was a Catholic argument for Catholic minds, and as such it was a fruitful and effective way of defining the relationship between reason and faith. For *fin-de-siècle* minds, however, the antagonistic relationship between faith and reason could only be happily resolved if the "battleground dead" included scholastic rationalism.[61] Blondel offered, in its place, a neo-Pascalian philosophy that demonstrated the reasonableness of faith to those for whom Christian dogma had no meaning; he argued the futility of reason and scientific knowledge to generate the answers to deeply human questions. Blondel, like Pascal, had a high view of human nature in its essential calling, but a low view of the individual's ability to achieve that calling. In the face of Darwinist determinism (random evolution) and pessimism (absence of a supernatural goal), Blondel presented a philosophical methodology that, he hoped, might rekindle spiritual hope and buttress the authority of the Church, an authority that, for Blondel, could only be recognized as the culmination rather than the commencement of faith.

---

61. Ibid., 346.

# 6

## Wagering on *Fin-de-siècle* Probabilities

IF, IN THEIR EPISTEMOLOGICAL explorations, Maurice Blondel challenged the academic community and Pierre Duhem disturbed the scientific community, Lucien Laberthonnière, a philosopher-priest, encroached on more dangerous grounds, breaching ecclesiastical boundaries in his apologetic efforts. While the Church worked to centralize authority and homogenize theological methodologies, everything Laberthonnière wrote was intended to thwart this authoritarianism. While Duhem and Blondel were laymen, Laberthonnière's clerical status made him more vulnerable to the antimodernist backlash that swept him up and, ultimately, silenced him.

In this chapter and the next, we will consider the ways that Laberthonnière contributed to the rise, and then the fall, of neo-Pascalian thought at the turn of the century. Here we will look most closely at three of his works which were central to his argument: "Le problème religieux" (1897), a three-part article "Le Dogmatisme moral" (1898–1899), and "Pour le Dogmatisme moral" (1899–1900), all of which were published in the *Annales de philosophie chrétienne*. In the next chapter, we will return to Blondel and continue with Laberthonnière, focusing particularly on certain of their works that addressed developments in historical studies.

Like Duhem and Blondel, Laberthonnière was heavily invested in reinvigorating a Catholic apologetic that eliminated the conflicts between faith and reason and restored epistemological centrality to the role of the individual. Like the others, Laberthonnière appropriated Pascalian ideas about the hiddenness of God, the divine destiny of the human individual, and the necessity of a personal hermeneutic in the exercise of faith. Laberthonnière pushed deeper, however, into the discussion about the relationship between the natural and the supernatural. As we shall see, his efforts to redefine such philosophically and theologically loaded terms as *idealism, realism,* and *dogmatism* led him to a realignment of ideological allegiances. Laberthonnière, more than the others, was labeled a neo-Kantian, a label that dogged all his works and made them untrustworthy in the eyes of the Church. And while he rejected Kantian ideas about the inaccessibility of supernatural knowledge, his emphasis on Pascalian arguments for the personal, inner experience and its ability *alone* to access the supernatural marked him in ways that threatened the clerical establishment. Laberthonnière was adamantly anti-Thomistic and, according to some of his colleagues, lacked the tactfulness that might have saved him from the Vatican's wrath.

Lucien Laberthonnière, like Duhem and Blondel, grew up in the context of the increasingly uneasy state of Roman Catholic political and internal affairs. Born in 1860, the same year that Piedmont defeated the papal armies and the pope lost most of the papal dominions, to a poor, pious Catholic family in the l'Indre region of France, Laberthonnière grew up under the Syllabus of Errors (1864) and entered higher education just as Catholics were given permission to set up their own university system (1875). He spent his early adulthood negotiating a transition into the clerical life during the growing anticlerical atmosphere of the 1880s. Educated at the Seminary of Bourges, Laberthonnière joined the Oratorians in 1886, an order dedicated to the perfection of the priesthood, its purification from any spiritual, moral, or intellectual deficiencies.

We have already described the ways that seminary education failed to satisfy the intellectual and vocational needs of many of its students. Laberthonnière found that it also failed to meet his philosophical and theological needs. Gabriel Daly writes that, in the last quarter of the nineteenth century, Roman textbooks mandated "a propositional view of revelation, deductive method in theology, and an ever-increasing concern to identify and label doctrinal assertions according to the degree of their ecclesiastical authority."[1] Laberthonnière, it seems, would spend the rest of his professional career resisting much of what he had learned in his clerical education. Ironically, he thus articulated his own brand of anticlericalism, one that shared the Republic's distrust of Roman hegemony and protested its lack of intellectual freedom. Nevertheless, he completed his studies at the University of Paris and served for a time as

1. Daly, *Transcendence and Immanence*, 12.

a professor of philosophy at the Collège de Juilly, submitting a doctoral thesis to Émile Boutroux, philosophy chair at the Sorbonne, in 1899.

Laberthonnière entered the journalistic discourse about the vitality of the Church after reading Blondel's *L'Action*, which resonated with his own concerns about the intellectual direction of the Church and the pre-eminence granted to scholastic thought. Early in 1894, Laberthonnière wrote to Blondel, gushing with praise for *L'Action*, calling it a "scientific and original systematization of an ensemble of truths garnered from Descartes, Pascal, Kant, and others."[2] He reiterated the comparison with Pascal in his next letter and some time later made reference to Pascal as his own philosophical tutor: "Pascal has been my philosophical inspiration; and I do not believe it is possible in this world to have a state of soul like that of one who has the serene possession of truth."[3]

We have seen how Blondel placed himself squarely in the stream of Pascalian thought; Laberthonnière's reference to his own Pascalian loyalties seemed to serve as a sort of shibboleth, cementing their common affinities. With these early letters of mutual admiration, Blondel and Laberthonnière began a long friendship and partnership in philosophical studies. They engaged in a regular thirty-year correspondence regarding the philosophical and theological issues of the day and together they explored the options to scholasticism and developed many of the ideas that they proceeded to publish, often in the *Annales*.[4] Their philosophical and personal compatibility became even more evident upon the death of Abbé Denis, the editor of the *Annales de philosophie chrétienne*. Blondel secretly bought the journal after Denis's death and instated Laberthonnière as its editor.

Much later, however, the relationship soured and the correspondence ceased. Laberthonnière's acerbic manner, his adamant resistance to the Church's authoritarian rhetoric, and his insistence on the Church's need to consider alternative perspectives grated on Blondel's spirit of restraint with adversaries and his commitment to persuasion rather than to antagonism. They were, in Blondel's assessment, "Two philosophical temperaments: one more 'prophetic,' the other more conciliating and more

---

2. Blondel and Laberthonnière, *Correspondance Philosophique*, 66.

3. Ibid., 72, 90. "C'est avec Pascal que j'ai commencé à philosopher; et je ne comprends pas qu'il puisse y avoir en ce monde un état d'âme correspondent à la possession sereine de la vérité."

4. Ibid., 37.

thoughtful."[5] Nevertheless, during the years under focus, Laberthonnière and Blondel were linked professionally, theologically, and philosophically, to the degree that Loisy could comment that "Laberthonnière's system ... is Maurice Blondel translated into French and without the latter's learned pretensions ..."[6]

Despite Loisy's disparagement of Laberthonnière's originality, the latter, inspired perhaps by Blondel, did in fact have much of his own to contribute to the intellectual discourse of the day. Laberthonnière honed in on society's pressing need to define "truth," a definition that shaped the crux of the arguments about morality and the pursuit of the good. Like Blondel, he focused on methodology rather than content, always upholding the Church's dogma as the proper end. Both Blondel and Laberthonnière insisted on the significance of the intellectual process as the critical ingredient in orthodoxy, whereas scholastics tended rather to underscore a simple adherence to the correct conclusions. In the eyes of the Pascalisants, those conclusions failed to satisfy the increasingly literate, world-weary, and cynical seekers of truth. Those religious conclusions no longer had any intellectual or emotional relevance to the realities people faced.

The Third Republic, as we have seen, was dealing with disappointing results to the exceptional agenda for social, moral, and economic progress that science had promised. Brunetière's 1895 "bankruptcy of science" speech summarized for many the disillusionment they felt in view of unmet expectations. A widespread but low-grade economic depression during the 1870s and 1880s, disguised by high production but apparent in disappointing profits,[7] seemed to parallel the Republic's apparent inability to settle down. While standards of living rose for a slice of society, the processes of industrialization had displaced many and the labor force was still restructuring. Many felt they were cut adrift without community support or vocational opportunities. For intellectual observers, the future seemed grim rather than rosy. Many seemed to be feeling what Pascal had expressed so well: "One needs no great sublimity of soul

---

5. Ibid., 52. Blondel seemed to have accepted the Church's hostilities toward his work as a part of his own spiritual development, a kind of intellectual mortification. See p. 241. "Deux tempéraments philosophiques : l'un plus 'prophétique,' l'autre plus conciliant et plus philosophe."

6. Loisy, *Choses passées*, 307; quoted in O'Connell, *Critics on Trial*, 304.

7. Hobsbawm, *Age of Empire*, 36.

to realize that in this life there is no true and solid satisfaction, that all our pleasures are mere vanity, that our afflictions are infinite, and finally that death which threatens us at every moment must in a few years infallibly face us with the inescapable and appalling alternative of being annihilated or wretched throughout eternity" (f. 427).

Religion, too, seemed incapable of finding a solid place of legitimacy. Its losses under the Ferry Laws in the 1880s and then the escalating political hostility building up to the Law of Separation worked to marginalize its role in civil discourse. The Dreyfus Affair had besmirched the Church's reputation in its blind support for the army, and the growing support for Charles Maurras and his utilitarian view of religion, which came out of the Affair, did nothing to advance either the cause of genuine piety or the Church's efforts to rally Catholics to the Republic. It seemed that best efforts changed nothing, and that perhaps the "right choice"—whether political, economic, social, or religious—was an ephemeral goal more related to antiquated ways of looking at human nature than to modern ideas of progress, ideas that issued out of historical materialism: "the dominant politico-Darwinist trend in Europe saw [Darwinism] as reinforcing Marx's view that evolutionary processes in nature and society take place regardless of men's will and consciousness..."[8]

Many Catholic leaders were also concerned about the renewed philosophical interest in Kant and what Catholics believed to be a subsequent subjectivism. Integralists, those who argued that the entire corpus of belief and practice was a solid entity and that the diminishment of any single part of that corpus threatened the whole, were afraid of relative truth, self-defined gods, and culturally delineated faiths.[9] Truth, for them, was the right answer to the right question. Any other definition threatened the authority of the Church, shattered confidence in the *magisterium*, and suggested Protestant individualism and subjectivity.

Amidst this highly charged intellectual atmosphere, Laberthonnière strove hard to restore certainty to the arena that Pascal had argued for: religious faith. In doing so, Laberthonnière redefined "truth" and thus realigned previously accepted notions of religious legitimacy, demonstrating that advocates of opposing arguments were actually allied in their common rejection of "truth." With Blondel, he urged a focus on the internal realities before settling on the external expressions of those

---

8. Ibid., 254.
9. Daly, *Transcendance and Immanence*, 7.

realities, but he pushed further by underscoring both the orthodoxy and the immediacy of such a focus. Laberthonnière had long cherished a passion for recovering the vitality of Augustinian thought, a stream of theological philosophy that had advocated an essential relationship between intellect and desire. He was convinced that Aquinas's synthesis of Greek philosophy and Christian theology had polluted the latter by granting dogmatic status to the speculative side of faith and undervaluing the experiential side of faith.[10] As one writer put it, "in the writings of the Angelic Doctor all the questions are asked in Christian language but all the answers are given with a pagan meaning."[11] According to Laberthonnière, this severing of two vital components of faith had left modern believers with the choice between a dry intellectual assent or a vacuous emotional commitment. Laberthonnière was determined to reunite both the speculative and experiential elements.

## CONSTRUCTS OF TRUTH VIA WILL AND DESIRE

In September 1896, Father Schwalm, a Dominican priest and neo-Thomist philosopher and author, wrote a scathing attack on Blondel's thesis because of its anti-Thomistic ramifications. The whole idea of immanence was dangerous territory, permeated with Kantian notions about the kind of transcendence that makes supernatural knowledge unattainable and leaves the seeker trapped in the imaginations and ignorance of immanence. Kant's philosophy had also become the basis for a set of philosophical and political principles that contributed to the development of individual freedom and personal moral responsibility. Though, as Martha Hanna points out, political Kantianism was not the primary objection of the neo-Thomists, this concept of individual autonomy in the political world had its corollaries in the religious world. "By situating moral authority in the hands of the autonomous moral agent, Kant undermined hierarchy and endorsed principles of revolutionary governance."[12] Kant's political views were merely Luther in a new guise. Kant's epistemological ideas were even more dangerous, for they circumvented the need for and indeed the possibility of genuine theological knowledge. That rejection of supernatural truth laid the ground-

---

10. Ibid., 92.
11. Sutton, *Nationalism*, 256.
12. Hanna, *Mobilization of Intellect*, 107.

work for an agnosticism that left the individual dependent on his or her own highest moral judgment, a subjectivist notion of authority that, in the eyes of the Catholic hierarchy, could only lead to chaos.[13]

After Schwalm's attack on Blondel, Laberthonnière wrote a defense and elaboration of Blondel's thought published as "Le problème religieux" in the *Annales* (1897). In it Laberthonnière referred to *L'Action* as a work containing "pages that overflowed with intense life, in which reverberate the accents of a soul fully Christian, reminiscent of the breath of Pascal and of Saint Bernard."[14] Pascalian thought penetrated both Blondel's *L'Action* and Laberthonnière's analysis; both were concerned to recover Pascal's understanding of the relationship between faith and reason. Schwalm's objections centered on what he perceived to be fideism in Blondel's focus, the Kantian sickness; Schwalm felt that Blondel abandoned reason altogether as an avenue of accessing supernatural revelation and preached faith as an individual's blind groping for truth. Ironically, Pascal, too, was accused both of fideism and skepticism.

Laberthonnière began his argument by underscoring the places he concurred with Schwalm's thought, primarily affirming that faith must indeed be a reasonable commitment to supernatural truths known by revelation. In assuming that were faith unreasonable, it would not be a human act, Laberthonnière reiterated Pascal's idea that the essential dignity of humanity, the defining element, is the ability to think: "Man is only a reed, the weakest in nature, but he is a thinking reed . . . Thus all our dignity consists in thought . . . Let us then strive to think well; that is the basic principle of morality" (f. 200). (Of course, Pascal did not believe man capable of thinking *well*, though that was his purpose in existing, and that chasm between purpose and ability was his key antinomy.) Faith, then, must be reasonable for it to fulfill man's highest calling.

For Laberthonnière, the problem resided not in giving reason a role, but in clarifying that role. How does one reasonably access supernatural truths that are inaccessible to reason itself? If reason presumes rights *not* appropriate to it, the believer will be forced into rationalism, and that rationalism terminates in a desiccated faith. If reason neglects obligations that *are* appropriate to it, the believer will be forced into fideism, and the

---

13. Ibid., 117.

14. Laberthonnière, "Le Problème religieux," 497 n. 3. "pages qui débordent de vie intense, où résonne l'accent d'une âme si chrétienne et où a passé à la fois comme un soufflé de Pascal et de S. Bernard."

abandonment of reason in the face of the proliferation of knowledge in the modern world will eventually erode any possibility of believing. This, according to Laberthonnière, was the crux of the religious problem. While Blondel looked at the problem from the bottom up (that is, from the spark of faith in the soul of the individual), Laberthonnière proposed to consider the problem from the top down (that is, working backward from the desired end—Christian dogma—to its place of origin).[15]

Laberthonnière recognized that faith has two facets: the objective one containing creedal material composed of supernatural truths and revelations; and the subjective one of the act of believing. Theology works with the objective facet of faith, and constructs a logical and organic system. This system, however, has no direct connection to the individual. The challenge, according to Laberthonnière, was to properly define the relationship between the first and the second facets of faith.[16]

Laberthonnière was sure that this relationship would come into focus when the two orders of truth, supernatural and natural, were properly related. For the scholastic, the supernatural order of truth was juxtaposed to the natural order, the gap between the two being closed by the act of reason, divinely enhanced, comprehending revelation. For Laberthonnière, this dichotomy isolated both the natural and the supernatural order of truth from the actual experience of the individual. He cited a commonly heard proposition—"reason brings man to the faith"—and pointed out its obvious flaw: it suggested that by reason alone a natural thing, a person, could elevate himself to an understanding of the supernatural, an implication that is itself unreasonable since the supernatural by definition is beyond natural capabilities. Laberthonnière, like Pascal, used the example of geometric equations to demonstrate that, while such natural logic is useful in natural arenas, supernatural truth cannot be deduced logically.[17] Supernatural truth, Laberthonnière argued, can only be accessed when it is unified with the natural order of truth, not by a logical and necessary interdependence, but by a living unity experienced in the life of the individual. The one cannot be tacked onto the end of the other like an extension ladder reaching into heaven; the two must merge in such a way that the supernatural infused the natural, making possible the exercise of a faith that was congruent with rea-

15. Daly, *Transcendance and Immanence*, 94.
16. Laberthonnière, "Le Problème religieux," 500.
17. Ibid., 503.

son rather than the declaration of a faith in spite of reason. Reason's job, then, was to reach a synthetic understanding of this organic unity. And the goal of this entire endeavor, critical to Laberthonnière's argument, was the act of persuasion (true conversion), again underscoring Pascal's intense commitment to addressing the attitudes of the dilettantes and unbelievers (f. 427). For Laberthonnière, arguing about correct doctrine within a community of the faithful was merely rearranging the furniture in a dusty living room that no one wants to enter.

A misplaced confidence in the ability of reason to attain faith through the appropriation of supernatural truths was what Blondel called intellectualism. Such an operation of reason buys into the scientific methodology, but Laberthonnière was convinced that this use of reason could not resolve the religious problem. Scientific methodologies, Laberthonnière believed, led to scientific conclusions, and such conclusions were of their nature impersonal, universal, and abstract; they were focused on the relationships between phenomena but gave no clues about the truth behind them. Thus Laberthonnière echoed the arguments of Duhem, who, with Poincaré, insisted on the binary nature of knowledge and truth. In the scientific world, natural laws described a systematic knowledge of empirical facts and a true knowledge of the relations between things, but could not generate knowledge about the "truth" behind the phenomena.[18] In the same way, systematic, or speculative, theology gave a certain kind of abstract and conceptual knowledge whereas positive, or experiential, theology gave a concrete and living kind of knowledge, i.e., truth. "One can with Pascal call the one the knowledge of the heart, and the other knowledge by the intellect."[19] Because this heart-knowledge is genuinely experiential, it is of necessity individual and personal rather than universal and abstract. "If in one sense to think is to think for everyone, to believe is not for anyone but for one's self, because to believe is to live, and no one can live another's life."[20] Here, too, Laberthonnière echoed Pascal's recognition of the solitary nature of discovering truth: "It is absurd of us to rely on the company of our

---

18. Copleston, *History of Philosophy*, 274.

19. Laberthonnière, "Le Problème religieux," 507 n. 1. "On peut appeler l'une avec Pascal connaissance par le Coeur, et l'autre connaissance par l'entendement."

20. Ibid., 508. "Si en un sens penser c'est penser pour tout le monde, croire ce n'est toujours que croire pour soi, parce que croire c'est vivre, et que personne ne peut vivre à la place de personne."

fellows, as wretched and helpless as we are; they will not help us; we shall die alone. We must act then as if we were alone ... We should unhesitatingly look for the truth" (f. 151).

In drawing attention to the role of the individual, Laberthonnière effectively rejected a determinist view of the universe. The choice of the individual, he insisted, is meaningful; it creates a destiny that would not otherwise exist. A person's future is contingent, not determined. It holds a certain amount of probabilities, but very few certainties. Choices must be made, choices that could change the course of a life. Laberthonnière, like Pascal, was concerned that people made genuine choices that had real results. The Church, by clinging to scholasticism, was depriving the individual of choice, and thrusting upon him or her a static system that, while logical and coherent, was ineffective in generating faith.

This argument resurrected the debate about grace that raged during Pascal's day. In *The Provincial Letters*, Pascal had addressed the pivotal religious question of his time: "What is the real condition of human nature since its corruption?" He described the squabbling between the Dominicans and the Jesuits about sufficient grace and efficacious grace. Pascal, however, brought the debate down to the experience of the individual by means of a parable about a wounded man seeking medical advice from three different physicians. Each of the physicians gave the man different advice about his condition, but they were all more interested in the correctness of their opinions than they were in giving the man the help he needed.[21]

Schwalm had accused Blondel of inserting action as the necessary and efficient mediator between knowledge and reality, thereby suggesting that the individual created his own "truth," and falling into Kantian subjectivism. Laberthonnière, rejecting Kantianism, still asserted that action was the crucial factor. The individual must choose to believe or not to believe; the decision must be made, and even the decision not to decide, to reject the need for decision, was a decision. Laberthonnière harnessed optimism (that the individual has the ability to choose) for the sake of pessimism (that the human individual's destiny teeters on the edge of either divine life or wretchedness) in order to challenge the dilettante's ambivalence. Truth, then, was accessed by the individual's commitment to its pursuit, not by a merely rational or intellectual assent to the Church's teaching. Fideists, however, were as misled as the

21. Pascal, *Provincial Letters*, 16–17.

rationalists, for clearly knowledge/intellect/reason played a role in the direction the seeker would take. If fideism were a valid option, any wild belief would do. "Some forget that thought alone cannot achieve everything; others forget that the will is not willed except by thought, for the will is a moral activity. Some suppress thought; others make it nothing more than an instinct. Whether falling in one extreme or the other, the result is the same: it is an avoidance of responsibility."[22]

Thus Laberthonnière brought the reader to the role of desire in the exercise of the will and the attainment of supernatural truth. He named the mystics as exemplars of this intuitive power and supported his emphasis on internal dissatisfaction with their experience. "Augustine had linked hunger of the heart with the quest for truth, virtually sacramentalizing both the hunger and the quest. The role which Laberthonnière gave to disquiet (l'inquiétude) in his own life and thought was exactly similar."[23] This distressing desire, he argued, was the key to the understanding of the work of God within, the exercise of the individual's choice, and the destiny that together they create. "Is it not God who also works within us by means of this disquiet, by this hunger, by this need of the infinite that prevents us from finding rest and that gives us the motivation to go farther and higher?"[24]

Laberthonnière began with the assumption that all human beings were called to live a supernatural life, and that this innate quality was evidenced by humanity's search for God and constant efforts to *be* God. Thus human nature itself revealed the "need for the supernatural."[25] Only by integrating this natural inclination with the divine invitation could the individual make possible the act of faith. "In the highest forms of intuition the synthetic principle may become self-cognizant and more visibly personal by being related to desire ... with Pascal the primary aim

---

22. Laberthonnière, "Le Problème religieux," 510. "Mais les uns oublient que la pensée pour être quelque chose n'est pas tout; les autres oublient que la volonté n'est volonté, c'est-à-dire activité morale, que par la pensée. Les uns tendent à la supprimer, les autres à en faire un instinct. D'une part comme de l'autre, le résultat serait le même: ce serait la suppression de la responsabilité."

23. Daly, *Transcendance and Immanence,* 116.

24. Laberthonnière, "Le Problème religieux," 616. "N'est-ce pas Dieu aussi qui agit en nous tous par cette inquiétude, par cet inassouvissement, par ce besoin d'infini qui nous empêche partout de trouver le repos et qui nous donne toujours du mouvement pour aller plus loin et plus haut?"

25. Ibid., 617.

of the *ordre du coeur* was to 'kindle' rather than to 'instruct,' and that in the religious domain at least, where intuition must always be in the nature of a personal discovery, he had regarded knowledge not as a purely representational operation, but as an act of love."[26] In sharp contrast with the scholastic reactive emphases, Laberthonnière reiterated Pascal's proactive apologetic, one that imparted authentic truth insofar as the heart, the *coeur,* synthesized and cooperated with knowledge by faith. Thus Laberthonnière saw two kinds of apologetic: the one presented religious knowledge as something transcendent, external to human life and beyond the human ability to grasp; this demanded that such knowledge be reconciled to the immanent, natural truths that dominated reality, making apologists work incessantly to integrate the religious truth with the scientific or philosophical developments of the day and leaving people in a duality. The other method, Laberthonnière's and Pascal's,[27] was to explain that transcendence infused immanence, not as a superimposition upon the natural life, but as a full integration of the human personality and the divine life.[28] "Thus there is no more reason for seeking to reconcile natural knowledge with supernatural faith than there would be for seeking to reconcile mathematics with morality."[29]

For the scholastics, this focus on a methodology leading to the individual's experience of truth could only be a form of neo-Kantianism. Laberthonnière rejected the charge, pointing out that the methodology would lead to the traditional expression of truth, not a subjective, self-defined, or relative expression of truth. "The meaning that each of us deep within attaches to the revealed doctrine is relative to who he is. But this is not to say that the truth depends on us, or that each can create his own truth."[30] Where Kant separated the phenomena from the noumena, Laberthonnière found them to be a synthetic whole, the latter found within the former.[31] Neither would Laberthonnière accept the

26. Eastwood, *Revival of Pascal,* 61.

27. Pascal, *Pensées,* f. 564. "But as we cannot love what is outside us, we must love a being who is within us but is not our own self. And this is true for every single person."

28. Eastwood, *Revival of Pascal,* 138.

29. Daly, *Transcendance and Immanence,* 108.

30. Lucien Laberthonnière, *Essais de philosophie religieuse,* 161. "Le sens que chacun de nous en son for intérieur attache à la doctrine révélée est relative à ce qu'il est. Mais ceci ne veut pas dire que la vérité dépend en nous, et que chacun peut se faire à son gré sa vérité."

31. Daly, *Transcendance and Immanence,* 101.

skeptic label, for a skeptic was someone who had abandoned the search for truth.[32]

Truth required an act of hermeneutics, an interpretive choice that implicated the individual. The individual, faced with the natural incomprehensibility of divine truth, entered into this "union of contending principles,"[33] and, through the inductive and experiential act of the will, stemming from desire, reached the certainty of truth, a certainty that could be reached no other way. That place of certainty, according to Laberthonnière, would lead to an internal acquiescence to the Christian dogmas, thus moving from the inner appropriation of truth to the external acknowledgement of truth.

The disparity between this apologetic and that of Thomistic scholasticism, "a theological perspective which saw revelation as assertion, faith as intellectual assent, and theology as a mainly deductive procedure,"[34] cannot be overestimated. Thomistic scholars argued that truth produced faith; yet Laberthonnière reversed the formula, arguing that faith could bring the individual to truth. The insistence that proofs of the Christian religion were apodictic did nothing to produce faith, and this alone should be the apologist's first concern.[35] Yet even Loisy, repudiated by the Church, could voice the hierarchy's concern, but not without adding a comment on his own disillusionment:

> Laberthonnière's system ... is simply a renewal of Protestant illuminism. It is the essential denial of theological dogma transmitted by tradition and by the authority of the church, which is its sovereign guarantee. These people believe all the dogmas of the church, but they do not believe them in the way that is necessary, in accord, that is, with an objective revelation and on the testimony of the church. They have for their only warrant their internal

---

32. Ibid., 98.

33. Eastwood, *Revival of Pascal*, 7. See, too, Pascal's expression of this human dilemma: "Incomprehensible that God should exist and incomprehensible that he should not; that the soul should be joined to the body, that we should have no soul; that the world should be created, that is should not; that original sin should exist and that it should not" (f. 809).

34. Daly, *Transcendance and Immanence*, 15.

35. See Pascal, *Pensées*, f. 190: "The metaphysical proofs for the existence of God are so remote from human reasoning and so involved that they make little impact, and, even if they did help some people, it would only be for the moment during which they watched the demonstration, because an hour later they would be afraid they had made a mistake."

experience, just like the Protestants. They are subjectivists. They are not orthodox. But then, nobody is orthodox. Orthodoxy is a fantasy of people who do not think.[36]

Laberthonnière might have agreed with Loisy's conclusions about orthodoxy, though in a different sense. For in Laberthonnière's opinion, those who did not think, with the mind of the heart as well with the reason of the mind, could not possibly come to the knowledge of the truth, a knowledge that depended upon action. Thus the disposition of the heart determined the act of faith. Such good will made certain knowledge accessible, if not immediately possessed, because it recognized both the inadequacy of its understanding and the imperative of the search for divine reality. Laberthonnière's conclusions about the adequacy of reason in the search for truth echoed Pascal's : "Reason's last step is the recognition that there are an infinite number of things which are beyond it" (f. 188).

## SHIFTING IDEOLOGICAL ALLEGIANCES

Laberthonnière coined a new term to describe his philosophy of the cooperation between faith and reason: "moral dogmatism." Some of his critics said that this philosophy was nothing more than voluntarism, the theory that makes will the fundamental epistemological principle; that is, that an individual's will defines knowledge in its exercise of choice. Others accused Laberthonnière of "dogmatism of the heart," a subjectivist endorsement of individual feelings rather than the affirmation of objective truth. Laberthonnière vehemently rejected the two labels; he insisted that they both resulted in dangerous individualistic tendencies, egoistical definitions of reality. Ultimately, when shorn of any transcendent definition of truth, they were nothing but a contemporary form of skepticism[37] (neither of them affirming the universal accessibility of absolute truth) whereas he adamantly defended the objective reality of truth. In his three-part article, "Le Dogmatisme moral," Laberthonnière carefully considered different ideological positions regarding the possibility of genuine knowledge and argues that, despite the traditional oppositional relationship between skepticism and a commonly-understood

---

36. Loisy, *Choses passées*, 307–8; quoted in O'Connell, *Critics on Trial*, 304.
37. Laberthonnière, "Pour le Dogmatisme moral," 398.

dogmatism, they were more similar than different in their openness to truth.

With "Le Dogmatisme moral," Laberthonnière entered into a tricky realignment of terms that was meant to demonstrate the orthodoxy of his thought and the actual flawed nature of philosophical positions traditionally accepted by the Church. He began by considering the conventional understanding of idealism, which is the denial of the reality of things in themselves. This is in contrast to realism, the affirmation of the reality of things in themselves, whether or not knowledge of that reality is accessible. According to this conventional understanding, Plato, then would be a realist.

Laberthonnière proceeded to the finer philosophical distinctions of his day. Working with this primary definition, Laberthonnière demonstrated that empiricists, those pragmatic so-called realists, who believed that the senses gave complete knowledge about things, were not however true realists, because they did not believe that any truth about the essence of things genuinely existed. Dogmatists, who would surely seem to be realists because they did affirm an essential reality, did not, however, automatically fall into the realist camp either. There are, Laberthonnière argued, two kinds of dogmatists. Empirical dogmatists, who assert that the only reality of things is that reality which is available through the senses, are ultimately skeptics because they disbelieve in an essential reality; intellectual dogmatists assert that the reality of things in themselves exists and that it is accessible not through the senses but through the intellect, but they merely substitute their idea of the reality for the reality itself. From the perspective of an empirical dogmatist, intellectual dogmatism is a form of idealism.[38] Actually, according to Laberthonnière, both kinds of dogmatists were idealists, for neither accepted the essential existence of a reality beyond the perceptions granted by the senses or circumscribed by the intellect.

Laberthonnière's arguments were even further nuanced. The difficulty, he asserted, came when the philosopher needed to delineate not only the possibility of a reality in itself, but also the nature of that reality. Many great philosophers, despite the differences in their systems, were realists in their affirmation of the reality-of-things-in-themselves, but that when their assertions about the *nature* of that reality were examined, many of them turned out to be idealists because they believed that the

---

38. Laberthonnière, "Le Dogmatisme moral," 537–38.

reality-of-things-in-themselves was completely expressed in their ideas about those realities. Thus, Descartes, who did believe in the reality-of-things-in-themselves, was actually an idealist because he believed that his ideas were the exact representations of that reality, while Kant, who believed that his ideas about the reality-of-thing-in-themselves were merely abstractions or designations of that reality, was a true realist. Such realists might argue about the nature of the essence or whether the essence could be known, but they never questioned the existence of that essence.[39] While Laberthonnière's semantics served his clear purposes of differentiating between individuals who believed in a reality beyond what was accessible to reason or sensory perception, which could not be reduced to any mere formula, and those who rejected the possibility of an ineffable reality, his definitions were not common fare. They served to thrust neo-Thomists, who were ostensible realists, into the idealist camp, for, according to Laberthonnière, they believed that their ideas about reality did in fact capture the essence of that reality.

Skeptics used all this confusion to confirm their rejection of any reality; the divisions and differences between the idealists supported their argument that truth is a moving target, not a fixed reality, and that we wander in a world of appearances from which we have merely deduced abstract notions of "reality."[40] This question of essence was not, however, according to Laberthonnière, an exercise in speculative reflection, but a question of vital urgency. Only the affirmation of an essential reality could offer an exit from the shifting phenomena. Were the only reality the phenomenal, whether defined by sensory perception or intellectual definition, then the managers of the phenomena—scientists, artists, theorists of every field, politicians—would be forever caught in dispute about the "truth." Skepticism, then, the rejection of reality, would be a deadly social option; dogmatism, the unqualified identification of reality and perception (empirical or intellectual), also had grave social risks.

Laberthonnière believed that a deep-seated human fear of being duped lay behind every choice of belief. Skeptics avoided gullibility by refusing to make any assertions, letting each individual choose according to appearance. "No one has the right to speak thus: this is. We can only say simply: this appears to me. If your 'appearances' agree with mine, so much the better! If they do not agree with mine, we can't do anything

39. Ibid., 539–40.
40. Ibid., 541.

about it, for each person, as they say, must 'stay in his own skin.'"[41] The essence of wisdom for a skeptic is not to affirm anything. Laberthonnière called this egotistical dogmatism.[42] Skeptics made the "I" the fixed point of knowledge, with all other bits and pieces of appearances or claims by others relative to the "I." Both fanatics, whom he called illusory dogmatists, and skeptics believed they had all the information they needed in their own self-awareness. They were, Laberthonnière says with a wry irony, lingering geocentrists, mere men who still insisted that they were the center of the universe.[43]

To do otherwise, to make the "I" adapt to the possibility of new knowledge, knowledge that did not issue from the self (whether through sensory perceptions or intellectual definitions), is moral dogmatism, the choice to "sortir de soi" (go out from the self). Laberthonnière's moral dogmatism began with an honest appraisal of the self, with its limitations and shortcomings, and the decision to resist egoism in favor of a greater end. In contrast to moral dogmatism, illusory dogmatism attaches itself to the phenomenon, to the relative, as though it were the essence. This position falls apart when it becomes obvious that, if sensations or ideas were indeed reality, we would all have the same such sensations or ideas. Truth, then, cannot be attained through the senses, and neither can it be pinned down through ideas. To make an idea, a belief, a dogma, or an intellectual assertion the essence of the reality is to make personal transformation and growth unnecessary—it is possessed and the journey is complete. "We want what we love to be good and what we think to be true. Consequently, we judge that everything must change in order to conform to what we love and what we think, without thinking that really we must change ourselves."[44] Laberthonnière recognized that the skeptic sees only temporality and cannot affirm the eternal; the false dogmatist sees the eternal but wrongly attributes it to the experiences or ideas that express it, thus absolutizing the relative. Nevertheless, both the

---

41. Ibid., 544. "Personne n'a le droit de dire: cela est; mais simplement: cela m'apparaît; si vos apparences concordent avec les miennes, tant mieux! Si elles ne concordent pas nous n'y pouvons rien: car chacun est forcé, comme on dit, de rester dans sa peau."

42. Ibid.

43. Ibid., 546.

44. Ibid., 555. "Nous voulons que ce que nous aimons soit le bien et que ce que nous pensons soit la vérité. Et en conséquence nous jugeons que tout doit changer pour se conformer à ce que nous aimons et à ce que nous pensons, sans que nous ayons à changer nous-mêmes."

dogmatist and the skeptic "have a fundamental identity: each expresses that secret desire in all of us, that what we love shall be good, and what we think shall be true, and in his implicit denial of Being each affirms himself."[45] In affirming the self and rejecting the probabilities of a greater reality, the skeptic and the false dogmatist embrace the contingent as the necessary and deny the essential as relative.

Thus Laberthonnière worked his argument: Truth is not mere knowledge, which may deal with appearances; truth is the reality-of-things-in-themselves; truth is not limited to our perceptions of truth, whether those perceptions are intellectual or sensory; truth is not what I merely wish it to be; truth requires an initial denial of my own definitions and a secondary commitment to a search for it outside of myself. Truth, then, is granted only to those who seek for it. Those who believe they possess it in its fullness have lost it. Laberthonnière sought allies in all who made truth a dynamic, transformative reality, and described as adversaries all who made truth a closed system or empty room. Both dogmatists and skeptics fell in the latter camp. The great men of the past, whether scientific or spiritual, made many mistakes, but history has affirmed their greatness in spite of their errors because of their willingness to sacrifice their ideas in the search for truth.

> This is why and how, if they can and should be guides for us, it is less a matter of what they thought or believed than it is what they wanted to think. It is their attitude that we must imitate. It is not what they said that we must cling to; we must emulate the spirit that animated them, not by a simple reiteration of their words, but in a full contemporary expression of the truth they expressed and the correction of those things they would correct if they lived today.[46]

---

45. Eastwood, *Revival of Pascal*, 121.

46. Laberthonnière, "Le Dogmatisme moral," 559. "Voilà pourquoi et comment, s'ils peuvent et s'ils doivent être pour nous des guides, c'est moins par ce qu'ils ont pensé que par ce qu'ils ont voulu penser. C'est leur attitude que nous avons à imiter. Ce n'est pas à ce qu'ils ont dit qu'il faut nous attacher; c'est à l'esprit qui les a animés et qui nous fera, non pas répéter, mais redire pour notre compte ce qu'ils ont dit avec vérité, et rectifier ce qu'ils rectifieraient s'ils vivaient à notre place ... Même avec des illusions ils étaient dans la vérité; ou plutôt la vérité était en eux, au cœur même de leur vie, acceptée, voulue et aimée. Aussi ce qui les caractérise c'est qu'ils ont toujours été en progrès sur eux-mêmes."

This attitude Laberthonnière called "good will," which was not a property or quality, but a habit. The new boundary, then, was between those who were in "philosophical motion"—in the unceasing search for truth—and those who were not. Those who were not in motion, whether skeptics or dogmatists, rejected tension. They sought resolution, a completion of thought and belief. Pascal and Laberthonnière were willing to remain on the path of inquiry. Each of the Pascalisants were intellectuals who were not content with answers, who continued to wrestle, and who were convinced there was an infinity left to understand. "By intellectual and moral shocks, warmed by irony, sarcasm, indignation, or charity, [Pascal] intends to bring the unbeliever to the point of accepting the proposition that one must search."[47] This necessity—Laberthonnière's "good will"—made possible the attainment of genuine knowledge. Is it possible to know the truth without good will? Laberthonnière answered: It is possible to express the truth and adhere to it abstractly, as to a logical set of ideas, but without good will, it is an expression in the process of being lost.[48] Such logical adherence, a systematic knowledge, accentuated a cuckolded God who could be manipulated, rearranged, and categorized according to the need of the believer. A free God must be pursued amidst vast uncertainties and the darkness of probability. "Truly, as Pascal said, it is at least a risk that a person should take, for eventually you will have nothing to lose that you would not have lost anyway."[49]

The kind of pursuit that Laberthonnière advocated galled his clerical contemporaries. Late nineteenth-century theologians felt compelled, as a defensive measure before the positivist onslaught, to systematize the historical and supernatural character of revelation; thus they hoped to give intellectual credence to material that failed the rationalist standard. This resulted in a speculative dogma, one based on abstractions and summations, rather than a positive one that focused on individual encounters with Christian revelation.

Hegel had argued that such systematization was futile. "To enter into a speculative system, positive revelation must be 'sublated' and absorbed into the higher synthesis of philosophy. You could have either positive revelation or systematic knowledge, since religion and philoso-

---

47. Davidson, *Origins of Certainty*, 46.

48. Laberthonnière, "Le Dogmatisme moral," 561.

49. Ibid., 32. "Et vraiment, comme dirait Pascal, c'est au moins une chance qu'on peut courir puis-qu'en définitive on n'a rien à perdre qu'on ne perdrait sans cela."

phy operated upon different levels of intellectual consciousness. But you could not have both simultaneously ... Faith and Kantian reason, the tradition of positive Christian revelation and Hegelian speculative system: these were the antitheses which the philosophers and theologians of the Catholic revival had to try to reconcile."[50]

Laberthonnière's adversaries believed his methodology left him with nothing but uncertainty, but he rebutted this with the Pascalian differentiation between metaphysical certainty and logical certainty. The latter, mathematical and natural, had nothing to do with the *finesse* of the former.

> Nothing expresses [this *finesse*] better than the song in Pascal's heart during that famous night when his words mixed with sobs that were both cries of pain and cries of joy ... Proud philosophers, self-assured in their bourgeois dogmatism, declare that Pascal was a skeptic, though it was never true, for his thought was concentrated, unified, fixed on the One with all the powers of his soul. Ah! It is true, he did not believe in this world, he did not believe in the idols of the senses or of the mind, which men adore. But at the same time, he couldn't believe in them and yet have indestructible certainty.[51]

Certainty, Laberthonnière concluded, came by a personal commitment to seek God, not by assent to knowledge about God. Yet the act of seeking itself was inadequate, for it must be an informed search, a directed choice. Thus to believe was a moral act informed by reason. Skeptics dismissed reason; dogmatists rejected the moral act. Neither, according to Laberthonnière, could gain access to truth.

---

50. McCool, *Catholic Theology*, 34.

51. Laberthonnière, "Le Dogmatisme moral," 40. "Rien n'exprime mieux ce qu'elle est que l'hymne qui jaillit du coeur de Pascal pendant une nuit fameuse, et dont les accents entrecoupés comme des sanglots, ressemblent à la fois à des cris de douleurs et à des cris de joie ... Il s'est trouvé des philosophes fiers et sûrs d'eux-mêmes dans leur dogmatisme bourgeois pour déclarer que Pascal était sceptique, lui croyant s'il en fut jamais, et qui avait concentré, unifié et fixé en Celui qui est toutes les puissances de son âme. Ah! c'est vrai, il ne croyait pas à la figure de ce monde, il ne croyait pas aux multiples idoles, ceux des sens et ceux de l'esprit, que les homes adorent. Mais justement il faut n'y pas croire pour être et pour avoir la certitude d'être indéfectiblement."

### EXTERNAL EXPRESSIONS VERSUS INTERNAL REALITIES

Prior to the last quarter of the nineteenth century, the Catholic hierarchy had been less concerned about methodology and process in the definition of supernatural reality and theological formulas. A certain generosity of thought had been allowed, granting a spirit of open-mindedness about the "how" as long as the "what" remained constant. With the rise of biblical criticism and the growing efforts to establish history as a scientific endeavor, the hierarchy recognized the dangers inherent in processes that valued particular ends (empirical) over others. *Providentissimus* reflected a new concern with the processes of thought and the means of discovery. In the years between *Providentissimus* and *Pascendi*, Catholic leadership narrowed the intellectual discourse to eliminate the diversity of process. The fact that Loisy freely accepted Catholic dogma in its entirety failed to secure him immunity from persecution; his processes, born of internal convictions about the nature of historical knowledge and its relationship to truth, mattered in ways earlier Church watchdogs had never considered.

In "Pour le Dogmatisme moral" (1899–1900), Laberthonnière explored the ramifications of his methodology as an instrument of faith. Over and over again, Laberthonnière made clear that he spurned the subjectivism and sentimentality of the Protestants while simultaneously resisting the intellectualism and aridity of the Thomists. The key to finding one's way between the Charybdis of individualism and the Scylla of authoritarianism, according to Laberthonnière, was the proper use of reason in the pursuit of the supernatural. Granting it excessive or inappropriate influence led to intellectualism; granting it inadequate or diluted influence led to superstition. Both methods were stagnant and useless. In support, Laberthonnière cited Thomas Aquinas's famed conclusion to his great theological works: "Everything I have written now seems to me nothing but straw."[52] It was common knowledge that, toward the end of Aquinas's life, he experienced increasingly ecstatic times of prayer. After one such mystical experience in December 1273, Aquinas refused to write any more, leaving his great "Summa theologica" unfinished. Even Aquinas, Laberthonnière seemed to imply, recognized the futility of his own systematic synthesis.

52. Laberthonnière, "Pour le Dogmatisme moral," 402. "Tout ce que j'ai écrit ne me semble que de la paille."

Insofar as the individual relied on something exterior to himself—whether reason or blind hope—he gave credence to science's claim that rational answers were the key to finding God. The scholastic did so by intellectual acclamation; the fideist did so by intellectual despair. Nor could access to God be achieved through sheer willing it to be, for the will itself must be directed and informed. Thus reason does have an active role. Thinking and willing must go hand in hand.[53]

Laberthonnière argued that directed, informed, and motivated reason gladly accepted the incompleteness of knowledge, even while it clings to the certainty of that partial knowledge. To insist that a dogmatic statement about God, however orthodox, captured the fullness of knowledge about that aspect of God was idolatry. Truth must remain open-ended; the act of solidifying it made it false. The one who says he knows enough about God, reduces God.[54]

Laberthonnière drew heavily on Pascalian thought about the hiddenness of God as a primary characteristic of human experience of the divine. Pascal would write about it thus: "[This religion] says that men are in darkness and remote from God, that he has hidden himself from their understanding, that this is the very name which he gives himself in Scripture: *Deus absconditus* ... that shall be recognized by those who genuinely seek him, and that he has none the less hidden them in such a way that he will only be perceived by those who seek him with all their heart ..." (f. 427). Laberthonnière echoed him when he wrote, "God gives himself, but it is necessary that we find him, and to find him we must search, and such a search is always just beginning, for we do not find him once and for all."[55]

This divine quest originated in the interior experience of despair and desire. Pascal: "We desire truth and find in ourselves nothing but uncertainty. We seek happiness and find only wretchedness and death. We are incapable of not desiring truth and happiness and incapable of either certainty or happiness. We have been left with this desire as much as a punishment as to make us feel how far we have fallen" (f. 401). And Laberthonnière agreed: "Before being able to call [on God] we sense

---

53. Ibid., 409.

54. Ibid., 411.

55. Ibid., 414. "[Dieu] se donne, mais il faut que nous le trouvions, et pour le trouver il faut que nous le cherchions, et c'est toujours à recommencer: car nous ne le trouvons pas une fois pour toutes."

him in the infinity of our hopes, in the unceasing discontent in which we find ourselves, in all that we do and all that we are, in the feeling of the inadequacy of everything."[56] Thus, in the search for certain knowledge—about God, about self, about the natural world—the individual must learn to exercise reason and faith, affirmation and understanding, simultaneously, as one fluid motion of desire. Reason (philosophical knowledge) cannot precede faith (theological knowledge), but neither can faith alone lead to knowledge. Laberthonnière called for a synthetic unity of "agir" and "connaître" rather than an oppositional or linear relationship between the two.[57]

This synthetic action is, Laberthonnière claimed, essentially moral, but it is not logical, linear, or systematic. On the contrary, it is a groping forward, hampered by weaknesses, distractions, forgetfulness, and shadows. "It is a constant struggle for our whole lives, in thinking, in acting, in loving."[58] It should be the most fundamental drive of life. In this, Laberthonnière placed himself firmly in the existentialist camp, echoing, perhaps unintentionally, the Danish philosopher, Søren Kierkegaard, in his insistence on the sole validity of the individual's choice. He also anticipated the twentieth-century existentialist call to *engagement*, though he does so in the light of religious faith rather than in the face of universal nothingness.

> Virtue can be rightly said to begin and end in knowledge, when knowledge is conceived not in restrictively discursive terms, but as an expression of the whole man who thinks and acts in accordance with his principles. Pascal's doctrine that it is the heart which recognizes and responds to principles is central to that stream of thought which stems from Augustine, which was driven underground mainly by the pressure of Christian Aristotelianism, but which surfaced again in the writings of Pascal, Kierkegaard, Coleridge, Newman, Maurice, and the modernists. In this way of thinking, reason may supply supportive "proofs" for various reli-

---

56. Ibid., 416. "Avant de pouvoir le nommer nous le pressentons dans l'infini de nos aspirations, dans le mécontentement incessant de ce que nous avons, de ce que nous faisons et de ce que nous sommes, dans le sentiment de l'insuffisance de tout."

57. Ibid., 418.

58. Ibid., 423. "C'est laborieusement par toute notre vie, en pensant, en agissant, en aimant."

gious claims, but it is the heart which "grasps their significance, and effects their synthesis."[59]

Such thinking appalled the scholastics, who insisted, with Aristotle, that all genuine knowledge must be derived from the information granted through the senses. Any appeal to internal experiences or intuitions obfuscated the clear path of learning. Revelation, the disclosure of the supernatural, must reach the individual through the senses, a position that makes the "proofs"—natural (God's message writ large in the created order) or supernatural (miracles, fulfilled prophecies)—binding and their interpretation properly administered by those who could interpret them correctly. Such proofs, wielded in the hands of authority, compelled reason to yield. Eastwood points out that such a position introduced an agnostic element into scholasticism. The believer cannot really *know*; he can only acquiesce. The one who refused to acquiesce would fall into darkness. According to Laberthonnière, such a reward/punishment approach to faith distorted the religious imagination by generating an image of God that had no real connection to the God described in scripture. Rather, such a faith was "something entirely extraneous to human life, constituting therefore a heteronomy, an enslavement, so that God appears as an arbitrary power, a *volonté de puissance* who demands on our part a passive submission."[60] Scholastics dichotomized knowledge; philosophy (human knowledge) and theology (divine knowledge) were two separate branches of truth, and humanity could only penetrate the former; the latter remained in shadow. "Faith (*fides*) and reason exist side by side as two entirely distinct and indeed mutually exclusive principles, in accordance with the Thomist axiom 'What is known cannot be believed.'"[61]

Laberthonnière's antipathy for scholasticism can hardly be overestimated. This externalism of revelation, what Blondel would call "extrinsicism," was destroying the truth about Christianity and the hope of the Church for the future. Revelation was a bottom-up proposition, not a top-down imposition. Daly summarizes this attitude thus: "In [Laberthonnière's] opinion scholasticism failed completely to appreciate that divine authority as a motive for faith, not merely can, but must,

59. J. Chevalier, *Pascal* (London: 1930), 272–73. Quoted in Daly, *Transcendence and Immanence*, 24.
60. Eastwood, *Revival of Pascal*, 134.
61. Ibid., 131.

have an interior reference which takes precedence over any external manifestation which may be present."[62] This "interior reference" led to Laberthonnière's overt challenge of Church authority, and led him to pursue a redefinition of role of the individual in the life of the Christian community.

## CONCLUSION

The three articles we have examined, "Le Problème religieux," "Le Dogmatisme moral," and "Pour le dogmatisme moral," set the tone of the debate between Laberthonnière and the ecclesiastical authorities. While Duhem kept his philosophical arguments within the context of scientific theories, and Blondel directed his comments to the philosophical world, Laberthonnière made direct challenges to the dogmatic assumptions and authoritarian pretensions of the Church hierarchy. Arcane as his arguments might seem today, at the time Laberthonnière's delineation of the two-part nature of truth (separating truth from knowledge), his redefinitions of philosophical postures (demonstrating the fundamental skepticism of most dogmatic positions), and his affirmation of the primacy of internal realities over external expressions clearly outraged the neo-Thomists. Laberthonnière had the audacity to challenge the hermeneutical primacy of the Church; he advocated, most dangerously, an exegesis of the individual. In a letter to Laberthonnière, dated 31 July 1904, a colleague wrote: "Monseigneur Duchesne said the other day that you were at the point of being condemned. He added that the pope has prepared a new Syllabus . . ."[63] And whereas Blondel tried to couch his remarks in ways that might persuade without insulting, Laberthonnière's words had no diplomatic veneer. Blondel recognized this, and worried about the association. After the purchase of the *Annales*, Blondel wrote: "With the *Annales*, Laberthonnière has in hand a powerful instrument for good, but he must handle with prudence . . . the 'pyrotechnic laboratory.' There are enough bombs around us."[64] Another Pascalisant, mathematician Edouard Le Roy, called the journal under Laberthonnière's guidance, a Trojan horse.

62. Daly, *Transcendence and Immanence*, 107.

63. *Laberthonnière et ses amis*, 45. "Mgr Duchesne disait l'autre jour que vous aviez été sur le point d'être condamné: il ajoutait que le pape tenait tout prêt un nouveau Syllabus . . ."

64. Ibid., 59 n. 21.

Shortly before *Pascendi* was issued, Laberthonnière's works were put on the Index of Prohibited Books.[65] Father Lapidi, the consultant to the Congregation of the Holy Office and of the Index, wrote about this decision: "If Blondel remained protected, it is because he is a young lay professor; we can tolerate his poor theological ideas; but we cannot accept from a priest, who should be a precise and rigorous theologian, what we can tolerate from a layman." And Lapidi went on to make three demands of Laberthonnière: 1) abstain from attacking scholasticism; 2) make his method a mere recommendation rather than a general substitute; 3) above all, rid his thinking of Kantian ideas—showing the clear connection between the supernatural and the natural.[66] While Laberthonnière formally submitted to Rome's mandates (unlike English Jesuit and "modernist" George Tyrell, who defied the authorities) by acquiescing to the directive never to publish again, he never renounced his convictions. Laberthonnière's ideas were too dangerous to the Roman Catholic Church's centralizing and homogenizing goals.

65. These included Laberthonnière's *Essais de philosophie religieuse*, which was a compilation of his articles, and *Réalisme chrétienne*, which we will address in the next chapter.

66. Ibid., 91.

# 7

# Telling Stories about Authenticity

THE ROMAN CATHOLIC CHURCH'S centralizing and homogenizing goals during the nineteenth century, so threatened by the neo-Pascalian ideas discussed heretofore, now need to be examined more closely in order to understand the complexity of the Church's strategy and of the diverse expressions of resistance to it. As we look at the ways the Church had narrowed orthodoxy and resisted every aspect of liberalism, it becomes obvious that the role of historical studies—their defined boundaries and proper methodologies—hits the heart of the Church's concerns. The questions of historical knowledge and veracity that challenged the claims of authentic truth and the subsequent right to shape the future involved both the Church and the State.

In this chapter, we take a step back to look at the larger policies at work behind the Vatican and the Third Republic objectives over the years in question. The historical question, so integrally a part of both the Republic's strategies and the Vatican's goals at the end of the century, became inflamed by the University system's efforts to manage the political aspects of historical studies in ways that incorporated scientific methods of study. Though republican politicians attempted to structure an "objective" historical profession, free of ideology, they succeeded primarily in crafting a historicity that catered to the Third Republic's ideology.[1] Those efforts, influenced by the German model of historical research, infiltrated the study of religious history, and the result was a burgeoning defiance of the static neo-scholastic use of history as evidential support to religious claims.

The fact that this dispute, building just at the turn of the century, coincided with the Vatican's conciliatory attempt to embrace the

---

1. See Talar, "Innovation and Biblical Interpretation," 194–95.

Republic and with the disastrous Dreyfus Affair is no mere historical twist of fate. In this chapter, we go on to consider the ways Leo XIII's *ralliement*, in itself an effort to recover lost political ground in French affairs, exacerbated the religious angst that ended with the vilification of the modernists. The *ralliement* threw the Catholic royalists' conventionally accepted historical model of throne-and-altar out and revised the historical perspective of Catholic French identity by separating it from its perceived French roots and aligning it more closely to Roman authority. It also refocused attention on the Roman Catholic claims to a vital role in the moral development of the nation, a role based on the Church's historical position as the repository and administrator of divine truth. While the *ralliement* expressed political goals amenable to those who were eager to embrace modern ideas, it simultaneously revealed an underlying religious authoritarianism that splintered the French Catholic community and made more room for the rise of nationalist fervor in the guise of restoring an essential French identity.

After a look at the political backdrop of this debate, two key works that addressed the theological question of historical knowledge and veracity will be carefully examined: Blondel's "Histoire et dogme" (1904) and Laberthonnière's "Le Réalisme Chrétien et l'idéalisme grec" (1904). These two articles spoke to the confusion about the dependability of historical accounts and their relation to Catholic dogmatic claims, a confusion that permeated epistemological discourses. If theological knowledge/dogma was based on biblical accounts and subsequent events in Christian history, and those accounts and events were proved unreliable, then what happened to that knowledge and the faith that was based on it? The development of historical studies using a scientific methodology and purportedly achieving "scientific" results—accuracy, truth, certainty—was a much-disputed issue in both academic and political circles. As the Dreyfus Affair and its aftermath accelerated the split between the Church and the State, the Church's claims to historical veracity (the basis of its right to moral authority) and the State's claims to retell the story of French identity (the basis of its right to secularize) collided.

Finally, we will consider the ways the Pascalisants' understanding of historical truth shaped their imagination and reinforced their sense of destiny. The neo-Pascalian teleological emphases were both an outgrowth of historical positions and a starting point that directed the Pascalisants' historical convictions.

## THE RALLIEMENT AND HISTORICAL TRUTH

The *ralliement* of 1890, Leo XIII's call to French Catholics to rally to the Republic and abandon monarchist agitation, failed. Intended to bridge the gap between the clearly established republican government and the festering monarchism that sidelined Catholics in their rejection of political participation, the *ralliement* ended up splitting the Catholic faction. Many Catholic Legitimists (convinced that their faithfulness to the monarchy was an essential part of faithfulness to the Church), felt that the Vatican had betrayed them. Some were so outraged by the pope's about-face that they simply refused to believe the directive really came from him. Rumors swirled about a duped pope whose secretary of state deceived him; other rumors even suggested that the pope had been kidnapped by Freemasons.[2] The political conflict fused with the intellectual conflicts in such a way that the French Catholic community became increasingly fractured. Ultramontanists, who traditionally supported the Roman authority, often became anti-*ralliement*; moderate and liberal Catholics, who systematically resisted Roman hegemony, most eagerly embraced the *ralliement*.

Though most historians have argued that the failure of the *ralliement* was due to Catholic political intransigence, it stemmed primarily from the inherent incompatibility of intellectual principles between integralist French Catholics (politically reactionary) and liberal French Catholics (politically progressive). Harvey Hill points out, as well, that Leo XIII's strategy was ultimately "a calculated strategy for bolstering the Church's political influence." Insofar as he could convince Catholics to participate in governmental affairs, he could mitigate anticlerical legislation and, perhaps, even rally French governmental support for the restoration of the lost Papal states.[3] Boundaries of identity became more

---

2. Wright, *France in Modern Times*, 238.

3. The terms "liberal" and "conservative" become increasingly difficult to use with clarity. Mgr. d'Hulst exemplifies this confusion. D'Hulst was simultaneously a moderate theological Catholic in the vein of Dupanloup (who had resisted the proclamation of the infallibility dogma), a philosophical supporter of Leo XIII's neo-Thomist agenda, and an ardent monarchist, thus making him a "liberal conservative." See Hill, *Politics of Modernism*, 93.

fluid, and Catholics on both sides of the political fence found allies in former adversaries. The *ralliement* asked French Catholics to relinquish their vision of historical national identity, one that was rooted in stories of royal glory and that was projected into a rosy future built on the partnership of throne and altar.[4]

Modernists served as the flashpoint of this conflict, for the modernist controversy brought to the forefront of the discussion the possibility of being Catholic without giving credence to the historical veracity of the Church's claims. While the Church was declaring the possibility of being Catholic without adhering to royalist traditions, the modernists were declaring the possibility of being Catholic without adhering to the historical reality of the creeds and confessions of the Church. Scripture, according to Alfred Loisy, lacked historical integrity, though it retained dogmatic validity. That is, Loisy argued that the Church had the authority to develop dogmatic beliefs that had no basis in history.

Integralist Catholics, who supported the papal right to dictate policy, had linked the authenticity of their religious story to their right to interpret national identity, to recover France's position as the "eldest daughter of the Church." If the telling of the story were disrupted by the suggestion that the accounts had been manipulated by the guardians of scripture (the Church), the right to intervene in the moral affairs of the nation was jeopardized. The integralists were caught between ultramontanist sentiment and a nationalist conceit based on royalist tradition. Progressive Catholics, on the other hand, who were more willing to jettison the nation's historical identity as Rome's faithful daughter, tried to separate the Church's history from the State's history, clinging to the authenticity of the former while retelling the latter. These disparate loyalties generated intellectual chaos, and the confusion, which pervaded the discourse at every level, did not end even when the *ralliement* attempt seemed to fade away.

This persistent unrest was summarized and analyzed in the 1901–1902 editorial comments of Abbé Charles Denis, then editor of the *Annales de philosophie chrétienne*. Denis published in his journal a three-part series of articles entitled "L'Église et l'État: Les Leçons de l'heure présente." He followed up with another article later in 1902, "Situation politique, sociale et intellectuelle du clergé français, Avril 1884–Septembre 1902." Both lengthy works probed the dis-ease that per-

4. Hill, *Politics of Modernism*, 92–93.

vaded the French Catholic Church and its internal and external relationships. Denis's articles were not philosophical or theological treatises but pastoral analyses designed to clarify rather than to remedy the situation that confronted French Catholics torn between papal loyalties, nationalist sentiment, and traditional identity. Denis gave a historical perspective of the dilemmas facing the French Catholic Church, and in doing so defined some of the political and cultural obstacles that French Catholics faced in the intellectual gulf between the Republic and Rome. A major obstacle, as we have seen, was the debate raging about the scientific nature of history, a question foremost in the minds of both republicans and Roman authorities and a question addressed prominently in Leo XIII's *Providentissimus Deus*.

Denis's articles touched on each of the facets that contributed to the larger issue of authenticity: the nature of truth in relationship to dogma, the conflicts between social identities and individual liberties, the apposite function of authority, and the role of imagination in the appropriation of truth. This discourse about legitimacy drew on the raging debates in the public sphere about epistemological certainty and its increasingly elusive quality both in scientific circles and in religious circles. As a priest, a philosopher, and an editor of a distinguished intellectual journal, Denis was well positioned to describe the situation as it appeared at the turn of the century. His articles demonstrate for us the chaotic, fractured state of the French Catholic Church stemming from the failed *ralliement* and leading up to the *Pascendi* encyclical. After considering Denis's description of the pastoral context, we will be better able to discern the convoluted bond between the Vatican's political efforts and the epistemological disputes about history.

Denis's first article, "The Church and the State: Lessons from the Present Time," addressed the conflicts that wracked the Catholic community. He began with the frank admission that "Catholicism ... is in a lamentable situation."[5] His diagnosis rejected the more popular theory that schismatic behaviors and beliefs (like Loisy's publications and the philosophical resistance to neo-Thomist arguments) were wreaking havoc on the Church; rather, he attributed the Church's difficulties to an essential lack of vitality, which he believed had been caused by an inflexible attitude toward progress in science, society, and politics. The

---

5. Denis, "L'Église et l'État," 129. "Le catholicisme, dans les milieux latins, est dans une situation lamentable."

Church, Denis charged, had rejected action and leadership in favor of entrenchment behind dogmatic walls. The Church had substituted political and philosophical traditionalism for the gospel.

Denis continued with a review of the Church's relationship with the State throughout the nineteenth century, a relationship that, by the turn of the century and following the uproar over the Dreyfus Affair, was at its most problematic. Denis weighed the different offenses committed by both Church and State in the evolution from authoritarianism to individualism. Denis saw this transition as the inevitable outworking of scientific advances, which had caused a move from attitudes of subservience (political, social, and religious) to increasing independence. Individualism, with all its civic and religious duties, had, he contended, become an obligation. The State, however, in rejecting partnership with the Church in directing such individualism toward a moral community, had fallen into two traps: "fonctionnarisme" and "socialisme." The former mitigated the power of individuals by giving the State the power to exercise the individual's liberty of conscience through excessive legislation. The latter denied the individual's liberty by creating a collectivity that ultimately eviscerated the power of freedom.[6]

Denis argued that, amidst the diatribe caused by the political and religious extremes, the rights of the individual to contribute to the public sphere had become linked not to truth but to sincerity: Political, social, and even philosophical dialogue required of its participants not real knowledge but merely earnest opinions, which could justify a position despite their epistemological integrity or lack of it. This had resulted in a working equality between truth and error, a functional indifference to reality. The Church's only offensive strategy before such a trend was its advocacy of liberty of conscience, but to use this defense required it to appropriate liberalism. Denis chastised French Catholics for spurning the use of liberalism and faulted the clergy for making liberalism, and thus liberty, a sin.[7] The *ralliement* had been a lost cause because the Church had systematically weakened the people's ability to think for themselves.

Denis pointed out that there were essentially two kinds of believers: humble, passive souls who accepted authority without question and developed an inner piety that never quaked before the onslaughts of the

6. Ibid., 145.
7. Ibid., 157.

world; and "contextualizers," just as faithful to the "papal command" but simultaneously aware of and engaged with contemporary contingencies. This second category of believers understood that evangelization was a new endeavor, for which the method, not the content, was in question. Earlier apologetic efforts, such as the prolonged conflicts with the Huguenots, had focused on the substance of the faith, putting it into sharp contrast with differing core themes, such as apostolic succession, biblical authority, and individual choice. Now, however, the substance of faith was only a secondary problem; the primary one was methodological. "It is not the purpose of the Encyclicals that is in question, but the manner in which they are presented . . ."[8] Denis was voicing the concerns so intricately argued by Blondel and Laberthonnière: that the fundamental objection was methodological rather than substantial, and that Rome's authoritarian manner of imposing truth as an institutional mandate crippled genuine faith. Like the Pascalisants, Denis believed that the historical truths put forward by the Church were not the problem, but the manner of their transmission was. While he did not specify any Encyclicals, Denis's comments surely included *Au milieu des sollicitudes* (1892), Leo XIII's call to *ralliement*, along with the others that had proved so problematic in their rejection of modern political, social, and intellectual developments.[9]

Church leadership, however, disdained this new apologetic focus, and in doing so, impugned the ability of the individual to work through the process of faith; the need to engage in the art of persuasion threatened their authoritative stance. Denis argued that a spirit of elitism had isolated the clergy and imbued them with a sense of esoteric self-righteousness, leaving them out of the more effective and challenging intellectual work that, lamentably, was being done solely by the laity. Contemporary clergy knew nothing about the "science of the soul," and

---

8. Ibid., 332. "Ce n'est pas l'objet des Encycliques qui est en question, mais la manière de les proposer selon qu'on s'adresse à ceux-ci ou à ceux-là ."

9. Encyclicals of the past century that had proven divisive in some manner included Gregory XVI's *Singulari Nos* (1834), which rejected Lammenais's liberalizing program; Pius IX's *Qui Pluribus* (1846), which pointed toward "infallible authority" in the pontiff; Pius IX's *Ubi Primium* (1849), which made dogmatic Mary's immaculate conception; Pius IX's *Inter Multiplices* (1853), which advocated ultramontanism; Pius IX's *Quanta Cura* (1864) with its Syllabus of Errors; and the papal bull "Apostolicae Curae" (1896) in which Leo XIII definitively rejected the validity of Anglican orders, a great blow to many who were working for institutional reunion between the Anglican Church and the Roman Church.

their efforts, focusing on force-feeding doctrine rather than persuasion, only served to antagonize rather than to convert. Thus they betrayed the heritage of the Church, which, Denis claimed, had always embraced liberty against oppression.[10] The Church persisted in seeing the threat as a substantial one rather than a methodological one.[11]

In his second article, "The political, social, and intellectual situation of the French clergy, April 1894–September 1902,"[12] Denis zeroed in on his analysis of the intellectual affairs of the Church and how they had reached the morass they were in. According to Denis, Pope Leo XIII's introduction of Thomism, ostensibly an effort to unite Catholic intellectuals under one philosophical banner, had actually introduced an antagonistic spirit of division between the seculars (both secular clergy and lay Catholic universities), whom the new papal emphasis had not reached and who were doing cutting-edge work in different directions, and the academic clergy (primarily in seminaries), who had become "parrots" of Thomism. He named as examples of the former Ollé-Laprune, Georges Fonsegrive (editor of *La Quinzaine*), and Blondel—"the neo-apologist core."[13] This intellectual antagonism became increasingly "uncharitable" in tone and had developed into a full-blown dichotomy between tradition and dissidence:

> For the [neo-Thomists], certainty was exclusively an objective order, historical . . . ; they invariably confused objective truth with subjective certainty; for the neo-apologists Catholicism was not necessarily dependent on any period of Church history; they gave to the phrase "autonomy of human thought" a sense as comprehensive as possible, but with the fundamental conviction that it was not in contradiction with the autonomy of the supernatural.[14]

Denis then linked the neo-Thomist controversy to the political debate being waged about the *ralliement*. He diagnosed the intellectual dispute between these two camps as a split parallel to the political one.

---

10. Ibid., 454ff.

11. Of course, the threat *was* substantial and not merely methodological, but the fact that the Church failed to delineate between the two led to the wholesale condemnation of *Pascendi*.

12. Denis, "Situation politique, social et intellectuelle du clergé français," 513–86/28.

13. Ibid., 517.

14. Ibid., 518.

His thesis was that the clergy, deprived of intellectual independence because of the neo-Thomist philosophical hegemony, lacked the ability to resist the verbal onslaught of the militant Catholic press, which rejected the papal injunction to make peace with the Republic.

Denis defended the pope's position, arguing that Leo's *ralliement* was impossible to most French clergy because the militant, refractory press, supported by recalcitrant cardinals, undermined papal authority at every turn. Denis suggested that the Vatican itself was racked with the same dualism that afflicted the French clergy. "Réfractarisme" promoted political traditionalism, the hard-line authoritarianism of congregations, clergy, and provincial officials, and resisted progress and lay involvement at any level of leadership. Congregations (religious orders), having been banned under Waldeck-Rousseau's post-Dreyfus reprisals, had become exiles, and as exiles, they could not submit to the *ralliement* and were thus relegated to refractory positions.[15] The fusing of conservative/monarchist interests with those of rich, militant congregations had resulted in the myth of the enslaved pope, duped by his secretary of state. This rumor exacerbated suspicion and revived a Gallican spirit among provincial clerics. Secular clergy supported the *ralliement*, but religious clergy resisted it, and the refractory press aggravated confusion and distrust by carelessly naming as heresy any new social, philosophical, or exegetical idea.[16]

Those who resisted these "réfractoires"—the dissident neo-apologetic historians, critics, sociologists—operated with a different vision of truth, a vision that enabled them to relate knowledge to truth without substituting the one for the other. While the debate about the *ralliement* raged, calling into question the historical realities that defined Catholic French identity, the dissidents were introducing a new historical hermeneutic, an interpretive guide that incorporated the best of modern science in order to arrive at the ancient truth. Their alternative vision of truth was fluid, and did not reside solely in the repositories of past definitions, but was equally present in the contemporary outworking of knowledge-

---

15. While contemporary historical studies focus on the *ralliement*'s defunct status by the end of the century, the fact that Denis continued to consider its relevance for the French Catholic community in the early years of the twentieth century demonstrated its ongoing power to disrupt dialogue between different Catholic factions. While the *ralliement* had lost any political profile, it continued to exercise a more subtle socio-religious significance in the intra-Catholic disputes.

16. Denis, "Situation politique, social et intellectuelle du clergé français," 530f.

production in science and philosophy, leading to "a philosophical movement that was simultaneously parallel and independent."[17]

## FROM THE RALLIEMENT TO NATIONALISM VIA THE HISTORICAL QUESTION

McManners reviews the split in the Catholic response to the *ralliement* and the despair with which many received the papal call to relinquish their campaign for a restored monarchy. The *ralliement* triggered a discourse both within the Catholic community and within republican circles about the limits that should be set on papal influence in the matters of secular government. Early overtures on the part of the Republic's Opportunists to collaborate with pro-*ralliement* Catholics were more a measure of the threat from the Left and the Opportunists' need to consolidate power than a positive response to the *ralliement*. By 1898, however, Opportunists had found new allies in the Radicals whose leftist orientation appeared moderate (and hence more palatable) when compared with the more radical ideology of the socialists.[18] Radicals and Opportunists found a more centrist common ground as they resisted both the virulent anti-Dreyfusards and the forceful socialists; neither of the political groups was dependent upon the Catholic vote, and, indeed, Waldeck-Rousseau's 1899 Radical-weighted government shed the *ralliement* idea like a husk.

As the *ralliement* faded from the political landscape, its demise exacerbated by the Dreyfus struggle, two voices competed for the right to express French Catholic spirituality, both of which based their authenticity on their historical vision. The intransigent Catholics, who could not let go of their traditional identity, rallied around an emerging nationalist rhetoric as a solution to the painful dissonance between the failed papal call to *ralliement* and the increasingly anticlerical administration of Émile Combes (which would lead finally to the Law of Separation). The modernists/Pascalisants, on the other hand, attempted to inject a contemporary historical justification and relevance into Catholic faith and dogma in order to draw believers back into a harmonious relationship with French culture, society, and politics.

---

17. Ibid., 542.
18. McManners, *Church and State*, 75.

Modernists/Pascalisants—a difficult classification in light of the tenuous connections between those who became identified solely by *Pascendi*, a post-development document, and its vilification of those who in any way advocated cooperation with liberal values[19]—competed with the increasingly more organized voice of right-wing nationalism via Charles Maurras. Michael Sutton traces the rise of Charles Maurras and his monarchist campaign of the Action française that stood for anti-individualism and for a revival of classical Hellenism. His platform directly contradicted the Pascalisants' (particularly Laberthonnière's) rejection of Greek influences on Christianity and their call for a method of immanence that began the search for God and truth within the individual. Maurras took advantage of the confusion that reigned within the French Catholic community and infused the political arena with a new version of mystical and spiritual Catholicism, a version that simultaneously applauded Roman authority and enhanced French identity. Maurras's conviction that the "lack of submission [to the proper authorities, as he defined them] . . . is causing the disintegration of the modern world—in politics, in ethics and in the realm of knowledge"[20] stemmed from the Revolution with its call to rebellion and indeed from the Reformation with its call to individualism. In Maurras's mind, a return to a spirit of classical antiquity, with its clear-cut sense of order and intellectual hegemony, combined with Rome's exercise of moral dominion was France's only hope. An atheist himself, Maurras's ideas, traditional enough to appeal to Catholics, were not inherently Catholic themselves. Yet few recognized or appreciated Maurras's core unbelief. Abbé Delfour, a clergyman and author recognized by the Académie Française said of Maurras: "No one is more Catholic—I was about to write as Catholic—as this aggressive atheist named Charles Maurras."[21] Maurras insisted that the ultimate root of individualism and the liberalism that issued from it was Judaism, and that the Protestants had appropriated this through

---

19. We must persist in recognizing the Pascalisants as a subset of the modernists, though neither was a recognized association of individuals and the two groups were often at odds. Their common element, again, was their resistance to undue Roman authority, exercised through an enforced scholasticism and its insistence on external priorities rather than internal ones, and a desire to reform the Church. See Jodock, *Catholicism Contending with Modernity*, 3.

20. Sutton, *Nationalism, Positivism and Catholicism*, 16.

21. Ibid., 196.

their renewed emphasis on scripture.[22] Maurras's solution include recourse to Thomistic thought, thereby mitigating the liberalizing influence of scripture by subjugating it to Roman authority.[23] Maurras could effectively merge a rabid ultramontanism with nationalism, thus simultaneously evoking Catholic devotion and French honor. It was a heady mix. Maurras offered his solution as a way out of what he took to be the moral darkness caused by a political order without traditional mores and the increasingly ominous political shadows cast by hardening diplomatic alliances.

O'Connell points out, too, that at this time the Vatican began to enter into increasingly direct negotiations with the governments of Catholic-based countries, circumventing the more established but crumbling centers of ecclesiastical authority, including France. This, combined with the increasing divisions between higher and lower clergy, the latter calling for mediation by Rome, furthered the absolute authority complex.[24] Denis had pointed out how the *réfractoires* took advantage of every conflict between bishop and clergy, and did so by portraying the bishops as "creatures" of the government.[25] "Leo XIII . . . began to restructure the Church's consciousness of the papacy with respect to holding territory. He began to think of the ecclesial territory more explicitly in terms of people's souls and consciences, at least until adequate territory could be returned to the papacy."[26] The papal territorial losses contributed to a sense of attrition, and the goal of territorial retention, at nearly any cost, became a priority. David Schultenover suggests that Leo's sponsorship of Thomism satisfied the papacy's sense of "dyadic agonism," the belief that "to admit one reality is to deny its apparent opposite, to acknowledge outside authority is to deny inside authority." The political realities—loss of power, land, and membership—were, in the hierarchy's mind, due to individualism, and the solution was to deny the latter in order to regain the former. "Thus the counter-Reformation popes argued that to allow validity to individual sentiment and internal guidance of the Holy Spirit

---

22. Ibid., 38.
23. Ibid., 81.
24. O'Connell, *Critics on Trial*, 26ff.
25. Denis, "Situation politique," 586 n. 2.
26. Schultenover, *View from Rome*, 235.

is to deny the necessity of external authority, and so the upshot must be atheism and anarchy."[27]

Gary Lease concurs, arguing that the international affairs of the *fin-de-siècle* affected the Vatican's philosophical policies. Church leaders could no longer manage their constituency in recognizably authoritative ways. "As that struggle became more and more impossible, there occurred a retreat from all effective foreign policy and a concentration upon the inner forum: the minds, hearts, wills and consciences of the institution's members . . . the anti-Modernist spasm at the turn of the century represents the final stage of a failed foreign policy program of almost a century's duration."[28] He suggests that because the Triple Alliance included recalcitrant Italy and Protestant Germany, Leo XIII felt even more threatened and his acute need for France's loyalty provoked the *ralliement*. It was his last hope of regaining the papal states.[29] Piux X held the same ambition, but chose to pursue it by demanding of Catholics an intellectual submission, which, he hoped, would lead to greater political clout. Maurras highly applauded these goals.[30]

Laberthonnière recognized the spirit of the day when he wrote to Blondel (21 August 1904): "It seems that all Christianity consists of is to prostrate oneself before the Pope while bellowing out one's submission . . . All this is conducive to a regime of spiritual Prussianism which frightens me."[31] In contrast, he and Blondel delineated a different approach to papal authority in their inaugural article to the *Annales de philosophie chrétienne* following Denis's death, Blondel's purchase of the journal, and Laberthonnière's installation as its editor. Blondel (the primary author) began "Notre Programme" with a quote from Augustine: "We search as those who must find, and we find as those who must still search; for as it is said, 'the man who comes to the end must simply begin again.'" Blondel attempted to work out the apparent conflict between Catholic fidelity and intellectual freedom by beginning with the assertion that those who chose dogmatic loyalty without reflection on their faith reduced truth and made its viability moot. Religious authority is real, but it is of its essence non-constraining, something completely different from

---

27. Ibid., 236.
28. Lease, "Vatican foreign policy and the origins of Modernism," 32.
29. Ibid., 46.
30. Ibid., 49.
31. Quoted in Sutton, *Nationalism, Positivism and Catholicism*, 173.

caesarism. "One can force heads to bow, knees to kneel, lips to speak, but one cannot force the mind to think, the will to desire, the heart to love." Any submission that does not come from the heart, Blondel argued, was false.[32] External authority could not accomplish what needed to happen within the life of the individual. Nor could that authority be used to support arguments in its own defense, because it had no power over the unpersuaded. Rather, there must be a fusion between the authority that teaches and the interior authority that wills to be taught. Official teachings, definitions, and dogma are problems to be resolved rather than solutions,[33] and therefore the *Annales de philosophie chrétienne*, under Laberthonnière and Blondel, would aim at exciting the curiosity of those who seek the truth rather than quenching it with answers.

Nevertheless, the *Annales de philosophie chrétienne* felt that it was part of its duty to defend the honor of the Church and to serve its interests. Therefore, its editors wished to make it "a center of *ralliement*... a steady, positive work of synthesis."[34] The only risk of such an endeavor was that of complacency in the knowledge of the truth. Only mobile truth, vital truth, indeed, humble truth—one that recognized its incompleteness and its need for ongoing discovery—was genuine truth. "The Church in the world is not the perfect realization of this idea: otherwise, once lodged in its breast, we would have nothing left to do. But the Church is the organ by which the idea [of truth] is realized in humanity."[35]

Such a redefinition of Church authority triggered what Victor Giraud, editor of the *Revue des deux mondes*, called "the fear of laicism and of the laity,"[36] a consideration that returns us to Pascal, an "honnête homme" rather than a professional theologian. In his reflections on the contemporary relevancy of Pascal, Giraud explored the correspondence

---

32. [Maurice Blondel], "Notre programme," 15. "Cherchons donc comme cherchent ceux qui doivent trouver, et trouvons comme trouvent ceux qui doivent chercher encore; car il est dit : l'homme qui est arrivé au terme ne fait que commencer.'" and "On peut forcer les fronts à se courber, les genoux à plier, les lèvres à parler, mais on ne peut pas forcer l'esprit à penser, la volonté à vouloir, le coeur à aimer."

33. Ibid., 19.

34. Ibid., 22. "un centre de ralliement... on pût y opérer lentement un travail positif de synthèse."

35. Ibid., 27. "L'Église en ce monde n'est pas la réalisation consommé de cet ideal: autrement, une fois dans son sein, on n'aurait plus rien à faire. Mais elle est l'organe par lequel il se réalise dans l'humanité."

36. Victor Giraud, "Anticléricalisme et Catholicisme," 864.

between Pascal's ideas and those of his own generation. Giraud found Pascal's thoughts "the echo of all our concerns," particularly that of religious unrest. Giraud pinpointed a key part of Pascal's popularity in his lay status, a significantly more persuasive voice than that of trained experts who understood nothing of the life most people led.[37] Giraud suggested that Pascal saw the health of the Church, the cure of unbelief, in the renewal of the laity and its gifts for the Church.[38] Insofar as individuals freely chose the authority of the Church, the Church would thrive. Clearly, the dignity granted to the individual and the responsibility of freedom of choice was a sharp contrast to the centralizing, formalizing corporate emphasis of Maurras's nationalist ideas.

This focus on authenticity within the individual was, according to many of the Pascalisants,[39] the thread of genuine French spirituality, expressed most eloquently by Pascal who not only argued from a spiritual/mystical approach, but also defended his convictions with rational, even scientific, explanations. All of these Pascalisants adhered to Pascal's three orders of knowledge—sense, reason, heart—and employed them in their efforts to recover a French religious voice that had been lost under layers of scholasticism. The shadow of skepticism that lay over Pascal's work eclipsed his claims to certain knowledge through the three orders.

Ironically, Pascal's "epistemological skepticism" had triggered Maurras's rejection of faith. Pascal's "elliptical mysticism" left Maurras cold and turned him toward the clarity of positivism.[40] Pascal's appreciation of Old Testament prophecies and Jewish history also would have aggravated the sense of antipathy that Maurras would feel toward the individualism promoted by scripture. Pascal's mysticism, hidden behind a mask of skepticism, also kindled an antipathy toward the suspect philosopher in the attitudes of the scholastics. Neither nationalists nor Romanists/ultramontanists, in their repudiation of liberalism, had a place for Pascalian thought or for Pascalian disciples.

Here, then, is where the tangled web of criticism leads: Modernists (Loisy, et. al.) and ultramontanists agreed that the translation of revelation required an authoritative hermeneutical function, though they

37. Giraud, "De la Modernité des 'Pensées' de Pascal," 604.

38. Giraud, *Pascal*, 220.

39. See also G. Lechartier's "Pascal d'après Em. Boutroux," 616; J. Bourdeau's, *Pragmatisme et Modernisme*, 133; and Adolphe Hatzfeld's *Pascal*, vii.

40. Sutton, *Nationalism, Positivism and Catholicism*, 232ff.

disagreed about who should exercise that role (the latter holding to the ecclesial authorities, the former holding to trained historical critics); both groups promoted a spiritual elitism. Integralists/ultramontanists rejected modernists' call for historical criticism because it made implicit the need for a privileged *magisterium* beyond their jurisdiction.[41] Pascalisants and modernists agreed that scholasticism closed the door to an individual's ability to benefit from historical revelation. Ultramodernists and Pascalisants agreed that the dogmas of the Church were divinely revealed and gave meaning to the private experience. The Ariadne thread through this maze that guided the Pascalisants amidst redoubtable challenges and eventually defined their contribution to the discourse, was their dual focus on 1) the intimate connection between dynamic truth-telling and dogma, and 2) the authenticity of the individual's religious imagination with its call to ultimate human destiny.

## STATIC VERSUS DYNAMIC TRUTH-TELLING: THE VITALITY OF DOGMA

The issue of the connection between authenticity and history and identity begins to clarify the constructed nature of "modernism" as it was shaped in the *Lamentabili Sane* decree of 3 July 1907 and the *Pascendi* encyclical of 8 September 1907. While the neo-Thomists reified biblical history through the imposition of static Church authority, making intellectual discovery and creativity impossible,[42] the dissidents (both modernists and Pascalisants) posited a different approach to the study of history, one that incorporated contemporary developments in science and thought in order to present a version of history that was more palatable to the non-Christian intellectual world. The modernists' position, however, was not merely hermeneutically heterodox, but it resulted in heretical conclusions about the veracity of Church tradition. Loisy, following in the steps of Renan, called into question the Virgin Birth, Jesus' self-awareness as Messiah, and the Bible's teaching about the Parousia (the full establishment of the kingdom of God in the future).

41. Schultenover, 230.

42. Many later twentieth-century neo-Thomists (notably Jacques Maritain and Étienne Gilson) moved past the early strictures of neo-Thomism, which had included a rigid thirteenth-century organization of knowledge. The Pascalisants might not have resisted the more broad-minded neo-Thomism of their philosophical successors. Indeed, Blondel himself made significant overtures toward neo-Thomism in his later career.

The position of the Pascalisants, on the other hand, was one of unwavering fidelity to the Church and incontestable adherence to its historical conclusions, though they, too, offered a different hermeneutic, one which they hoped would satisfy the ecclesiastical authorities because of its traditional conclusions but still incorporated contemporary thought. Neo-Thomists, modernists, and Pascalisants all struggled to make sense of the cacophony of arguments. From their point of view, the correct historical perspective could clarify positions of authority.

We turn now to look more closely at the disputes about history between the modernists and the Pascalisants. In the articles under consideration in this chapter, the Pascalisants strove to differentiate themselves from the modernists. While they both opposed neo-Thomist hegemony, they disagreed with one another about both the intellectual process and its conclusions. Ultimately, their critical differences only served to fortify Rome's resistance. We see in their disagreement that the process of defining historical truth and reifying it via dogma, identity, authority, and imagination made erstwhile adversaries into common enemies of Rome.

Ernest Renan's *Vie de Jésus*, published in 1863, rocked both the popular and the exegetical world. It introduced the possibility that the scriptures, long promoted by the Church as the true account of the life and mission of Jesus, had been systematically glossed, enhanced by years of self-preserving institutional leaders. Beneath all that polish lay the real Jesus, a simple first-century Jewish peasant who had some good things to say . . . he was not, however, in Renan's controversial judgment, a Messiah, but only a rabbi. Adolf Harnack, German professor of theology and church history, had brought the discussion started by Renan into the academic world with his multi-volume work *Lehrbuch der Dogmengeschichte* (1886–90), *History of Dogma*, in which he rejected dogma as an imposition on the biblical text and called for the stripping away of cult and institution to find the primitive core of Christianity, the "real truth," by discerning the original gospel within the multi-layered historical accounts in the Bible. In response to Harnack's thesis, and, he believed, in defense of Catholic dogma, Loisy (who had studied for a short time under Renan at the Collège de France[43]) wrote

---

43. Reardon, *Liberalism and Tradition*, 258. See also Talar, "Innovation and Biblical Interpretation," 199. Talar explains that Loisy's writings indicate that Renan had exposed him to German scholarship. Thus, Loisy demonstrates for us the binary struggle

his *L'Évangile et l'Église* (1902) in which he argued that, though Harnack was right about the historical development of dogma and its essential absence from the gospel accounts, he was wrong about its speciousness. The seed of the dogma lay hidden in the simplicity of the gospel, and while the man Jesus knew little or nothing about the greater truths of the Roman Catholic Church and was, in fact, wrong about such facts as the *parousia* (Christian teaching about the imminent return of Christ), Catholics could nevertheless adhere to Roman dogma as truth because it had evolved to become truth. Biblical criticism was about knowledge—facts about the authorship, historical context, and reliability of records; the "domain of revealed truth"—supernatural assertions—was inaccessible to human reason and thus disconnected from knowledge per se.[44] Loisy felt safe because he held fast to Church doctrine though he rejected the historicity of scripture. He was, however, deluded about his ecclesiastical security; Alexander Dru deems Loisy's book the equivalent of "putting a pistol to the heads of the authorities."[45] Talar points out the ways that neo-Thomistic historical studies relegated biblical exegesis to a mere evidential role. Scripture was not explored on its own terms, but only in relation to and in support of the dogma that was built upon it. "The proof-texting role assigned to exegesis recapitulates the ahistorical, 'essentialist' character of neo-scholasticism generally and neo-Thomism more particularly."[46]

Blondel, already under ecclesiastical suspicion because of his determined work on the method of immanence, felt the need to firmly separate himself from association with Loisy's line of thinking. In response to Loisy's *L'Évangile et l'Église*, he wrote "Histoire et Dogme," published in *La Quinzaine* (January–February 1904). In this article, Blondel defined the two extremes that were eroding the Church's intellectual foundation, extremes that had resulted in two "quite incompatible 'catholic mentalities,' particularly in France."[47]

---

of Catholic intellectuals who on one hand struggled to accommodate traditionalist expectations from their clerical colleagues while endeavoring to stay abreast of academic trends in the secular community.

44. O'Connell, *Critics on Trial,* 219.
45. Dru, "Prefatory Note," in *The Letter,* 211.
46. Talar, "Innovation and Biblical Interpretation," 197.
47. Blondel, *The Letter,* 221.

On the one hand, according to Blondel, was extrinsicism (the neo-Thomist's hermeneutic), an adamant insistence on the one-to-one relationship between biblical facts and Christian faith that focused purely on the accidental, extrinsic character of those facts. For example, extrinsicists argued that the biblical accounts of Jesus' miracles were historical proof of his miraculous power; as such they could justly be used to authenticate the dogma of his divinity and therefore compel belief. This positivist approach relegated dogma to a museum and deprived it of any vital power. Scholarly efforts of the mid to late nineteenth century to build a recognizably scientific basis to the study of history, however, had ultimately resulted in the clear recognition that historical facts could not produce faith. The more vociferously scholars argued the absolute historical reliability of such supernatural biblical accounts as the seven-day creation, the parting of the Red Sea, or the raising of the dead, the less they seemed able to convince the nonbeliever. Extrinsicists, however, according to Blondel, refused to believe this to their own shame, "taking refuge in an ostrich-like policy, shutting their eyes and not even allowing themselves to face too plainly the embarrassing literalness which they continue to teach the simple."[48] In the face of such historical skepticism, many were left with a historicism that defined faith as a human construct based on inspirations or a pure fideism.[49]

The historicist method (represented by Loisy's hermeneutic), however, Blondel argued, was equally sterile, for it merely examined the content of knowledge, whereas what must happen is the "critique of knowledge itself."[50] According to Blondel, historicism was a positivist approach to historical studies. It included a weighing of historical accounts by contemporary measures, which relegated phenomena that could not be scientifically demonstrated to the realm of the extra-historical. These extra-historical elements were in turn of historical interest as a "composite effigy" of a living reality that disclosed the intents and purposes of authors, but not the facts. History, then, was a study of the logical development of events without the attribution of cause or meaning.[51] This, Blondel argued, was a simplistic contempt for the more complex

---

48. Ibid., 230.
49. Ibid., 226ff.
50. Ibid., 234.
51. Ibid., 240ff.

understanding of historical knowledge as a synthesis of human experiences and the accounts of them.

Blondel insisted that, as a modern science, history, too, must recognize its own limitations, that it could not speak to anything but the phenomenon, and that any simple historical fact was only a part of the intricate chain of human experience, which he believed was itself a supremely metaphysical realm of inquiry. Loisy had isolated historical fact from its human context, which eviscerated the fact of its epistemological value, leaving only a false reification of one perspective of an event, the substitution of a bare reduction for the fullness of the historical reality. Loisy's hermeneutic would take a biblical event, like the feeding of the five thousand, and cut it off from any relationship to the psychological and moral realities of human lives that really lived and experienced the event. To isolate a "fact" as an objective historical observation without recognizing its place as a link in the chain of human experience is to reject the metaphysical reality of that experience.[52] Historicism "claims to have penetrated the spiritual secret of the living chain of souls because it has verified the external joints of the links which are no more than its corpse."[53] Blondel thus presents an early deconstruction of history as an intellectual enterprise:

> In default of an explicit philosophy, a man ordinarily has an unconscious one. And what one takes for simple observations of fact are often simply constructions. The observer, the narrator, is always more or less of a poet; for behind what he sees the witness puts an action and a soul so as to give the fact a meaning; behind the witness and his testimony, if they are really to enter history, the critic puts an interpretation, a relation, a synthesis; behind these critical data the historian inserts a general view and wider human preoccupations; which is to say that man with his beliefs, his metaphysical ideas, and his religious solutions conditions all the subordinate researches of his science as much as he is conditioned by them.[54]

Accepting such knowledge as the fullness of truth, Blondel argued, would only lead to ideologies rather than to reality. The only viable ideology of faith that could subsist under historicism would be fideism, a

52. Ibid., 239.
53. Ibid., 240.
54. Ibid., 237–38.

relinquishment of the requirements of reason in favor of religion. Both historicism and extrinsicism have rejected the role of interpretation.

What, then, according to Blondel, is the link between fact and faith, between truth and belief, between certainty and conviction? It must be something other than a mechanical relationship, for otherwise facts would convince everyone and all would be believers. Yet to sever the ties between fact and faith would leave dogma wandering in a mythical no-man's-land and faith, then, would be a merely symbolic system of spirituality. This, ironically enough despite his pro-Catholic stance, seemed to be exactly Maurras's ambition: the creation of a symbolic system of spirituality that lent itself to political manipulation but that had no actual claims to an authenticity that would have made intellectual demands. Blondel's solution, delineated in "Histoire et dogme," is a Hegelian-like movement between history and dogma resulting in an active, organic synthesis of form and substance that eliminated the possibility of neutrality.

Blondel called this method of integration and cooperation Tradition, though he carefully differentiated his meaning from the weapon-like use of tradition among Catholic reactionaries after the Revolution. The problematic nature of Tradition, Blondel explained, stemmed from the traditionalist use of Aristotelian scientific methodologies, which piece together bits of information to form a contiguous and definitive whole, whereas modern scientific methodologies collaborate and conflict in a constant, fluid relationship that never collapses because they never attempt to speak the whole truth (the essence) about any matter.[55] On the contrary, science is merely an abstraction of a line of thought about reality, a method and process rather than a solution or conclusion about anything. (Here, clearly, Blondel reiterated the new scientific theories of Duhem and Poincaré rather than drawing on positivist notions about absolute scientific truth.) Tradition, as Blondel defined it, offers a middle way, a synthesis between the facts and the ideas.

Tradition needs the participation of the individual, something which both historicism and extrinsicism neglected. Historicism disconnected past events from present human actions; with this methodology doctrines proceeding from the intellectual work of the Church were mere impositions of authoritative inferences on simple historical facts.[56]

---

55. Ibid., 236.
56. Reardon, *Liberalism and Tradition*, 274.

Extrinsicism rejected the need for the individual's engagement in and interpretation of those events; thus, with this methodology doctrines were merely assertions of institutional authority over the individual. Both historicism and extrinsicism dispensed dogma and expected faith in return. Both extremes catered to a "religious aristocracy," fostering "an intellectual privilege which only exists as such, in opposition to, and as external to, the common state."[57]

With Tradition, on the other hand, the believer moved from faith to dogma rather than from dogma to faith. Thus its genesis was in the individual, not in the institution and not in the science. Echoing Pascal's advice to "quiet reason," Blondel returned the focus to the practice of the Christian life, something that, in his view, came not from an intellectual adherence to facts, but from "acts at first perhaps difficult, obscure and enforced," permitting the individual to rise "to the light through a practical verification of speculative truths."[58] Thus did the individual, in a synergy of faith and certainty, make real the claims of the Church. "The infallible *Magisterium* is the higher and really supernatural guarantee of a function which has as its natural foundation in the concert of all the powers of each Christian and of all Christianity."[59]

Blondel's article, and Laberthonnière's subsequent supporting articles on Christian history, ruffled the feathers of many "modernists" who contended that an insistence on biblical authenticity betrayed the goals of reconciling faith with modern expressions of reason. Loisy himself objected to Blondel's implicit rejection of the role of authority in the definition of truth. He, oddly similar to Maurras, willingly embraced the hegemonic role of the Church in the realm of dogma.[60] This from a man who privately concluded that "If I am anything in religion, it is more pantheist-positivist-humanitarian than Christian."[61] Loisy easily segregated truth from doctrine, "the former being the divine reality which is disclosed over the ages, the latter the formulation of that reality made under the conditions obtaining at the time and therefore subject to change with time."[62] Truth was inaccessible, but doctrines, mere human

57. Blondel, *The Letter*, 283.
58. Ibid., 274.
59. Ibid., 277.
60. Loisy, *Choses passées*, 307–8, quoted in O'Connell, *Critics on Trial*, 304.
61. Reardon, *Liberalism and Tradition*, 278.
62. Ibid., 265.

formulas, could be accessed by reason because they were the results of reasonable actions.

Loisy also accused Blondel of trying to deal with history from a philosophical point of view instead of from a historian's perspective. What could a philosopher know about historical studies? Loisy wished to be, so he said, nothing but an historian; his work had nothing to say about theology. Yet both Blondel and Laberthonnière agreed that these claims were disingenuous, and that the method of interpretation was itself a theological assertion.[63] This reiterated Blondel's primary contention that methodology bore the weight of faith.

Though Blondel had defended the essential truth of Tradition, his rejection of the one-to-one correspondence between fact and faith, between scriptural accounts and revelatory claims, made him equally questionable in the eyes of the neo-Thomists. For them, "Nothing more was required for knowing God's mind and will than a simple reading of scripture and the church's tradition—although authorities did not encourage private reading by the laity, as that smacked of Protestantism."[64] According to the neo-Thomists, only one testimony was needed: that of the Church. That alone should be adequate to compel faith.

Yet according to Blondel, this testimony, like that of those who witnessed miracles, seemed inadequate. Obviously, many witnesses of miraculous acts and witnesses of the Christ himself did not believe. Why? Why was testimony itself insufficient in the production of certainty? Because the individual must become involved. "We must always respond *within* to the 'proofs,' for as luminous as they are externally, they fail to manufacture faith in spite of ourselves and without our participation."[65]

This hermeneutic of the individual, which we have seen has been the Pascalisant theme, was reiterated by others who recognized its importance in historical studies. In his 1905 book on *The True Religion according to Pascal*, René Sully-Prudhomme (poet, Nobel laureate, and literary critic) reiterated this emphasis on the role of the individual in the interpretation of scripture. About Pascal he wrote, "It follows that

---

63. Daly, *Transcendence and Immanence*, 57.

64. Schultenover, *View from Rome*, 229.

65. Blondel, *Lettres Philosophiques*, 132. "C'est que toujours nous aurions eu et nous avons à répondre *du dedans* aux preuves 'très certaines,' à la portée de tous qui, brillant *au-dehors*, doivent suffire à déterminer notre foi sans réussir à la déterminer *en fait* malgré nous et sans nous."

faith has as its object, other than the dogma itself, the historical foundation of the dogma, not only the mysteries, but, before all, the accounts that call us to belief . . ."[66] Such a faith did not imply an incompatibility with the discoveries of modern science, Sully-Prudhomme argued, when like Pascal the critic strictly separates the intellectual exercises of metaphysical interpretation from those of scientific inquiry, just as Pascal kept separate the exercises of geometric deduction from those of empirical observation.[67]

Brunetière, another Pascalisant, also addressed this effort to discern the truth amidst the claims of dogma and science. The problem, he argued, is that people want to make history into a science and it cannot be done. History cannot be science, for science is about establishing laws and reoccurring patterns, and history is about accidental events that occur once. According to Brunetière, history was philosophy; any historical representation said more about the historian's perception than about the factual content of the representation. Quoting Pascal, Brunetiè re reminded the reader that reasonable reason will recognize this and apply itself accordingly.[68]

Dogma, then, became something other than a scientific result to an empirically based study of scripture. It was an answer to the question of the human experience, an answer in dramatic form rather than in prosaic form. Sully-Prudhomme drew this conclusion from the *Penseés*, arguing that Pascal wished to present the hiddenness and obscurity of the revelation as a means of drawing the individual, whose understanding had been shattered by original sin, into the story and thereby engaging him in its completion.[69]

The story, however, in its dogmatic form, had been corrupted, according to Laberthonnière. In his 1904 book, *Le Réalisme Chrétien et l'idéalisme grec*, Laberthonnière entered the dogma/history controversies with a gauntlet that challenged both Third Republic ambitions and those of the neo-scholastics. As we have seen, many Third Republic leaders were dedicated to the recognition of history as a science. William

---

66. Sully-Prudhomme, *La Vraie Religion selon Pascal*, 333. "Il s'ensuit que la foi a pour objet, outre le dogme même, le fondement historique du dogme, non pas uniquement les mystères, mais avant tout les récits qui les proposent à la créance . . ."
67. Ibid., 365.
68. Brunetière, *Questions Actuelles*, 23.
69. Sully-Prudhomme, *La Vraie Religion selon Pascal*, 259.

Keylor describes the concerns of several Second Empire *normaliens* who became increasingly concerned about the desperately inadequate role of history in secondary education. The 1870 defeat only underscored for them the superiority of the German system and the need to revitalize and, indeed, reinvent history for French students. Historical studies became the key to the unity of a nation insofar as it resurrected a sense of pride in French grandeur and prescribed an identity that could guide citizens in rebuilding their future. Historical studies became a pedagogical tool for Third Republic ideology.[70]

Harry Paul describes this late nineteenth-century storytelling that began with Greek beginnings and the reintroduction of Greek thought by the Arabs, that continued with the darkness of the Middle Ages under the aegis of the Church and the regeneration of Greek wisdom during the Renaissance. The story then moved to the seventeenth-century French victory over dead scholasticism under the Enlightenment masters and the birth of true science in the eighteenth century.[71] Jules Michelet (1798–1874) exemplified this new emphasis on historical revision.[72] His multi-volume *History of France* incorporated the best of French Romanticism's focus on a national mystique that yet awaited a grand destiny to be inaugurated by France's own self-creative act. His mid-century *History of the Revolution* retold the story of the French Revolution as an exploration of humanist glories confronting Catholic obduracy, a traditionalist attitude that had held France back since the Middle Ages. By the *fin-de-siècle*, it had become commonplace in historical circles to argue that the Church had been the bane of French history and had obstructed its intellectual, scientific, and social progress.

Laberthonnière rejected this account and told a different story, one that presented a foundational opposition between Greek philosophy and Christianity.[73] Thus Laberthonnière both contradicted secularized accounts of the ways the Church had suppressed the advancement of knowledge and rebuffed the Thomistic synthesis between Aristotelian

---

70. Keylor, *Academy and Community*, 41.
71. Paul, "Scholarship and Ideology," 378.
72. Keylor, *Academy and Community*, 49.
73. Duhem, too, gave a great deal of his time and energy exploring scientific history under the premise that the Church had actually been the instigator rather than the antagonist of scientific progress. Before his death, he wrote five of a planned ten volumes entitled *Le Système du monde, Histoire des doctrines cosmologiques, de Platon à Copernic*.

philosophy and Christian theology. According to Laberthonnière, the Renaissance was no rebirth, but a dark return to paganism, one in which the reintroduction of Greek values under the guise of Christian orthodoxy was artificial.[74]

Greek philosophy linked truth to knowledge; ignorance was the true evil. The difficulties that arose in pinning down the truth drove the Greeks to abstractions, which could serve as static formulas of truth and thus of virtue. Experience, which was ephemeral, contradictory, and temporal, could never lead to truth because it could not be reproduced. Thought alone could transcend experience. Thus most individuals, stuck in the transient material world, could never attain truth. Such a definition of truth led to an aristocratic elite composed of philosophers who, supported by artisans, soldiers, and slaves, could indulge in the search for wisdom with material care.[75]

According to Laberthonnière, Christianity had an entirely different approach; it looked at the world around it and called its followers to examine themselves, their interior realities, and their destinies. Christian revelation, Laberthonnière explained, took place in a world of time and space, and so it was historical, yet it was more than history. The historical facts, real events, became concrete and living representations of truth as the individual interpreted them. When Laberthonnière wrote that the accuracy of the details was immaterial as long as they expressed the truth of what really happened, he posited a vital, organic theory of truth, one that was tied to history but was also fluid, contemporary, and linked to the individual's interpretation.[76] Tradition was merely the extension of the individual's experience; human life, a brief and inadequate experience, needs Tradition to make sense of its part of the drama. Thus Laberthonnière removed Tradition from the hands of authority and placed it in the hands of the individual: "And so doctrine, whose traditional character is like a common patrimony of truth, takes in each person a subjective and personal form of knowledge, adapted to

---

74. Laberthonnière, *Le Réalisme Chrétien et l'idéalisme grec*, 11.

75. Ibid., 14–30. F. Ravaisson had also pointed out the contemporary obsession with generalization and abstraction, practices that separate truth reality. He, too, underscores Pascal's importance as a clear thinker who carefully delineated the differences between mathematical truths (which issue from logical functions but which are abridgments of reality) and spiritual truths (which issue from encounters with the divine and yield certainties in their own field). See Ravaisson, "La Philosophie de Pascal," 401ff.

76. Ibid., 62.

that person's capacity at the time."⁷⁷ The Greeks believed actual events to be mere accidents of abstract realities. Laberthonnière believed that Christianity presented the actual events as the outside of an inside truth, a truth made available not only to the elites but to each individual: "Behind the events or more truthfully in the events one discovers God with his infinite power and his goodness. That is why and how, as I have indicated, interpretation becomes the essential mode of the activity of the spirit."⁷⁸

The Church, however, in its late nineteenth century fever of historical objectivity, dealt only with the verification of facts and the authentication of texts. It may be argued that in Laberthonnière's day, historical criticism had taken the place of natural theology—metaphysical answers about the work of God were sought no longer in the world around them, as they had been in Pascal's time, but in the documents that recounted the work of God. Laberthonnière's arguments, then, about the insufficiency of historical verification replicated Pascal's rejection of natural theology as an adequate apologetic for the truth.

Truth, for the Pascalisants, was positive, not speculative. It dealt with the active experiences of the individual, not the abstract formulas of the institution. Even Duhem argued that the most basic methods of knowing, such as sight and touch, could yield greater certainty than the most scientific experiments. The latter drew in a plethora of theories, some overt, some covert, and required confidence in each of them in order to grant certainty. Truth must make room for "that rare subtle quality" that Pascal called "l'esprit de finesse."⁷⁹ Pascalian truth was vital, persuasive, and compelling, yet simultaneously elusive, hidden, and pursued. It was, in fact, a drama in which the audience played as actors. "Pascal never addressed himself to abstract reason, but to the real and complex individual, capable of thought and of fear, of hope, of love, and of desire. He did not aim at resolving problems theoretically by means of rules of

---

77. Ibid., 77. "Et ainsi la doctrine, qui par son caractère traditionnel est comme un patrimoine commun de vérité, prend en chacun la forme d'une connaissance subjective et personnelle, appropriée à sa capacité du moment."

78. Ibid., 81. "Derrière les événements ou plutôt en elles on découvre Dieu avec l'infinité de sa puissance et de sa bonté. Voilà pourquoi et comment, ainsi que nous l'avons déjà signalé, l'*interprétation* devient ici le mode essentiel de l'activité de l'esprit."

79. Duhem, "Some Reflections on the Subject of Experimental Physics," in *Essays*, 98.

logic... We are engaged in a drama."⁸⁰ As in any good drama, the balance of tension between precision and paradox, between certainty and faith, is tenuous. It lies suspended, like Pascal's man, between the two abysses of "grandeur" and "ignominy," "reuniting the two incompatible parts, the reason troubled by their inexplicable contradictions and the heart by their painful conflict."⁸¹

This suspense, however, was for the Pascalisants not one of contradiction, but of life-giving tension. Blondel was adamant that any genuine thought about metaphysics began with paradox and that the effort to resolve it or to choose one position as the correct one would lead to despair.⁸² Rather, Blondel encouraged the seeker to discover truth from the inside out. Apodictic demonstrations cannot grant philosophical or theological certainties; truth must move from observation to participation. From his perspective, there were no longer any windows into truth, only doors.⁸³

Another Pascalisant, Fortunat Strowski, wrote a three-volume work, *Pascal et Son Temps,* first published in 1903, addressing Pascal's method of reaching certain truth. Like Blondel and Laberthonnière, Strowski presented Pascal's process of using reason to accomplish goals of faith, rather than using revelation to accomplish the goals of reason. According to Strowski, Pascal argued that most of our greatest certainties are founded on a small number of proofs that, separated, are not infallible, but which become so when added together.⁸⁴ Pascal applied this line of thinking to religion, layering testimony upon testimony (evident in miraculous accounts and most clearly in prophetic proclamations), none of which was conclusive when it stood alone, but which had the po-

80. Friedel, *Pages choisies du Père Laberthonnière*, 13 n. 1; quoted in Gélinas, "La Restauration du Thomisme sous Léon XIII et les Philosophies Nouvelles" (PhD diss., Catholic University of America, 1959), 206. "Pascal ne s'adresse jamais à une raison abstraite, mais à l'homme réel et complexe, capable assurément de penser, mais aussi de craindre, d'espérer, s'aimer, de vouloir. Il ne s'agit pas pour lui de résoudre théoriquement un problème conformément aux règles de la logique.... Nous sommes engagés dans un drame."

81. Hatzfeld, *Pascal*, 272. Hatzfeld, another Pascalisant, was a Jew who converted to Catholicism through studying Pascal's *Pensées.* See Giraud's *Pascal: L'Homme, l'oeuvre, l'influence,* 201. "partout réunis bien qu'ils s'excluent, troublant la raison par leur contradiction inexplicable, et le Coeur par leur conflit douloureux."

82. Blondel, "L'Illusion Idéaliste," 726.

83. Ibid., 742.

84. Strowski, *Pascal et Son Temps,* 289.

tential to convince when added together. This process of addition, however, required the function of the heart's reason, "source of knowledge." When probabilities led to certainties, they demonstrated a passage from one order to another, impossible from a purely geometrical perspective without "le coeur." "The role is the same throughout: whether it produces common sense, whether it produces geometric principles, whether it produces love, whether it produces faith, it is the essential element of induction, of synthesis or, to speak like Pascal, of the passage from one order to another."[85] This movement, so incomprehensible to rationalists, could not take place for those who refused to acknowledge the very real ways it conforms to the evidence and yields results. According to J. Roger Charbonnel, another self-proclaimed "disciple of Pascal," the Pascalian methodology of reaching certain truth was more scientifically coherent than any other theory.[86] It achieved a level of truth inaccessible to geometric methods, which involved the insertion of arbitrary principles and observations that cannot be proven.[87] This accomplishment, however, belongs to the individual, not to the institution. It is a creative function, vital, ongoing, dramatic, and Strowski reiterated the role of the "coeur" of the human individual—every conversion is an "histoire personnelle."[88]

## IMAGINATION AND DESTINY

Laberthonnière's differentiation between the Greek worldview and that of the early Christians focused on the difference between abstract realities, captured in ideals such as beauty, and concrete realities, captured in human experience. The Christian belief that the events of the Old Testament were historical and that the life and death of Jesus Christ took place in actual human time distinguished the dramatic nature of the Christian faith from the one-dimensional, ideological nature of religion as symbolism. It was, according to Laberthonnière, a teaching about be-

---

85. Ibid., 292–93. This theme is echoed in Bazaillas's book, *La Crise de la Croyance*, an examination of the philosophical influences of Ollé-Laprune, Newman, and Balfour. See p. 75. "Son rôle est donc le même partout: qu'il crée le sens commun, qu'il crée les principes géométriques, qu'il crée l'amour, qu'il crée la foi, il est l'instrument essentiel de l'induction, de la synthèse ou, pour parler comme Pascal, du passage d'un ordre à l'autre."

86. Charbonnel, "A Propos de Pascal," 637–38.

87. Strowski, *Pascal et Son Temps*, 272.

88. Ibid., 297.

ginnings and ends, about sources and destinies.[89] Time was the medium in which humans experienced reality, and the brevity of experience was supplemented by the larger experience that the Church called Tradition. This Tradition infused the individual Christian's life with the knowledge of his end, his destiny.

This struggle to understand the meaning of life in terms of its goal, its purpose, had become exponentially greater with the inculcation of Darwinian ideas of evolution. The idea of human perfectibility as the inevitable end of evolution shared an uneasy partnership with the naturalist focus on the randomness of evolution, which suggested that there was no end, no direction, no purpose whatsoever. Gélinas agrees that "the focal point of the conflict [in the nineteenth century] was the conscience of man, the problem of his final end."[90] This enigma shaped the discourses about morality, about scientific progress, about the possibility of the supernatural, about the essence of human nature. Questions about the human future could not be answered by science.

The human experience, and reflection upon it, was meant to lead to ever-greater action that focused on its future. The Pascalisants continually drew this facet of the argument into any discussion about truth. Brunetière, in his description of the bankruptcy of science, pointed out that science could not, and would never be able to, solve the ultimate question about human destiny, the question of "where we're going."[91] Blondel was adamant that philosophical reflection demanded a teleological perspective. "We cannot look back to our beginnings without also being called toward our end . . ."[92] Such an effort required imagination, the ability that defined the human identity. "Man is gifted with the great ability to interpret forms . . . his imagination surpasses the real and leads on a ladder toward a life superior to the one we now live." This imagination informs destiny, the outcome of evolution: "Astronomy and geology witness to the truth that, since an incalculable time, nature has worked to produce life, and we see its fruit most clearly when we realize that there lies within an obscure, but undeniable ideal; we feel ourselves

---

89. Laberthonnière, *Le Réalisme Chrétien*, 72.
90. Gélinas, "La Restauration du Thomisme," 330.
91. Brunetière, *Questions Actuelles*, 12ff.
92. Blondel, "L'Illusion Idéaliste," 741. "Nous ne pouvons regarder en arrière vers notre source sans être appelés en avant vers notre fin . . ."

drawn with a powerful desire toward a sublime goal."[93] Evolution, the Pascalisants argued, must be interpreted as a divine appointment, and, as Pascal explained, we are engaged in the conflict, whether we will or not.

Blondel was adamant that the end for which humanity was destined was divinization. In commenting on Blondel's and Laberthonnière's correspondence, Claude Tresmontant underscores their insistence that the world itself is an Action, a divine creative work in progress that invites human participation. He identifies in their private reflections their main question: "How is this divinization of a human being possible? What are the metaphysical, ascetic, mystical conditions of this divinization of a creature made out of nothing?"[94] It is the ultimate drama, "the drama of our souls,"[95] an improvisational script engaging the audience in a vital part of the resolution of the plot. The plot is fraught with anguish and seeming impossibilities, but Blondel's conscience was clear about the task: "I remain convinced, with Pascal, that there is an indescribable mix of obscurities and illuminations, of cowardice and of courage, that we must make use of in order to detach ourselves from Earth and make our way to Heaven."[96] The ultimate contingency is the one in the human soul, the gap between what the individual aspires to be and what he actually is, between what he hopes for and what he experiences. The individual must choose; he must "pronounce upon the problem of his destiny."[97]

The Pascalisant discourse is replete with images of human anguish, the Pascalian "terror" at his untethered place in the universe and "this

---

93. Sully-Prudhomme, *La Vraie Religion selon Pascal*, 289. "L'homme, en outré, est doué de la plus grande aptitude à l'interprétation des formes . . . son imagination dépasse le réel et tend vers un échelon de la vie supérieur à celui qu'il occupe." and "L'astronomie et la géologie nous attestent que, depuis un temps incalculable, la nature en travail fait oeuvre de vie, et nous la voyons élaborer encore ses productions pour réaliser quelque idéal obscur, mais indéniable; nous nous sentons entraînés dans cet élan gigantesque vers un but sublime."

94. Tresmontant, Introduction to *Correspondance Philosophique*, 54. "Comment cette divinization d'un être créé est-elle possible? Quelles sont les conditions métaphysiques, ascétiques, mystiques, de cette divinisation d'un être créé de rien?"

95. Blondel, *The Letter*, 260.

96. Blondel to Laberthonnière, 12 March 1920, *Correspondance Philosophique*, 256. "je reste convaincu, avec Pascal, qu'il y a partout un mélange indicible d'obscurités et de clartés, de turpitudes et d'héroïsmes, dont nous devons nous servir pour nous détacher de la Terre et nous faire aspirer au Ciel."

97. Blondel, *The Letter*, 162.

necessary struggle of light and darkness."[98] Pascal's nineteenth-century disciples agreed with him: "When I see the blind and wretched state of man, when I survey the whole universe in its dumbness and man left to himself with no light, as though lost in this corner of the universe, without knowing who put him there, what he has come to do, what will become of him when he dies, incapable of knowing anything, I am moved to terror . . ." (f. 198). According to the Pascalisants, this pivotal recognition is the climax of each individual's "role," and the conflict must be resolved by means of the imagination, the ability to integrate the cool demands of reason, which calls the individual to make a shrewd gamble on the possibility of the existence of God, with the passionate experiences of both misery and grandeur. This essential antimony must push the individual to an act of the will that issued from the *coeur*, that interior (and superior) form of intelligence that propels him toward a future different from that which would evolve were he to rely solely on reason or experience.

And thus we return to Goldmann's theory of Pascal's tragic vision, his conclusion that Pascal had boxed himself into a corner with a God who allowed no compromises and offered no way out of the conundrum of human experience. According to Goldmann, the tragic vision embraced absolute values that were impossible to attain. The human condition could never achieve its vision. "It is this rejection of any notion of progression or of degree which distinguishes the tragic mind from spirituality or mysticism."[99] Even Goldmann's recognition that, in the tragic vision, the human aspiration toward moral goodness must make reference to eternity, to destiny, misinterprets Pascal's emphasis. Goldmann argues that Pascal's rejection of the world and simultaneous choice to remain in it left him paralyzed by his own futility. "Pascal finds everything in the world inadequate and sees no rest for man as long as he remains in this life. He also, however, denies that man can find a certain and non-paradoxical proof of God's existence and that he can turn away from the world to seek refuge in solitude and eternity."[100]

Yet Goldmann fails to discern the dramatic nature of Pascal's paradox. For Pascal, like the Pascalisants 250 years later, recognized that the paradox was not in God, and not in nature, but in the contingencies of

---

98. Blondel, *L'Action*, 364 n. 1.

99. Goldmann, *Hidden God*, 63, 207.

100. Ibid., 284.

the human soul, and was resolved not by achieving moral perfection or attaining absolute knowledge but by directing the will toward its perfect end. This resolution would be a teleological one, an elucidation of the purpose of existence. It required a "willing will," issuing from a spiritual desire kindled by a *coeur*-inspired imagination that was authenticated but not determined by external authorities—dogmatic, papal, or political. "All that we have seen or felt of Him is only a means to go further. It is a road; therefore, we do not stop in it, otherwise it is no longer a road. To think of God is an action; yet we also do not act without cooperating with Him and without having Him collaborate with us by a sort of necessary *theergy* which integrates the part of the divine in the human operation, in order to achieve the equation of voluntary action in consciousness."[101]

Indeed, it may be argued that the stress the Pascalisants placed on the imagination enabled them to persevere as dissidents both within the smaller modernist camp and the much larger neo-Thomist faction. Identifying themselves as "reformers" granted them a position of some internal power that they derived from an inward calling to do the work of God. Duhem, sidelined by republican politics because of his legitimist leanings and rejected by neo-Thomists because of his unwillingness to subjugate physics to metaphysics, endured an unwarranted measure of professional obscurity with confidence in his role as a servant of God. "In the immense labor, there is no worker whose work has been lost. Not that that work has always served the purpose its author intended: the role it plays in science often differs from the role he attributed to it; it took the place marked in advance by Him who controls all this agitation."[102] As described in Chapter Four, Blondel absorbed both the academy's suspicion and the Church's censure as an act of self-mortification, a part of the divinization process in his own life. And Laberthonnière, perhaps the most intransigent of the three, accepted the Church's condemnation as an act of suffering for the sake of the truth. In a letter written to Hébert just before *Pascendi*, Laberthonnière describes his attitude: "We are at a particularly tragic moment. I am not complaining. How well I know that in one manner or another I will be crushed. But it is of no importance! What is important is not to be caught outside [the Church]. And I hope

---

101. Blondel, *L'Action*, 325.

102. Duhem, "L'Évolution des Théories Physiques," 499; quoted in Martin, *Pierre Duhem*, 213.

that I never will. It is my Catholicism itself that preserves me from the blows that you see coming, you and others, to me from Catholicism."[103]

Just as Pascal imagined himself poised between *l'infini* and *rien*, infinity and nothing, that act of imagination kindling within him both the desire to know truth and the power to confront truth (about himself, about God, about the world around him), so the Pascalisants integrated their imagination about the Church, about their destiny, and about their own identity into their protest.

## CONCLUSION

The three preceding chapters, covering the individual contributions of Duhem, Blondel, and Laberthonnière, zeroed in on the unique aspects of Pascalian thought each individual incorporated in his work and the ways their works affected the larger intellectual discourse. In this chapter, we have enlarged our perspective, looking at the ways the broader political context—wrestling with the historical question, the production of historical knowledge, and the power to shape identity—both contributed to and informed the ways the Pascalisants struggled to differentiate themselves from the neo-Thomists and from the modernists.

We have seen the ways that the State was investing itself in the pedagogical and ideological potential of French historical studies. Third Republic politicians and their academic colleagues in the universities, which, as we have seen, enjoyed a large overlap, intensified their efforts in the last decade of the nineteenth century to capture the imagination of the French people through a revisionist approach to history. It enabled them to vilify the Church as the ancient stumbling block to French progress and empowered them to create a new identity for the French citizen, one compelled by images of grandeur and liberty. These efforts were informed by German models of historical criticism, models that apparently had infused the German nation with the power that France so coveted.

Simultaneously, the Church, scrambling to retain its political clout, which was rooted in its historical role as France's "conscience," gambled

---

103. *Laberthonnière et ses amis*, 146. "Nous sommes à un moment particulièrement tragique. Je ne m'en plaindrai pas. Je sais bien que d'une manière ou de l'autre je serai écrasé. Mais qu'importe! Ce qui importe c'est de n'être pas atteint au-dedans. Et j'espère que je ne le serai pas. Et c'est mon catholicisme même qui me préservera des coups qui vous paraîtront, à vous et aux autres, me venir du catholicisme."

on a political reconciliation, the *ralliement*, in order to reinsert itself into French affairs, mitigate its losses, regain French favor, and, perhaps, recover the Papal States. The *ralliement* was a historical statement, severing France's monarchist past from its future French identity, and as such left the French Catholic Church in a state of disarray. On another level, the historical question was insidiously penetrating the Church's inner sanctums. The Church recognized that its simple definitions of historical facts and their links to Catholic dogma were being challenged by the same secular models of historical criticism that were leading the State to reshape its future. Loisy and other modernists (notably Tyrrell, von Hugel, and Le Roy) seemed willing to dissect Church dogma, retaining their symbolic and institutional value while discarding their historical foundations.

The Pascalisants sat in the eye of the storm. Academics themselves, they recognized the need to embrace all the advancements that science and philosophy could offer. Only insofar as the Church kept apace with the production of knowledge could it hope to engage people in faith. Yet they were simultaneously adamant about the need to uphold the historical authenticity of scripture and its underpinning for Catholic dogma. Nevertheless, their innovative ideas and willingness to embrace the modern world, at a time when the Church was at its most defensive and authoritarian, destined them to the same fate as the modernists: *Pascendi*.

# Interlude II

## *Pascendi Dominici Gregis* (1907)

THE DRAMA POSED BY the individuals we have examined and the raging debates in which they engaged came to an abrupt and draconian end. The death of Leo XIII in 1903 left the papal chair open, and Leo's reign, one characterized by intellectualism and political finesse as well as theological conservatism, was over. A new regime began, one that was far more interested in clearly drawn boundaries and homogeneous identities. This interlude will look at the new pope, Pius X, who reigned from 1903 to 1914, and at the agenda most connected with his memory—the battle against modernism. While, as I have pointed out earlier, the Pascalisants' works differed radically from more typical modernist arguments, they were grouped together as common enemies of the hierarchy's hegemonic position. Thus the anti-modernist encyclical, *Pascendi dominici gregis*, issued in 1907, shut down neo-Pascalian thought as well as modernist ideas.

Pius X was an unexpected ecclesial choice. Upon Leo XIII's death, most of the cardinals in the conclave favored his secretary of state, Cardinal Rampolla. It seemed clear that Rampolla would be the next pope, but the Austrian emperor, who had been disgruntled by Leo XIII's and Rampolla's fixation on France, exercised an obscure right of veto to block Rampolla's election. Despite the cardinals' protests, the subsequent rounds of voting moved away from Rampolla in search of a pope with a different style from Leo's. Giuseppe Melchiorre Sarto (b. 1858), patriarch of Venice, fit the requirements.[1]

Leo XIII had come from a family of lesser nobility; a highly educated ecclesial administrator, he had never served as a parochial priest. He was an intellectual who sought to address intellectuals; he was a politician, and eagerly participated in diplomatic maneuvering. In contrast, Sarto, born to a village postman and a seamstress, had had a simple local education followed by seminary and had then spent nearly a decade as a country curate. His interests were pastoral, and he devoted his energies to the revitalization of clerical life, the reorganization of internal Curial administrative functions, and the restoration of traditional Catholic piety.

Cardinal Sarto, patriarch of Venice, announced from the outset his determination to be a different kind of pope from his predecessor, a pastoral leader rather than a political one. Nevertheless, purported ambitions aside, Pius X's reign was highly politicized, and during his tenure he intervened in Italian politics by urging bishops to participate in elections; he intervened, to no avail, in the separation of Church and State in Portugal (1911); he offended Americans by refusing to receive Theodore Roosevelt who had been traveling and speaking in Rome (1910); and most importantly for our study, he lost Rome's tenuous, but traditional association with the Third Republic. Pius believed that Leo's style of political appeasement was a failure, and he redirected papal efforts to the advocacy of Church rights; his pastoral instincts were also dismayed by what he perceived to be a growing cancer in the Church: modernism. Pius gathered a description of these symptoms and in 1907 rendered a diagnosis, *Pascendi*, creating in the process the illness itself.

In his essay, "Catholic anti-Modernism: the ecclesial setting," Paul Misner points out the ways that anti-modernism preceded modernism. The spirit of anti-liberalism, in zeroing in on the issue of authority, had by default defined its opponents.[2] Darrell Jodock agrees, writing that "if Modernism is defined as a coherent system of thought, no such thing existed prior to the encyclical."[3] Pius's perceptions created the system called modernism and those who were guilty of its heresies became so only after the fact.

1. Lease, "Vatican foreign policy," 47.
2. Misner, "Catholic Anti-Modernism," 82.
3. Jodock, *Catholicism Contending with Modernity*, 2.

The encyclical was preceded by a decree, *Lamentabili*, released in the July prior to the September encyclical. Another Syllabus of Errors, the decree listed sixty-five heretical propositions that attacked sacramental practices, biblical exegesis, and Christian revelation.[4] There was barely time to absorb the clear condemnations of the decree when the Vatican issued *Pascendi*.

Those whose work became labeled modernist objected strenuously to the encyclical's branding and its accusation that the modernists were a covert but organized group dedicated to the systematic and intentional spreading of their doctrines in such a way that they would appear random and isolated. The encyclical claimed that these heretics were "the most pernicious of all the adversaries of the Church" and that they "employ a very clever artifice, namely to present their doctrines without order and systematic arrangement into one whole, scattered and disjointed one from another, so as to appear to be in doubt and uncertainty, while they are in reality firm and steadfast . . ."[5]

Modernism was a term generated by the encyclical and defined by the encyclical. Its heretical teachings included agnosticism (the inability of the natural reason to recognize or identify the supernatural), which, the encyclical argued, included the perverse suggestion that God could neither be the object of scientific or historical inquiry. Such agnosticism was merely a step on the way to full-blown atheism. The encyclical also named the heresy of vital immanence, which, in its definition, implied that the revelation of divinity is found in religious sentiment and is thus of human origin. Dogmatic formulas, then, are not statements of truth, but merely vessels of that religious sentiment. They are no different from "the Protestants and pseudo-mystics."[6]

The encyclical carefully worked through every article of "modernist" teaching, each of which echoed the issues we have discussed: individual experience, the relationship of faith and science, certainty of knowledge, scripture, the relations between Church and State, the *magisterium* of the Church, historical criticism, apologetics, and the desire to reform the Church. Throughout the encyclical, modernists were declaimed as duplicitous, jugglers of words, closet pantheists, subject to "perversion of mind" and blind pride. Modernism was denounced as the "synthesis

4. Kurtz, *Politics of Heresy*, 153.
5. *Papal Encyclicals*, 72.
6. Ibid., 76.

of all heresies."[7] Certainly the encyclical did accurately describe the goal of the modernists: "their one great anxiety is, in consequence, to find a way of conciliation between the authority of the Church and the liberty of believers."[8]

Pius's encyclical also prescribed the remedy for this theological cancer: 1) the study of scholastic philosophy; 2) the immediate dismissal of any educational directors or professors whose writing was tainted with modernist notions and the rejection of ordination for those candidates for Holy Orders who "extol the Modernists or excuse their culpable conduct"; 3) strict censorship of Catholic publications to prevent the spread of "pernicious" writings; 4) the prohibition of secular priests as editors without episcopal approval; 5) the cessation of Congresses, where these ideas might spread; 6) the creation of secret diocesan watch committees (Councils of Vigilance) to watch for any signs of modernist thinking in pulpits, publications, and classrooms; 7) a triennial report from every bishop on all these matters.[9]

Strong as it was, this Vatican response to the modernist heresy was followed up in November 1907 with a *motu proprio*, a papal decree of excommunication for anyone who opposed either *Lamentabili* or *Pascendi*.[10] And, finally, in 1910, Pius issued a requirement that every clergyman and holder of a position in a Catholic institution take an oath against modernism, submitting himself to "the condemnations, declarations, and all the prescriptions which are contained in the encyclical letter 'Pascendi' and in the decree 'Lamentabili' [which in 1907 had condemned 65 propositions considered to be Modernist errors] especially those which bear on what is called history of dogma."[11] The oath included this statement: "I profess that God, the beginning and end of all things, can be known with certainty and demonstrated by the natural light of reason from the things that have been made, that is, from the *visible* works of creation, as a cause known from its effect."[12] Further ramifications included the 1909 establishment of a secret search-and-seizure group, the *Sodalitium Pianum* (secretly known as the "Sapinière"), whose

7. Ibid., 89.
8. Ibid., 81.
9. Ibid., 92–97.
10. Hill, *Politics of Modernism*, 201.
11. Jodock, *Catholicism Contending with Modernity*, 7.
12. Daly, *Transcendence and Immanence*, 235.

purpose was to uncover any "crypto-Modernists"[13]; the establishment of an "international anti-Modernist network of 'integral Roman Catholics'; and the publication of a weekly newspaper entitled *La Vigie* to serve as a watchdog for orthodoxy. These clearly created an oppressive atmosphere in many academic and clerical circles, what Archbishop Mignot called "an ecclesiastical combisme" (referring to Émile Combes anticlerical harassment)."[14]

Pascal had defended Gallican liberties[15] and even placed in doubt the orthodoxy of the Pope, calling into question the hegemony of Roman authority when confronted with the power of an individual's conscience.[16] He had worked to restore Catholicism to its purity by challenging unwarranted Roman authority, particularly that exercised by the Jesuits. Pascal's condemnation of probabilism, casuistry, and formalism, of religion as a form of domination and of politics as a means of bringing on the kingdom of God remained effective as a subversive line of reasoning. Henri Bremond argued that France's greatest religious heritage—enhanced by the works of such spiritual giants as Fénelon, de Sales, de Caussade, and Pascal—had been stifled long ago, leading to the sterility of nineteenth-century religious life.[17]

Daly points out the ways that *Pascendi* "claims to unmask a system of thought, while its critics will maintain that it blatantly *creates* a system which it can then refute."[18] Modernism, and thus neo-Pascalianism, was suppressed not by reason but by brute authority, resulting in "the total outlawing of experience as a factor in religion, theology, and spirituality."[19] While Pascalisants had made significant efforts to differentiate themselves from modernists like Loisy, they were nevertheless caught in the clerical crossfire. The Vatican authorities, in their anxious bid to quell dissidence, impose uniformity of thought, and reestablish absolute au-

---

13. O'Connell, *Critics on Trial*, 363.

14. Ibid., 364.

15. "France is now almost the only place left where one is allowed to say that the council is above the Pope" (f. 604).

16. Strowski, *Pascal et Son Temps*, 367.

17. Bremond, *L'Histoire littéraire du sentiment religieux en France*, quoted in Dru and Trethowan's Introduction to Maurice Blondel's *The Letter on Apologetics* and *History and Dogma*, 22.

18. Ibid., 196.

19. Ibid., 216.

thority made no distinction between the factions. Neo-Pascalianism was certainly no accidental victim of the *Pascendi* encyclical, for the values that Pascal had infused into the Pascalisants—the separation of natural and supernatural, the inaccessibility of spiritual knowledge to reason, the role of the individual's choice, the role of the *magisterium* as a representative of truth rather than an administrator of it, the inefficacy of natural theology—were counterintuitive to all that the Vatican was trying to recover (i.e., the rationality of Christian faith, the authoritarian role of the *magisterium*, the nature of faith as intellectual assent, the subordination of the individual to the dictates of Rome, the right of the Church to dictate truth). Nevertheless, as Misner points out, anti-Modernism existed before modernism[20]; that is, the mentality and attitudes that culminated in the *Pascendi* encyclical had been evolving since the French Revolution, and the encyclical merely captured within its net all those ideas (some of which had once been considered orthodox) that challenged the reactionary momentum of the century. Anti-modernism, the primary reactionary movement, one that was a "program for preventing the dechristianizing of Europe,"[21] triggered a secondary reactionary movement: modernism. "Rome did much to create the monster it slew."[22]

---

20. Misner, "Catholic anti-Modernism: the ecclesial setting," 57.
21. Jodock, *Catholicism Contending with Modernity*, 13.
22. Daly, *Transcendence and Immanence*, 89.

# Conclusion

WE HAVE WORKED THROUGH a considerable quagmire of thought and discourse, but to what end? What do we gain in understanding about the Third Republic? about the French Catholic Church at the *fin-de-siècle*? about the role of Pascalian thought in French intellectual discourse during a time fraught with political and theological instability? In examining the high-intensity discourse between 1893 and 1907, we are afforded a nuanced understanding of the creative efforts of a handful of intellectuals who attempted to engage the Roman Catholic Church in a reform that would, on one hand, integrate the best of the modern world, and on the other hand, recover a spirit of deep piety and persuasive integrity. The nineteenth century had been one of increasing authoritarianism in both Catholic and positivist circles, the former grounded in the papal privilege to define truth and the latter grounded in scientific certainties to prove truth, and the individual became the pawn that threatened both Third Republic stabilities and clerical absolutes. The Pascalisants recognized that that pawn, the individual, could become the source both of French civic responsibility and of Catholic renewal insofar as he could be empowered to choose faith.

During the fifteen-year period under review, the Church and French state wrestled for control over the minds and imaginations of French citizens. The Church remained convinced of its prerogative to be the moral rudder of the nation and the State remained convinced of the Church's intent to interfere. Phyllis Kaminski describes these years as one in which a "transformation of consciousness" was taking place.[1] Intellectuals, both Catholic and secular, recognized that this transformation was occurring, and they strove to control its outcome. The transformation was the culmination of a centuries-long challenge to Catholic Christianity, one that began with the scientific revolution, intensified

---

1. Kaminski, "Seeking Transcendence," 116.

during the Enlightenment, and erupted in the French Revolution.[2] The Church, having only inadequately dealt with each of these developments, was scrambling during the nineteenth century to retain authority. As historians consider the collapsing certainties at the end of the nineteenth century, it is important to penetrate the broad classifications of positivism, secularism, modernism, and neo-Thomism to find within them the philosophical subtleties that are easily missed. While most historians' lists of modernists include Blondel and Laberthonnière, this book has attempted to prove that their devotion to the Church (along with Duhem's), their common inspiration in Pascal, their efforts to find a middle way between modern intellectual methodologies and traditional Church doctrines differentiated them from the modernists and from the neo-Thomists. They were a unique group of thinkers who found in Pascal an earlier French spirituality that empowered them to both persevere and protest in matters of faith. They were in search of a path of reconciliation and regeneration, one that, finally, clerical fear and republican resistance made impossible.

We have seen the ways that the social, political, and intellectual conditions of Third Republic France created an atmosphere in which devout French Catholics feared for the future of their Church. They were anxious about the relevance of Christian faith to the increasingly secularized ways of thinking promoted in government and academy, and many felt that the Church's tactics—more authoritarian than pastoral, more didactic than persuasive, more rational than intuitive—would result in further attrition rather than a strengthening of faith.

Scholasticism, the mandated orthodoxy of the Vatican, was simultaneously a method, a terminology, a philosophy, and a theology.[3] Its enforced imposition encompassed a vast network of fields in which diversity of thought, creativity, and imagination became stifled. While Catholic intellectuals earlier in the century had enjoyed a lenience in orthodox methodologies and broad philosophical freedoms, the nineteenth century had been one of tightening boundaries. The Vatican had traditionally permitted an open intellectual freedom in matters of history and philosophy, yet by the end of the nineteenth century, its multilayered losses (territorial, political, spiritual, sociocultural) generated a spirit of conservatism that could no longer afford such moderation.

2. Daly, *Transcendence and Immanence*, 91.
3. Gélinas, "La Restauration du Thomisme," 330.

Rome's interference in education and in clerical administration, culminating in *Pascendi*'s closure, effectively eliminated the possibility of the quest. O'Connell points out the ways that the Law of Separation in 1905, followed by *Pascendi* in 1907, triggered "a kind of terrorism," "a wind of mediocrity, of meanness, of spite."[4]

This "terrorism" was extremely effective in silencing the opposition. Many journals ceased to publish under the threat of papal denunciation, including *Demain, La Quinzaine,* and *La Revue d'Histoire.* and, in 1913, the *Annales de philosophie chrétienne.* By that time, Laberthonnière's works had already been Indexed, Loisy and Tyrrell had been excommunicated, and many had lost positions in Catholic educational institutions.

*Providentissimus* was ostensibly a document about biblical criticism, but ultimately it was a document about authority. In removing exegesis from a historical framework and thrusting it into a scholastic scaffolding, it established an autonomous basis that generated its own internal authority. "So that if the new critics had their way, they would become partners in dialogue with dogmatic theologians and authorities rather than simply servants to an externally imposed agenda. In other words, they ... would exercise their own internal authority. This would mean power-sharing, a concept distinctly Protestant and wholly repugnant to patriarchal thinking."[5]

Neo-Pascalians, a diverse group, had several common goals: the reformation and revitalization of the Church; the creation of a new apologetic that would speak to the liberal and modern understanding of unbelievers; and the mitigation of heavy ecclesiastical authoritarianism that dissipated the energy of faith. They shared these goals with the modernists, yet the Pascalisant methodologies led them to different conclusions. Ironically, heterodox methodology was the very point of contention for the Vatican. It subverted Vatican priorities and circumvented its authority.

In order to achieve their goals, the Pascalisants recovered the language, the ideology, and the passion of their seventeenth-century predecessor in faith: Blaise Pascal. Pascal, they concurred, offered a clear and compelling way out of the intellectual morass of the day. His focus on the individual not only recovered the older strain of French spirituality in its Augustinian form, it also corresponded to the Republic's call to

4. O'Connell, *Critics on Trial*, 328.
5. Schultenover, *View from Rome*, 238.

civic participation. His description of authentic knowledge-production as an operation primarily of the *coeur*, a reasonable and yet not merely rational means of certainty, afforded a way out of the positivist/scholastic conundrum. Pascal's status as a pre-Kantian philosopher whose emphases on avenues of knowledge beyond sense and reason and on the inadequacy of the phenomena to define reality mitigated the putative threat of Kantian relativism. Unfortunately, the Church did not see the Pascalian "solution" as anything but defiance to its uncompromising position of ecclesial authority and philosophical homogeneity.

It is curious to consider the ways that Pascal's experience with the Church authorities paralleled that of his late nineteenth-century disciples. One *fin-de-siècle* author wrote that modernists were Catholics who felt that the greatest threat came not from secularists, but from "the debilitating regime of an intransigent autocracy, from an intellectual isolation, from the shortcomings of the clergy, and from the passivity of the faithful."[6] The Jansenists could have said the exact same thing.

The Formulary of 1661, by which Jansenists were required to swear an oath against *Augustinus*, was not unlike the oath demanded of the modernists, and, like the modernists, Pascal objected vehemently to the abuse of power implied in that oath. Like the Jesuits' political efforts to eradicate their Jansenist enemies, the modernists and Pascalisants had a political enemy in Charles Maurras, who celebrated *Pascendi* as a triumph over decadent individualism. Sutton suggests that the Action française helped in the closing of the *Annales de philosophie chrétienne*, a likelihood in view of Blondel's 1910 *Annales* article denouncing Catholic-Maurras cooperation, "Une alliance avec l'Action française," and his 1911 book *Positivisme et Catholicisme* that analyzed the pagan foundations of the Action française.[7]

The problem could be found in the dense semantic jungle of *fin-de-siècle* discourse. Common philosophical and theological terms—reason, faith, knowledge, truth—became tangled with nuanced definitions that mislead others who infused their own definitions. Schultenover concludes that the modernist crisis was a "misjudgment of each other" which "came in thinking that if they spoke the same language, they meant the same thing by the same words. They did not."[8] Perhaps they once had. When

---

6. Bourdeau, *Pragmatisme et Modernisme*, 172.

7. Blondel, *Correspondance*, 213.

8. Schultenover, *View from Rome*, 242.

Leo XIII decided that Thomism was the answer to the philosophical diversity that threatened the Church's authority, he broke with the Church's tradition of "mild pluralism" in Catholic theology. As Daly describes it, "It was a particularly severe blow to the Augustinian-Franciscan school of thought which laid emphasis on the role of the will, of the affections (to use St. Augustine's term), and of feelings in general in matters of faith."[9] This Augustinian influence was the background to Jansenism and the inspiration for much of Pascalian thought. Linguistic differences became shibboleths for orthodoxy; the word "experience" became dangerous; the concept of faith was reduced to intellectual orthodoxy; history served only to prove theology, not, as Pascal had perceived it, as a confirmation of belief; and theology itself was a rational expression of supernatural truths divinely revealed and clerically managed.[10]

In the short term, the neo-Pascalian movement died away. Its demise was both an abrupt cessation of thought brought on by the *Pascendi* encyclical and a slow waning of inspiration caused by the tyrannical intellectual atmosphere in the decades following *Pascendi*. As we have seen, creative thought came under suspicion and was ruthlessly suppressed. While no one was named in the *Pascendi* encyclical, the thoughts of the different modernists were apparent in the text. Several of Loisy's works were quoted, and Blondel's and Laberthonnière's ideas about the method of immanence were excoriated. Comments about the Church's perspective on the relationship between faith and science lead to a rejection of the modernist separation of the two, which was reminiscent of Duhem's work. All three of the Pascalisants studied in this dissertation felt the brunt of the condemnation. Laberthonnière never published again, and Blondel carefully crafted his work in the years following the encyclical to accommodate neo-Thomistic structures.

Duhem, as a physicist rather than a philosopher, was less directly affected by the encyclical and lived only a few more years after its release, during which time he devoted his efforts to the completion of his *System of the World* history. Duhem saw his Pascalian inspiration justified in the national discourse about French science versus German science. Martha Hanna points out that "Pascal's distinction between the 'spirit of finesse' and the 'spirit of geometry,'" one of Duhem's most cherished philosophical distinctions, inspired a new level of scientific discourse at the outset

9. Daly, "Theological and philosophical Modernism," 96.
10. Ibid.

of the First World War.¹¹ Pascalian thought gained recognition within secular circles as a "priceless national legacy";¹² Pascal was lauded once again as a genuine French intellectual hero.

The Church, too, eventually instigated a slow recovery from the painful fallout of the *Pascendi*. The autocratic thrust of the scholastic movement was mitigated by the onset of the First World War. Benedict XV (reigned 1914–1922) stopped the Sapinière "witch-hunt" of suspected modernists. Scholasticism, too, moved on in diverse ways and shed many of the thirteenth-century anachronisms that had made it so unpalatable to *fin-de-siècle* thinkers. Both modernism and anti-Modernism need to remain historicized and contextualized, firmly rooted in the political, cultural, and religious circumstances that made the conflict possible.

Such a contextualization makes later developments more comprehensible. As heterodox thinking went underground and modernists explored more mature expressions of their ideas, so did the neo-Thomists mature and evolve. As the last hopes of papal prerogatives in State affairs vanished with the Law of Separation and the antagonism between Church and State dissipated through the greater trials of the war, the fears and hatred on both sides of the fence abated. By the middle of the twentieth century, philosophers were reengaging with many of the modernist ideas. Pope Pius XII's 1943 encyclical *Divino afflante spiritu* granted permission to incorporate critical exegetical ideas in scriptural studies.¹³ The thrust of Vatican Council II (1962–1965) included many of the aims of the neo-Pascalians: the use of the vernacular in liturgy was a conciliation to the needs of the laity; Catholic individuals were encouraged to read scripture; a revitalization of faith and practice called for individual participation. All of these emphases recovered that genuine strain of French spirituality that had been lost during the Church's severe responses to challenges to its authority.

Some of the Pascalisants were rehabilitated. The fact that Blondel retained a reputation that had been lost to Laberthonnière, due in part to his lay status, can also be attributed to Blondel's willingness to express himself in ways more conducive to Thomistic approval. Kaminski points out that Blondel's work continued to permeate Catholic thought in subtle ways, and many of his ideas "bore fruit in the Second Vatican

---

11. Hanna, *Mobilization of Intellect*, 199.
12. Ibid., 206.
13. Jodock, *Catholicism Contending with Modernity*, 12.

Council."[14] Tavard concurs, citing a 1944 letter from Cardinal Montini, who would later be known as Pope Paul VI, recognizing Blondel's contributions to Catholic philosophy.[15] He goes on to see reverberations of Blondel's work on *action* in John Paul II's *Fides et ratio*.[16]

While Pascalian thought, incarnated in his late nineteenth-century disciples, found new avenues of expression as both the Church and the state moved past this rancorous period of relationship, Pascal himself remained tainted in the eyes of many, both seculars and clerics, by his vehement protests against hierarchical abuses, by his rejection of natural theology, and by his refutation of reason as an authentic source of knowledge. Many contemporary French, whose knowledge of Pascal's ideas and Descartes's writings may be marginal, speak flippantly about whether a person is "Pascalian" or "Cartesian." In their jargon, a Pascalian personality is purely intuitive, imaginative, and slightly irresponsible; a Cartesian is a rationalist, logical and orderly. Pascal would have been disappointed in this legacy, for he believed in the power of reason to take the individual to the brink of the greatest truths and there humbly leave him to make far more wonderful discoveries. "Reason's last step is the recognition that there are an infinite number of things which are beyond it. It is merely feeble if it does not go as far as to realize that" (f. 188). The possibility that Pascal developed a supremely rational approach to reason and faith has largely been lost to popular knowledge.

---

14. Kaminski, "Seeking transcendence in the modern world," 115.
15. Tavard, "Blondel's *Action* and the problem of the University," 168.
16. Ibid.

# Selected Bibliography

## PRIMARY SOURCES

Bazaillas, Albert. *La Crise de la Croyance dans la Philosophie Contemporaine.* Paris: Perrin, 1901.

Benoist, Charles. "La France et le Pape Léon XIII." *Revue des deux mondes* 116 (March 15, 1893) 397–430.

Blondel, Maurice. *L'Action (1893): Essay on a Critique of Life and a Science of Practice.* Translated by Oliva Blanchette. Notre Dame: University of Notre Dame Press, 1984.

———. *Carnets Intimes (1883–1894).* Paris: Cerf, 1961.

———. "L'Illusion Idéaliste." *Revue de métaphysique et de morale* 5 (1898) 726–45.

———. *The Letter on Apologetics & History and Dogma.* Retrieval & Renewal: Ressourcement in Catholic Thought. Edited by David L. Schindler. Translated and Introduced by Alexander Dru and Illtyd Trethowan. Grand Rapids: Eerdmans, 1964.

———. "Lettre sur les exigences de la pensée contemporaine en matière d'apologétique et sur la méthode de la philosophie dans l'étude du problème religieux." *Annales de philosophie chrétienne* 33–34 n.s. (Octobre–Mars, Avril–Septembre) 1895–96.

———. *Lettres Philosophiques.* Paris: Aubier, 1961.

———. "Notre programme." *Annales de philosophie chrétienne* 4.1 (October–March 1905–1906) 5–31.

———. "Le Point de Départ de la Recherche Philosophique." *Annales de philosophie chrétienne* 4 (October–March, 1905–1906) 337–60.

Blondel, Maurice, and Lucien Laberthonnière. *Correspondence Philosophique.* Paris: Seuil, 1961.

Bourdeau, J. *Pragmatisme et Modernisme.* Paris: Alcan et Réunies, 1909.

Brunetière, Ferdinand. *Questions Actuelles: La Science et La Religion.* Paris: Perrin, 1916.

Charbonnel, J. Roger. "A Propos de Pascal." *Annales de philosophie chrétienne* 3.3 (October–March, 1903–1904) 634–38.

Dechamps, Victor Auguste. *L'Infaillibilité et le Concile Général: Étude de Science Religieuse.* Paris: Magnin, 1869.

Denis, Charles. "L'Église et l'État : Les Leçons de l'Heure Présente." *Annales de philosophie chrétienne* 45 (October–March 1901–1902) 129–58, 326–51, 452–82.

———. "Situation politique, sociale et intellectuelle du clergé français, Avril 1884–September 1902." *Annales de philosophie chrétienne* 46 (April–September, 1902) 513–86/28.

de Vogüé, Eugène-Melchoir. "Affaires de Rome." *Revue des deux mondes* 81 (15 June 1887) 815–53.

*Dogmatic Canons and Decrees*. New York: Devin-Adair, 1912.

Duhem, Pierre. *The Aim and Structure of Physical Theory*. 2nd ed. Translated by Philip P. Weiner. Princeton: Princeton University Press, 1954.

———. *Essays in the History and Philosophy of Science*. Translated and edited, with Introduction by Roger Ariew and Peter Barker. Indianapolis: Hackett, 1996.

———. "Quelques Réflexions au sujet de la physique expérimentale." *Revue des questions scientifiques* 6 (July 1894) 179–229.

———. "Physique de Croyant." *Annales de philosophie chrétienne* 4 (October–March 1905–1906) 44–67, 133–59.

———. "Physique et Métaphysique." *Annales de philosophie chrétienne* 28 (August–September 1893) 461–86.

———. "Les Théories de l'optique." *Revue des deux mondes* 123 (May 1894) 94–125.

———. "Une Nouvelle Théorie du monde inorganique." *Revue des questions scientifiques* 33 (January 1893) 90–133.

Giraud, Victor. "Anticléricalisme et Catholicisme." *Revue des deux mondes* 32 (15 April 1906) 851–70.

———. "De la Modernité des 'Pensées' de Pascal." *Annales de philosophie chrétienne* 4.2 (April–September 1906) 594–607.

———. *Pascal: L'Homme, l'oeuvre, l'influence: Notes d'un Cours professé à l'Université de Fribourg (Suisse) durant le semestre d'été 1898*. Paris: Anciennes Maison Thorin & Fontemoing, 1922.

Hatzfeld, Adolphe. *Pascal*. Paris: Alcan, 1901.

Laberthonnière, Lucien. "Le Dogmatisme moral." *Annales de philosophie chrétienne* 38–39 (April–September, October–March, 1898–99) 531–62, 27–45, 146–71.

———. *Laberthonnière et ses amis: Dossiers de correspondance (1905–1916)*. Edited by Marie-Thérèse Perrin. Paris: Beauchesne, 1975.

———. "Pour le Dogmatisme moral." *Annales de philosophie chrétienne* 41 (October–March, 1899–1900) 398–425.

———. "Le Problème religieux." *Annales de philosophie chrétienne* 35 (February–March, 1897) 497–511, 615–32.

———. *Le Réalisme chrétien et l'idéalisme grec*. Paris: Lethielleux, 1904.

Lechartier, G. "Pascal d'après Em. Boutroux." *Annales de philosophie chrétienne* 42 (April–September 1900) 598–617.

Leo XIII. *The Great Encyclical Letters of Pope Leo XIII*. New York: Benziger, 1903.

*The Papal Encyclicals: 1903–1939*. Raleigh, NC: McGrath, 1981.

Pascal, Blaise. "Entretien avec M. de Saci." In *Pascal: Oeuvres Complètes, Présentation et Notes de Louis Lafuma, l'Intégrale*. Edited by Luc Estang, 348–59. Paris: Seuil, 1963.

———. *The Essential Pascal*. Edited by Robert W. Gleason. Translated by G. F. Pullen. The New American Library. New York: Mentor-Omega, 1966.

———. "Expériences nouvelles touchant le vide." In *Pascal: Oeuvres Complètes, Présentation et Notes de Louis Lafuma, l'Intégrale*. Edited by Luc Estang, 195–98. Paris: Seuil, 1963.

———. *Pascal: Oeuvres Complètes*, Présentation et Notes de Louis Lafuma, l'Intégrale. Edited by Luc Estang. Paris: Seuil, 1963.

———. *Pensées*. Revised, edited, and translated with an Introduction by A. J. Krailsheimer. London: Penguin, 1995.

———. "Préface sur le traité du vide." In *Pascal: Oeuvres Complètes, Présentation et Notes de Louis Lafuma, l'Intégrale*. Edited by Luc Estang, 230–32. Paris: Seuil, 1963.

———. *The Provincial Letters*. Translated by Thomas M'Crie. Eugene, OR: Wipf & Stock, 1997.

———. "Réflexions sur la géométrie en general: de l'esprit géométrique et de l'art de persuader." In *Pascal: Oeuvres Complètes, Présentation et Notes de Louis Lafuma, l'Intégrale*, edited by Luc Estang, 348–59. Paris: Seuil, 1963.

Ravaisson, F. "La Philosophie de Pascal." *Revue des deux mondes* 80 (15 March 1887) 399–428.

Strowski, Fortunat. *Pascal et Son Temps*. 3rd ed. Vol. 3, *Troisième Partie, Les Provinciales et les Pensées. Histoire du Sentiment Religieux en France au XVIIe Siècle*. Paris: Plon-Nourrit, 1913.

Sully-Prudhomme, René. *La Vraie Religion selon Pascal: Recherche de l'ordonnance purement logique de ses Pensées relatives à la religion*. Ancienne Librairie Germer Baillière et Cie. Paris: Alcan, 1905.

## SECONDARY SOURCES

Acomb, Evelyn. *The French Laic Laws (1879–1889): The First Anti-Clerical Campaign of the Third French Republic*. New York: Octagon, 1967.

Anderson, R. D. *Education in France: 1848–1870*. Oxford: Clarendon, 1975.

Bouchilloux, Hélène. "Pascal and the Social World." In *The Cambridge Companion to Pascal*, edited by Nicholas Hammond. Cambridge: Cambridge University Press, 2003.

Bredin, Jean-Denis. *The Affair: The Case of Alfred Dreyfus*. Translated by Jeffrey Mehlman. New York: Braziller, 1986.

Cahm, Eric. *The Dreyfus Affair in French Society and Politics*. London: Longman, 1996.

Clarke, Desmond M. "Pascal's Philosophy of Science." In *The Cambridge Companion to Pascal*, edited by Nicholas Hammond. Cambridge: Cambridge University Press, 2003.

Copleston, Frederick. *A History of Philosophy. Volume IX, Modern Philosophy: From the French Revolution to Sartre, Camus, and Lévi-Strauss*. New York: Image, 1974.

Crosland, Maurice. *Science under Control: The French Academy of Sciences, 1795–1914*. Cambridge: Cambridge University Press, 1992.

Daly, Gabriel. "Theological and Philosophical Modernism." In *Catholicism Contending with Modernity: Roman Catholic Modernism and Anti-Modernism in Historical Context*, edited by Darrell Jodock, 88f. Cambridge: Cambridge University Press, 2000.

———. *Transcendence and Immanence: A Study in Catholic Modernism and Integralism*. Oxford: Clarendon, 1980.

Davidson, Hugh M. *The Origins of Certainty: Means and Meanings in Pascal's Pensées*. Chicago: University of Chicago Press, 1979.

Davies, Michael. *Partisans of Error: St. Pius X against the Modernists*. Commemorating the Seventy-fifth Anniversary of the Encyclical *Pascendi Gregis* of St. Pius X. Long Prairie, MN: Neumann, 1983.

Desan, Suzanne. *Reclaiming the Sacred: Lay Religion and Popular Politics in Revolutionary France*. Ithaca: Cornell University Press, 1990.

Dru, Alexander and Illtyd Trethowan. Introduction to *The Letter on Apologetics & History and Dogma*, by Maurice Blondel, Retrieval & Renewal: Ressourcement in Catholic Thought, ed. David L. Schindler. Grand Rapids: Eerdmans, 1964.

Eastwood, Dorothy Margaret. *The Revival of Pascal: A Study of His Relation to Modern French Thought*. Oxford Studies in Modern Languages and Literature. Oxford: Clarendon, 1936.

Fremantle, Anne. *The Papal Encyclicals in Their Historical Context*. New York: Mentor, 1956.

Gay, Peter, and R. K. Webb. *Modern Europe since 1815*. New York: Harper & Row, 1973.

Gélinas, Jean-Paul. "La Restauration du Thomisme sous Léon XIII et les Philosophies Nouvelles: Étude de la pensée de Maurice Blondel et du Père Laberthonnière à la lumière d'AETERNI PATRIS." PhD diss., Catholic University of America, 1959.

Gibson, Ralph. *A Social History of French Catholicism: 1789-1914*. London: Routledge, 1989.

Goldmann, Lucien. *The Hidden God: A Study of Tragic Vision in the* Pensées *of Pascal and the Tragedies of Racine*. International Library of Philosophy and Scientific Method. London: Routledge & Kegan Paul, 1964.

Griffiths, Richard. *The Reactionary Revolution: The Catholic Revival in French Literature, 1870-1914*. New York: Ungar, 1965.

Groothuis, Douglas. *On Pascal*. Wadsworth Philosopher Series. Belmont, CA: Thomson Learning, 2003.

Hammond, Nicholas, ed. *The Cambridge Companion to Pascal*. Cambridge: Cambridge University Press, 2003.

Hanna, Martha. *The Mobilization of Intellect: French Scholars and Writers During the Great War*. Cambridge: Harvard University Press, 1996.

Hill, Harvey. *The Politics of Modernism: Alfred Loisy and the Scientific Study of Religion*. Washington, DC: Catholic University of America Press, 2002.

Hobsbawm, Eric J. *The Age of Empire, 1875-1914*. New York: Vintage, 1987.

Hubert, Marie Louise. *Pascal's Unfinished Apology: A Study of His Plan*. Yale Romantic Studies: *Second Series*. New Haven: Yale University Press, 1952.

Jaki, Stanley L. *Uneasy Genius: The Life and Work of Pierre Duhem*. The Hague: Martinus Nijhoff, 1984.

Jodock, Darrell, editor. *Catholicism Contending with Modernity: Roman Catholic Modernism and Anti-Modernism in Historical Context*. Cambridge: Cambridge University Press, 2000.

———. "Introduction I: The Modernist Crisis." In *Catholicism Contending with Modernity: Roman Catholic Modernism and Anti-Modernism in Historical Context*, edited by Darrell Jodock, 1-18. Cambridge: Cambridge University Press, 2000.

———. "Introduction II: The Modernists and the anti-Modernists." In *Catholicism Contending with Modernity: Roman Catholic Modernism and Anti-Modernism in Historical Context*, edited by Darrell Jodock, 19-31. Cambridge: Cambridge University Press, 2000.

Jordan, Jeff, editor. *Gambling on God: Essays on Pascal's Wager*. Lanham, MD: Rowman & Littlefield, 1994.

Kaminski, Phyllis H. "Seeking Transcendence in the Modern World." In *Catholicism Contending with Modernity: Roman Catholic Modernism and Anti-Modernism in Historical Context*, edited by Darrell Jodock, 115-41. Cambridge: Cambridge University Press, 2000.

Keylor, William R. *Academy and Community: The Foundation of the French Historical Profession*. Cambridge: Harvard University Press, 1975.

Kselman, Thomas. "France: Religion and French Identity: The Origins of the *Union Sacrée*." In *Many Are Chosen: Divine Election and Western Nationalism*, edited by William R. Hutchison and Hartmut Lehmann, 57–79. Harvard Theological Studies 38. Minneapolis: Fortress, 1994.

Kurtz, Lester R. *The Politics of Heresy: The Modernist Crisis in Roman Catholicism*. Berkeley: University of California Press, 1986.

Larkin, Maurice. *Religion, Politics and Preferment in France Since 1890: La Belle Époque and Its Legacy*. Cambridge: Cambridge University Press, 1995.

Lease, Gary. "Vatican Foreign Policy and the Origins of Modernism." In *Catholicism Contending with Modernity: Roman Catholic Modernism and Anti-Modernism in Historical Context*, edited by Darrell Jodock, 32–56. Cambridge: Cambridge University Press, 2000.

Lowinger, Armand. *The Methodology of Pierre Duhem*. New York: Columbia University Press, 1941.

Martin, R. N. D. *Pierre Duhem: Philosophy and History in the Work of a Believing Physicist*. La Salle, IL: Open Court, 1991.

McCool, Gerald. *Catholic Theology in the Nineteenth Century: The Quest for a Unitary Method*. New York: Seabury, 1977.

———. *The Neo-Thomists*. Marquette Studies in Philosophy. Marquette, WI: Marquette University Press, 1994.

McKenna, Antony. "The Reception of Pascal's *Pensées* in the Seventeenth and Eighteenth Centuries." In *The Cambridge Companion to Pascal*, edited by Nicholas Hammond. Cambridge: Cambridge University Press, 2003.

McManners, John. *Church and State in France, 1870–1914*. New York: Harper & Row, 1972.

Miel, Jan. *Pascal and Theology*. Baltimore: Johns Hopkins Press, 1969.

Misner, Paul. "Catholic Anti-Modernism: The Ecclesial Setting." In *Catholicism Contending with Modernity: Roman Catholic Modernism and Anti-Modernism in Historical Context*, edited by Darrell Jodock, 57–87. Cambridge: Cambridge University Press, 2000.

Moody, Joseph N., ed. *Church and Society: Catholic Social and Political Thought and Movements, 1789–1950*. New York: Arts, 1953.

———. *French Education since Napoleon*. Syracuse, NY: Syracuse University Press, 1978.

Nye, Mary Jo. "Determinism of Nature: The Catholic Synthesis of Science and History in the *Revue des questions scientifiques*." *British Journal for the History of Science* 9/33 (1976) 274–92.

O'Connell, Marvin R. *Critics on Trial: An Introduction to the Catholic Modernist Crisis*. Washington, DC: Catholic University of America Press, 1994.

Paul, Harry. "The Crucifix and the Crucible: Catholic Scientists in the Third Republic." *Catholic Historical Review* 58/2 (1972) 195–219.

———. "The Debate over the Bankruptcy of Science in 1895." *French Historical Studies* 5/3 (1968) 299–327.

———. *The Edge of Contingency: French Catholic Reaction to Scientific Change from Darwin to Duhem*. Gainesville, FL: University Presses of Florida, 1979.

———. "Scholarship and Ideology: The Chair of the General History of Science at the Collège de France, 1892–1913." *Isis* 67 (1976) 376–97.

Phayer, Michael. "Politics and Popular Religion: The Cult of the Cross in France, 1815–1840." *Journal of Social History* 11/3 (1978) 347–65.

Phillips, Henry. "Pascal's Reading and the Inheritance of Montaigne and Descartes." In *The Cambridge Companion to Pascal*, edited by Nicholas Hammond, 33–34. Cambridge: Cambridge University Press, 2003.

Reardon, Bernard. *Liberalism and Tradition: Aspects of Catholic Thought in Nineteenth-Century France*. Cambridge: Cambridge University Press, 1975.

Schultenover, David. *A View from Rome on the Eve of the Modernist Crisis*. New York: Fordham University Press, 1993.

Silver, Brian. *The Ascent of Science*. New York: Oxford University Press, 1998.

Smith, Robert J. *The École Normale Supérieure and The Third Republic*. Albany: State University of New York Press, 1982.

Sutton, Michael. *Nationalism, Positivism and Catholicism: The Politics of Charles Maurras and French Catholics, 1890–1914*. Cambridge Studies in the History and Theory of Politics, Cambridge: Cambridge University Press, 1982.

*A Symposium on the Life and Work of Pope Pius X*. Washington, DC: Confraternity of Christian Doctrine, 1946.

Talar, C. J. T. "Innovation and Biblical Interpretation." In *Catholicism Contending with Modernity: Roman Catholic Modernism and Anti-Modernism in Historical Context*, edited by Darrell Jodock, 191–212. Cambridge: Cambridge University Press, 2000.

Tavard, George H. "Blondel's *Action* and the Problem of the University." In *Catholicism Contending with Modernity: Roman Catholic Modernism and Anti-Modernism in Historical Context*, edited by Darrell Jodock, 142–68. Cambridge: Cambridge University Press, 2000.

Vovelle, Michele. *The Revolution against the Church: From Reason to the Supreme Being*. Translated by Alan Jose. Columbus: Ohio State University Press, 1991.

Weber, Eugen. *Action Française: Royalism and Reaction in Twentieth-Century France*. Stanford: Stanford University Press, 1962.

———. *My France: Politics, Culture, Myth*. Cambridge, MA: Harvard University Press, 1991.

———. *Peasants into Frenchmen: The Modernization of Rural France, 1870–1914*. Stanford: Stanford University Press, 1976.

Weisz, George. *The Emergence of Modern Universities in France, 1863–1914*. Princeton, NJ: Princeton University Press, 1983.

Wilson, A. N. *God's Funeral: A Biography of Faith and Doubt in Western Civilization*. New York: Ballantine, 1999.

Wright, Gordon. *France in Modern Times: From the Enlightenment to the Present*. 5th ed. New York: Norton, 1995.

# Index

Abbé Charles Denis, 120–21, 130, 157–62, 165–66
Action française, 27n31, 30–31, 83, 84n6, 118n38, 164, 198
*Aeterni Patris* (1879), 5, 26, 41, 42, 58, 76
*Annales de philosophie chrétienne*, 8, 10, 82, 90, 120, 128, 130, 134, 152, 157, 166–67, 197–98
Anticlericalism, ix, xi, xii, xiv, xv, 2, 18–19, 21, 36, 129, 156, 163, 193
Apologetics, 2, 6, 8–9, 12, 14, 73, 85, 106, 121–26, 128, 139–40, 160, 180, 191, 197
Aquinas, Thomas, 5, 51, 58, 76–77, 90, 133, 148
Aristotle, 45, 46, 58, 90, 151
Augustine, 64, 71, 90, 119, 138, 150, 166, 199
*Au milieu des sollicitudes* (1892), 29, 160

Barrès, Maurice, 33
Bautain, Louis, 27
Benedict XV, Pope, 200
Bergson, Henri, 33, 58, 117
Bert, Paul, 17n4
Berthelot, Marcelin, 17n4, 82–84
Bismarck, Otto von, 19
Blondel, Maurice, x, 8, 10, 21, 36–38, 45, 73, 84n6, 106n1, 131, 131n5, 135–36, 152, 160–61, 166–67, 169n42, 171, 181, 183–84, 186, 196, 198–201
"L'Action" (1893), 106, 108, 110–20, 130, 133, 134, 137
"L'Lettre" (1896), 121–26
Theergy, 119, 186
"Histoire et Dogme" (1904), 155, 171, 173–76
Extrinsicism, 38, 151, 172, 174–75
Bonald, Louis de, 27, 38, 40
Boulanger, Georges General, 15–16
Bourget, Paul, 29, 33–34
Boutroux, Émile, 107–8, 120, 130
Brunetière, Ferdinand, 11, 34, 42–43, 116, 131, 177, 183

Cartesian thought, 7, 39, 47, 61, 75, 85, 89, 90, 93, 113, 201
Catholic universities, xiv, 17, 34, 41, 129, 161
Chateaubriand, Francois René de, 28, 38
Claudel, Paul, 1, 28
Clemenceau, Georges, 17n4
Combes, Émile, xv, 2, 17n4, 21, 76, 163, 193
Comte, Auguste, 16, 31, 44
Concordat of 1802, xv, 21–22
Contingency, 5, 9, 43, 52, 86, 103, 105, 118, 137, 145, 160, 184, 185
Cousin, Victor, 7, 8, 44, 108
*La Croix*, 31

Darwinianism, ix, 5, 41, 111, 112, 127, 132, 183
*Dei filius*, 40, 75
Descartes, René, 44, 46, 57, 59, 89, 100, 104, 130, 143, 201
D'Hulst, Maurice, Monsignor, 29, 156n3
Dogmatism, 45, 60, 63, 88, 99, 129, 141–44, 147
Dreyfus Affair, xiv, xv, 2, 31, 83, 132, 155, 159, 162–63
Duchesne, Abbé, 24, 76, 152
Duhem, Pierre, x, 8–11, 21, 36, 45, 58, 73, 82–108, 115–16, 126, 128–29, 136, 152, 174, 178n73, 180, 186–87, 196, 199
  "Physique et Métaphysique" (1893), 82, 86, 88, 90–91, 106, 116
  "Quelques réflexions au sujet des théories physique" (1892), 82, 86
  *Le Système du Monde*, 84
  "La Théorie physique: son object, sa structure" (1904–1905), 98–99
  "Quelques Réflexions au sujet de la physique expérimentale" (1894), 102
  "Physique du croyant" (1904), 91
  "Les théories de l'optique" (1894), 103

École des Hautes Études, 24, 35
École Normale Supérieure, 9, 10, 34–36, 82, 92, 107
École Polytechnique, 34
Epistemology, xv, 1, 4, 7–8, 10, 14, 25, 34, 36, 39, 41, 43–45, 58–59, 61, 78, 80, 82, 86, 89, 90–91, 106, 115–16, 124–26, 128, 133, 141, 155, 158–59, 168, 173

Falloux Law, 13, 17
Ferry, Jules, xi, 17, 23
Ferry Laws, 17, 132
Fideism, 6, 39, 55, 58, 64, 88, 114, 117, 134, 137–38, 149, 172–73
France, Anatole, 32
French Revolution, ix, xi, xv, 4, 14–15, 19, 22, 25, 27, 34, 83, 164, 174, 178, 194, 196
Freycinet, Charles de, 17n4

Gilson, Etienne, 169n42
Giraud, Victor, 8, 167–68, 181n81
Goldmann, Lucien, 7, 68–70, 72, 185
Goncourt brothers, 32

Harnack, Adolf, 170–71
Huysmans, J.-K., 29, 32

Idealism, 129, 142
Immanence, 72–73, 81, 85, 106, 120, 124–26, 133, 139, 164, 171, 191, 199
*Immortale Dei* (1885), 29
Institut Catholique, 4, 24, 29, 77, 91
Integralists, 20, 34, 38–40, 132, 156–57, 169
Intellectualism, 58, 71, 114n24, 117, 136, 148, 189

Jansenism, 6–7, 12, 22, 24, 45, 59, 64–67, 198–99
Jesuits, 45, 59, 60, 66–67, 137, 153, 193, 198

Kantianism, xiv, 34–36, 39, 42, 44, 89, 108, 113, 118, 120, 129–30, 132–34, 137, 139, 143, 147, 153, 198
Kierkegaard, Søren, 150

Laberthonnière, Lucien, x, 8,
   10–11, 21, 36n53, 45, 73, 106,
   128–53, 160, 164, 166–67,
   175–82, 184, 186–87, 196–97,
   199, 200
   "Le problème religieux" (1897),
      134
   "Le dogmatisme moral" (1898),
      141
   "Pour le dogmatisme moral"
      (1899), 148
   "Le réalism chrétienne et
      l'idéalisme grec" (1904), 155,
      177
Lamennais, Félicité Robert De, 25,
   38, 40
*Lamentabili Sane* (1907), 169, 191,
   192
Law of Separation, xv, 2, 3, 21, 23,
   132, 163, 197
Leo XIII, Pope, xii, 3, 5, 26–27, 29,
   41, 58, 74–80, 82–83, 106,
   155–56, 158, 160–62, 165–66,
   189–90, 199
Le Roy, Edouard, 152, 188
*Libertas* (1888), 27
Littré, Émile, 32
Loisy, Alfred, 4, 77–78, 80, 123, 131,
   140–41, 148, 157–58, 168–76,
   188, 193, 197, 199

Mach, Ernest, 85, 99
Maistre, Joseph de, 27, 38, 40
Maritain, Jacques, 169n42
Maurras, Charles, 30, 118n38, 132,
   164–66, 168, 174, 175, 198
Michelet, Jules, 178
*Mirari Vos* (1832), 25
Modernism, xv, 2, 5, 8, 10–12, 14,
   27, 34, 38, 77, 120, 128, 150,
   153, 155, 157, 163–70, 175,
   186–200
Montaigne, 51, 52, 60

Nihilism, 113, 114

Ollé-Laprune, Léon, 107–8, 161,
   182n85

Painlevé, Paul, 17n4
Pascal, Blaise, x, xv, xvi, 1, 6–13, 38,
   43–73, 80–81, 86, 89–90, 95,
   97–105, 108–10, 113, 115–16,
   119, 124–28, 130–41, 146–50,
   167–68, 175–77, 179n75,
   180–87, 193–201
   and Aristotle, 45, 51, 58
   and Torricelli, 46
   *Deus absconditus,* 43, 45, 68, 71,
      72, 81, 125, 128, 149
   *Esprit de finesse et de géométrie,*
      6, 36, 48, 62, 86, 95, 100, 103,
      147, 180
   Geometry, 48, 61
   *Infini-rien,* 54, 61, 63, 70, 116,
      187
   *Lettres provinciales,* 59, 61, 65, 67
   Orders of knowledge, x, 10, 45,
      61–62, 72, 86, 90, 168
   *Pensées,* 7–12, 53–57, 60–67,
      70–72, 86, 100, 119, 125, 132,
      134, 136–37, 141, 149, 177,
      185, 201
   Vacuum, 46
   Wager, 63, 72, 100, 109, 113
*Pascendi* (1907), xiv, 8, 11–12, 27,
   74, 148, 153, 158, 161n11,
   164, 169, 186, 188–200
Pasteur, Louis, xii, 5
*Pastor aeternus* (1870), 75
Péguy, Charles, 1, 28
Pius IX, Pope, 2, 16n2, 25, 26, 74–77,
   160n9
Pius X, Pope, 74, 189–92
Poincaré, Henri, 11, 33, 58, 85, 115,
   116, 136, 174

# Index

Positivism, 3, 5, 7, 12, 14, 16–18, 24, 28, 30–36, 42–43, 50, 58, 65, 84–91, 95, 98–99, 105, 107, 112, 115, 146, 168, 172, 174–75, 195–96, 198

*Providentissimus Deus* (1893), 8, 74–81, 106, 148, 197

*Quanta Cura* (1864), 26, 75, 160n9

Ralliement, ix, xii, 29, 83, 155–63, 166–67, 188
Rampolla, Cardinal, 189
Realism, 85, 129, 142
Renan, Ernest, 1, 23, 32–33, 44, 53, 76, 169, 170
*Rerum Novarum* (1891), 29
*Revue de philosophie*, 8, 98
*Revue des deux mondes*, 8, 34, 167
*Revue des questions scientifiques*, 8, 82
Rey, Abel, 91
Roman Catholic Church, 3, 9, 13, 19–21, 30, 41–43, 58, 75, 80, 84, 129, 153–58, 160n9, 164–65, 171, 193, 195

Scholasticism, 5, 41–42, 44, 46, 75–77, 81, 90, 98, 108, 124, 126–27, 130–31, 135, 137, 139–40, 149, 151, 153–54, 164n19, 168–69, 171, 177–78, 192, 196–200
Schwalm, Father, 133–34, 137
Scientism, xi, xii, xiii, xiv, 1, 12, 18, 28, 33–37
*Singulari Nos* (1834), 25, 160n9
Skepticism, 6, 11–12, 39, 41, 44–45, 49, 52, 60, 63–64, 88, 99, 104, 134, 141, 143, 152, 168, 172
Spencer, Herbert, 112

Strowski, Fortunat, 86, 181, 182
Syllabus of Errors, 2, 26, 41, 75, 129, 152, 160n9, 191
Taine, Hippolyte, 32
Third Republic (1870–1940), ix, xi, xii, xiv, 1–3, 12–13, 15–21, 29, 31, 34–36, 111, 129, 131–32, 154–58, 162–63, 177–78, 187, 190, 195–97
  Bonapartists, 15, 16
  Laic Laws, 18, 167
  Opportunists, xi, 15–16, 163
  Radicals, 15, 163
  Republicans, ix, xi, xiii, 18, 16–30, 83

Thomism, xiv, 2, 5, 8, 10–12, 14, 26–27, 29, 41, 50–51, 58, 69, 71, 73–74, 90, 99, 105, 111, 120, 123, 129, 133, 140, 143, 148, 151–52, 156n3, 158, 161–62, 165, 169–72, 176, 178, 186–87, 196, 199–200
Tyrrell, George, 188, 197

Ultramontanism, 25–26, 38, 75, 156–57, 160n9, 165, 168–69
*L'Univers*, 30

Vatican, ix, xiv, xv, 14, 19, 20, 31, 37, 42, 74, 78, 129, 154, 156, 158, 162, 165–66, 191–97, 200
Vatican Council (1870), 26–27, 40, 75, 77
Verlaine, Paul, 29, 33
Veuillot, Louis, 30
Vicaire, Eugène, 82, 88
Von Hugel, Baron Friedrich, 188

Zola, Émile, 1, 32

www.ingramcontent.com/pod-product-compliance
Lightning Source LLC
Chambersburg PA
CBHW050555240426
43664CB00049B/2490